THE EARLY YEARS
Volume II

Now, We Begin

Jeshua

Copyright © 2019 by Audio Enlightenment Press All rights reserved. No part of this publication may be reproduced, distributed, or transmitted in any form or by any means, including photocopying, recording, or other electronic or mechanical methods, without the prior written permission of the publisher, except in the case of brief quotations embodied in critical reviews and certain other non-commercial uses permitted by copyright law. Printed in the United States of America

0 1 2 3 4 5 6 7 8 9

First Printing, December 2019
ISBN 978-1-941489-47-5

WayofMastery.com

WayofMasteryBooks.com

Kindle/ePub / Audiobooks
Available on WayofMasteryBooks.com

First "AudioEnlightenmentPress.Com" Printing
December 2019

CONTENTS

Foreword .... *vii*

Mastering Communication 11

The Blessing of Forgiveness 25

The Divine Feminine 49

The Holy Instant 59

The Holy Spirit 83

The Light that You are 125

Walk with Me 171

Love Heals All Things 191

The Meaning of Ascension 241

Teach Only Love 271

The Heart of Freedom 305

The Master of Time 327

Foreword

The book you hold in your hand is a transcription of channelings given by Jeshua to public groups from the early years of my work with Him. These teachings are an extensive collection of Jeshua's wisdom, a vital part of The Way of Mastery Pathway, and are available here for the first time in book form.

As recounted in The Jeshua Letters, after my more personal initial communion with Jeshua, a new period of my studentship and work with Him shifted to a more public stage.

From 1988, until the time He began the three year course of The Way of Mastery: The Christ Mind Trilogy in 1994, He asked that I remain surrendered to Him. This included stepping into this more public role of channeling for groups, something I was very uncomfortable with to start with!

Regardless, however, as word got out, groups would increasingly gather at my home in Tacoma, Washington, and invitations, taking me farther and farther afield, came in as well. All this requiring that I surrender further and further to a process I did not understand at all!

This began with a first group gathering, in which He lifted me out of my body (or what I have come to see as 'the body'), and then entered into it to communicate with those in attendance.

I refer to this stage as the beginning of the 'channeling' phase of my work with Him, although it important for the reader to understand what is meant by that phrase.

Here is what would always happen:

I would close my eyes and initiate a simple prayer He had given me to do, and I would feel myself dropping into a deeply meditative space. Then, a peculiar vibration would begin, increasing, and I would be transported out, and above the body; I could see it below, along with the crowd gathered, as well as a circle of light beings fully encircling the group.

Things would accelerate, and I would experience a rapid movement through multi-colored light. I could witness the crowd, and then the house in which the crowd sat, and then further, wider, "telescoping" out until I could see planet Earth herself, and then rapidly even the physical universe itself would vanish, even as the pulsing, vibrating colored light increased!

Then, it would stop, and I would be aware of being with Jeshua, now together with Him in a field of Light.

He would teach me while I was there with Him, and yet…while all this was occurring, He was also moving into, and teaching through, 'my body' to the group gathered together!

At some point, He would tell me, 'It is finished now'. I would begin to feel a kind of vibrational change, and the reverse of the journey ensued until I 'zoomed' downward and landed - often with a kind of shock - in the body. It would often take as much as 30 minutes for me to be able to move a finger, or begin to make any sound as I slowly regained adaptation to the body.

After, it would be so charged with energy that I often would be up for hours, yet in an altered state. Everything shimmered in light, and often objects like buildings, trees, telephone poles, and more, were transparent. I could see right through them!

Foreword

One night, I was very sick with a fever and strep throat, and was 'so sure' the evening should be cancelled. He assured me there would be no problem, and – to everyone's shock – as I 'left' and Jeshua entered, I was told later that suddenly there was no trace at all of my sickness!!

Indeed, after returning, I experienced the body radiating in clarity and perfect health, only then to gradually feel it 'sink' as we all know of as the strep throat returned! When I asked Him what had happened, he replied:

'I would suggest that to be a very good question for you to dwell in. Why has what you call 'sickness' returned?'

It is the type of question He lovingly asks, yet it is apparent He is bringing attention and contrast as to why one might use the body for such a thing as sickness, which, apparently, His use of the body did not include!

The Way of Mastery: The Early Years (volumes I & II) transcriptions of these gatherings, originally recorded live, capture what Jeshua taught us all in these beautiful gatherings. The wisdom, guidance, and sheer brilliance of them is astounding; there is so much in these pages, dear reader, that will help you grow in understanding, support you to truly heal into peace, and more!

You might like to know this as well. Jeshua shared that while this mystical alchemy I was undergoing was part of my studentship, it was also His learning curve in acclimating to 'my' body, as well as merging with and learning to utilize the language structure of its 'brain-mind.'

Indeed, the first phases of this period would find Him often communicating in a slow, monotone voice, with no movement of the body at all. Gradually, over time, He could animate it, and seemed to enjoy using my American idioms that He has accessed through this process as well!

Our interactions were varied and amusing. I would often feel His presence as I, for example, watched a bit of television, and he would make comments of the shows and even commercials. He said He was learning of my world through the part of my soul fixated, and operating through, the body, that tiny thing which I was still mistakenly thinking to be 'me'!

The Early Years are filled with ancient wisdom, timeless Love, and even prophecy. In opening to this wonderful trove of material from Jeshua, may you enjoy these jewels that He has given us all!

Blessings to you,
Jayem

December, 2019

Mastering Communication

Now we begin.

You have asked in this hour for me to abide with you, to join with you yet again as your brother and as your friend, and perhaps as one still seen as one who has gone ahead a little bit. Yet I say unto you, always our minds are joined, always our hearts beat as one, always our very life is the life of the Love extended from the Mind of God that is the extension of Creation itself — and forever and always, the Son is One. And yet within Creation it can appear that I have gone ahead a little way, while you believe you yet linger, getting a final taste of shadows long since outgrown.

And yet we are a conspiracy. That is, we *breathe together* to bring light to every shadow and every illusion. *We breathe together* to bring forth the perfect remembrance of God. And God is but Love. And if we are to breathe together, if we are to embrace Creation and allow through us a transformation of Creation to occur so that all things are returned to the light of God's Love, it becomes necessary to look at what Creation is doing.

Where am I in this moment?

Do you abide in a world in which it is not necessary to speak words? Do you abide in a dimension in which it is not necessary to strive to communicate from one mind to another? Do you live in a world in which it is clear that there is no divisiveness between minds? Of course not. Therefore, if you would breathe with me, if you would desire truly to bring forth the Love of God and to transform the shadows, the illusions, the obstacles to the presence of Love, understand then that you are asked to assume responsibility for *what* you would choose to communicate and for *how* you would choose to do so.

Communication is a simple term. It simply means to create that experience in which two minds come into union so that one idea, one vibration, informs both minds and is valued equally by them. All of you have had the experience of genuine communication. For when communication succeeds, the mind is transcended, the heart opens, and there is a joining at the level of the Soul within the depth of the Mind that far transcends anything which can be uttered by words or even symbolized by words. So the goal of communication is always the same — to link two minds together at such a depth of union that separation is transcended and the Love of God remembered as the only reality. Communication: to establish communion.

I have shared with you before that there are four keys to the kingdom: Desire, Intention, Allowance, Surrender. Therefore, what you desire in any moment is of utmost importance, for from your desire you will begin to *move* Creation, move the energy of mind in a certain direction that will have a certain flavor, a certain vibration. If you desire to breathe with me, let your desire be singular of purpose.

> *Father, how might I extend my treasure this day? And my treasure is the gift of union with You that you have given to me before the foundation of all worlds. And I long that my brothers and sisters awaken to the remembrance of that union that lives within their own hearts and their own minds. Let my life in this world while it lasts be given only to the extension of the Good, the Holy, and the Beautiful.*

Mastering Communication

And if that is your desire, set it in stone, if you will, with your intention. An intention is simply a clear decision in the mind that the wholeness of your being will be committed to and dedicated to the fulfillment of your desire. In the realm of intention comes one simple question:

How can I communicate in this moment the depth of my intended desire to bless the world with the love of God?

You will always communicate what you most desire and intend to communicate. You are infallible at this in each moment, and you never blunder. Therefore, where communication seems to be *unclear*, you may rest assured that there has been an *unclear* intention and desire, perhaps even a *denial* of the desire to join in loving union with another: that is, to be the presence of Christ who blesses the world. This is why if you would truly master communication you *must seek first the Kingdom* that all these things might be added unto you.

What does that mean? The path of awakening requires discipline—and well do I know that many of you think that discipline is a heavy burden. It is not. Separation is a heavy burden. To be disciplined simply means to be 'a disciple of'. And of what? Of Love. To recognize that Love is the greatest good, that Wisdom your greatest power, that Union is your greatest truth; that you are as God created you to be, and why would you ever again want to waste a moment trying to be something you're not?

So discipline means to turn away from the illusion, the temptation of giving up your Christedness, and assuming the mantle of responsibility.

I will be a disciple of the truth and I will rest at its altar even prior to every breath. I will cultivate within myself the skill necessary to turn every decision over to the Comforter, the Holy Spirit. I will discipline my mind. I will learn to be a master of the kingdom given unto me...

which is simply your own mind, your own field of awareness...

And I will dedicate the fields in my kingdom to that which can bring forth great fruit, and offer it to my Creator.

What would your life be like if prior to every thought you remembered your primary desire and thereby remembered your purpose for incarnation? What would your life be like if you were so fully disciplined within your own mind that only loving thoughts were spoken with your words? If you remembered your Creator so thoroughly that before any situation, before anything is uttered or done, you ask within quietly:

Father, what would you have me do that love might be extended and offered?

Communication, then, requires *discipline*, and discipline grows from committed intention and a clarification of your deepest *desire*. You will always experience exactly what you're desiring.

Muddled communication? *Look within.* Is there a fear of genuine intimacy? Is there a reluctance towards forgiveness? Is there a blockage in the emotional body?

Here is a simple prayer that you can utilize each of your days, until it becomes second nature for you. When you rise in the morning, before you speak a single word or take a single action, go within the heart. Lay upon the altar of the Heart all that you think you've learned up to this point and remember that *you need do nothing*, remember that you *know nothing*, and then ask:

Father, this day I find myself in this world. What would you have me communicate this day with my actions, with my words, and with my very thoughts?

Then rest in silence and see what presents itself to the screen of your awareness. Trust that prayer. Learn to use it often until it's second nature — so that in any moment, at any time, that is as the soil from which each moment is springing.

Father, what would you have me communicate in this day or in this moment?

You see, the essence of genuine communication is the remembrance that you belong to *no one* but God. The essence of communication will flow more effortlessly when you behold the other as belonging *only* to God, not to the ego, not to illusion, not to you, not to another. They too are Gods, and therefore your Creator wishes only to communicate *through you* to his own. And nothing can have greater value than the communication of that which heals, that which enfolds and embraces, that which forgives, that which loves. For what you communicate one unto another, rest assured you immediately receive for yourself.

And here's the nub of the issue. If you want God, if you want to breathe one breath with your Creator, become so selfish in the domain of your own mind that all you communicate are your loving thoughts, that all you do is bless the world. For in this way you *are* blessed, and as you *give* Christ, you *remember* Christ, until Christ never fades from your awareness. And then, indeed, you are free.

Communication requires, then, in any given moment of relationship that someone assume responsibility for remembering that neither party knows anything. Now often we would see that in your relationships one would like to enter that state but is quite sure the other one doesn't want to, and so then needs to defend themselves and steps into ego consciousness—and off you go, spinning like your planet, getting nowhere. The purpose of communication is to teach only love. Therefore, wait on no one. Don't wait to see if your mate or friend wants to enter that place. Assume responsibility for doing it *for yourself* so that you can offer it freely to another. Rest assured that if you resent the fact that they haven't entered into it with you, you didn't offer it freely. Become selfish enough that you will not settle for communicating anything less than that which your Creator would extend through you, so that by doing so *you receive it yourself.*

Communication is life. Communication *is* relationship. It has nothing to do with the juxtaposition of bodies in space and time, since that is not what you are. *Communication is relationship.* Relationship is the means of your salvation.

Therefore, if I might paraphrase a phrase from your Bible: Count it all joy when those around you persecute you or attack you, for remember that in that moment you are given the power to teach only Love, to remember your desire to stay firm in your intention and thereby receive the gifts of being the one who blesses this world. Hmm. That rather makes sense, doesn't it?

> *Oh, that's right. What is it that I want to communicate? What is it I am most desirous of learning more thoroughly? . . . That only Love is real. I want it for myself, so deeply, so thoroughly, that nothing can enter into the field of awareness I call myself save the presence of God.*

Can you care enough about that, that you couldn't care less what anybody else on the planet wants? You become so selfish that you see that each moment of time is an incredible opportunity to remember the Truth by extending it. To remember that there is no such thing as 'time off'. Since each thought creates an experience, a domain, a world, that fills your awareness, what would you drink into your field of awareness? Pain and suffering; or joy and freedom, peace and the presence of Christ?

When I walked your planet as a man, I had need of learning exactly what I am seeking to communicate with you. And if there has been any power that has touched you in the few words that I've used so far, it is *only* because I have *cultivated* the clarity of my desire and *made concrete* my intention. And through the use of time as a man and through the use of communication since I left your planet with every mind that would open its heart to me, I have perfected the purity of one desire: *to teach only Love.*

The power of your communication, then, flows from the depth of your commitment and your discipline and the willingness to learn how to use the tools available to you, whether it be a pen and a piece of paper, whether it be a drawing or a painting, whether it be a hug or a handshake, whether it be a smile or a kiss upon the cheek. Can you use every gesture, every tool available in your world, to teach only Love, to discover what it means to lay your hand on the shoulder of a friend *out of* union with God, having asked first:

> *Father, what would you have me communicate? How can this hand be a vessel or a vehicle that extends the blessing of the Comforter?*

To learn how to speak in complete sentences. To learn how to take a thought and struggle with whatever you need to struggle with until you have crystallized it in the best words that you can find. Can you care enough about yourself to perfect and master the forms through which you can communicate while in this world? And can you ever come to an end to that? Of course not, since perfection is unlimited. Creation merely extends itself more and more and more and more, revealing the Good, the Holy, and the Beautiful. And all of you know what it's like to sit down and listen to someone who's just learning to play a violin. Hm! And you know what it's like to listen to a master. Something in what the master has accomplished can touch your heart more deeply, more purely, like a sword that cuts to the core reveals its gifts.

Would you be willing to become committed to One whose communication is so pure, so crystal clear, that when you communicate Love to another, *they get it*? They get it so profoundly that lifetimes of suffering is resolved in an instant, that merely by looking in your eyes they remember God. For that is the commitment of anyone who birthed Christ in their own awareness.

Oh yes, communication is very important. For what you communicate and how you choose to do so speaks to the world of what you most desire and what your deepest intention is *for yourself*. Therefore, in each word, in each gesture, in each activity you choose to participate in, you are speaking your message to the world — you are telling the world what your judgment of God is. Pure and simple.

Become, therefore, very, very selfish. Find your glory within yourself. Desire to communicate to this world the presence of God. Embrace the moments of time that you might use them constructively, that you might taste the perfect freedom of walking this plane as Christ incarnate— and never settle for less.

Now in the process of mastering communication there is an extremely important and very serious element—innocent play. Innocent play.

> *Well, I've decided to communicate Christ to the world. Hm, I have a feeling I have spent many lifetimes trying to do the opposite, but the past is passed away. Thank God for that. And today, I choose anew. Huh, how do I communicate Christ in this moment?*
>
> *Ah, I'll ask the Comforter. I'll give up my own thinking and simply ask what would be the best way to communicate Christ in this moment. If you really want to have fun, tell the one in front of you, "You know, I've decided to communicate Christ in this moment. Now just take a deep breath and give me some time, because I am learning by doing."*

Rest assured, that if you would begin each communication in that way, you will immediately disarm the one in front of you and you will have asked them to offer *you* the space of innocence. It makes it easier for them and easier for you. Then communicate whatever you will, and then ask them,

"Well, how did I do? Did you feel it? I really love you. That's my intention here. How did it come across?"

In other words, bring innocent playfulness to your communication. See yourself as a child who is on their way to remembrance of mastery. Have fun on your planet. Drop the seriousness. Drop the veils, the personas and the egos in which the world has taught you that you need to look like you're already an expert. What do you have the commercial 'Never let them see you sweat'. Why not let them see you sweat:

> "Look, I'm just here trying to embody Christ. That's all I'm committed to. I love you. You're innocent. Now just take a breath, give me a moment, and we'll see how I do."

Then touch them, and kiss them. Then if it is words that need to come, speak the words. If it is a feeling that needs to be shared, share the feeling from the place of your perfect innocence and the fact that you are a student in the University of God Consciousness. So much seriousness comes into your communications one with another. And seriousness is the opposite of the Kingdom.

Last of all, in this short communication, always begin by acknowledging your oneness, your union with the one to whom you would communicate, whether person, whether plant, whether mineral. Hm? When you go to water a flower, begin by acknowledging your oneness. Therefore, see the sacredness of the moment and give it over to the Comforter, who alone can guide it into bearing much good fruit. And yes, I know very much that in your world there are still a few minds on your planet that prefer conflict over peace, dissonance rather than resonance. Does it matter? If you wait for another mind to want what you want, you will never achieve what you want. *Be*, therefore, what you most desire, and you are Christ, you are the Light that lights the world, you are the field of Love that attracts others to release their illusions, to release their suffering, to let go of their seriousness, to let go of all attempts to defend their rightness. You become the field that attracts the seeker of Reality to itself, *because you have accepted it first for yourself.*

Many of you that will hear these words know that I have said that a teacher of God has one responsibility: to accept the atonement for him- or herself. If you are reluctant to master the forms of your communication, have you truthfully accepted the atonement? For the acceptance of the atonement pops the mind open and you realize that your brother or sister is yourself, and you can only have what you give away. That is why communication is sacred. That is why it has always been taught: Observe the thoughts in your mind and think before you speak. For each spoken word is as a pebble dropped in a pond; it creates a ripple and a vibration that returns to you immediately. Think only loving thoughts. Speak only with the wisdom of Christ. Celebrate and honor the one before you, asking only:

Father, what would you have me communicate?

And in this way, the pebbles that you drop in the pond of human consciousness become as diamonds shimmering in the light of God's Love, radiating Light in all directions, bringing joy and abundance and wealth to those that behold your presence.

Become the Love that you seek. Master communication. For the day will come when you no longer need the body, or space and time, as a teaching or learning device for you; and yet communication will continue unbroken according to the degree of your mastery. That mastery will carry you to where I am; to a place in which separation is impossible; to a place in which by simply turning your attention you are one with the soul of anyone who's present for you. In the twinkling of an eye you will travel through a multitude of dimensions and everywhere you go you will be the presence of Light and you will touch the farthest reaches of Creation—which, by the way, goes on and keeps expanding—and you will bless it with the Love of God, and you will know such bliss and such unlimitedness that you will wonder why you ever resisted taking responsibility for communication. And you will thank God that you became so selfish as to want to *truly* teach only Love.

For now, we will let that be enough on communication. Rest assured that if you will meditate on each word chosen — slowly, deliberately, carefully, innocently — the very vibration communicated in this short sharing will already do much to bring about a correction of vibration in the depth of your own mind — that your own communication almost magically, effortlessly, will begin to improve, will flow from a deeper depth and therefore be far more satisfying in your own heart.

A teacher of God is a master of communication. Communication is the bridge that brings you home to your brother or your sister. And in the perfection of communication, the Kingdom is remembered and restored.

So with that, blessings unto you, all those of you that will hear these words: Master your communication. Well do I know that whatever it is that I have accomplished, and even am still accomplishing, greater things than these can you bring forth. I am just a beginner in the Mind of my Father.

So. Hmm. Do you think that that will be sufficient?

Beloved sister?

I think it's wonderful. Thank you.

What would you wish to communicate in this moment?

I love you.

Now. Take a moment and go into the mind and simply ask:

Mastering Communication

Father what you have me communicate in this moment?

and when you're ready, say it again.

I love.

Mmmm... Now the rest of you here, did you feel the difference?

[Agreement]

A greater depth, a greater expanse, a greater *power?* . . . a greater *joining?* Did you feel it?

Yes.

Indeed. So just maybe that little prayer works. And did you notice how you changed it from "you" to *"I love"*?

Yes.

Indeed. That is the truth of who you are. Hmm. Thank you for providing an excellent example for those who will read these things.

Jeshua I'd like for you to address two sentences that I keep hearing in my mind as we go through this, directly out of your *Course in Miracles*. The first sentence is: "Never tell your brother that he is what you would not want to be". And the second one is: "Words are but symbols of symbols and therefore twice removed from reality." Would you elaborate on those two?

Certainly. Words are indeed symbols of symbols, since they represent an idea; and when a word is spoken it again gives the message that this is the idea that you are valuing. Hm?

Now that is why I asked you when we began: Do you live in a world where words are not necessary? Since you abide *here*, it must be the Father's Will that you be the one who finds way to communicate Love *here*. And the wise teacher speaks the language of the student. Therefore, words are necessary in this dimension as a way of pointing beyond themselves to the symbols they represent and even beyond the ideas to the direct experience of the revelation of Love's presence.

Now when you communicate to a brother or a sister in a way that indicates to them that you believe they are less than Christ, because of the power of thought and words you have immediately placed *yourself* in a position less than Christ. So that sentence refers to the divine selfishness that we have spoke of in this hour.

Do you want to be less than Christ? If not, then communicate in such a way that honours the truth of your brother or sister regardless of the degree of insanity they may temporarily be choosing. Honour that place first. We do not mean by that that you overlook the behaviour of insanity but that you *see through it and offer first the truth*.

Does that make sense for you?

Yes.

Does it help in regard to those two sentences that 'somebody' must have stuck in there by accident?

It's nice to know you have a sense of humour.

Beloved friend, the further you go into God the more you have to just laugh.

The Blessing of Forgiveness

Now we begin.

And, indeed, greetings unto you, beloved holy friends. Indeed, greetings to you, beloved and holy great Rays of Light shining eternally in the mind of our Father, bringing forth that which is Love, bringing forth that which is Light, bringing forth that which is Wisdom and Peace and Simplicity — and Forgiveness.

For in Truth, the world waits upon your forgiveness. It waits to be anointed by the Mind of Christ that would look upon all created things and grant it forgiveness. For your world lives steeped in fear. Your world is filled with many brothers and sisters that are plagued by a deep sense of unworthiness and guilt. Having fallen asleep, they continue to dream an illusory dream. But much like any dream, it holds the power to enchant the mind and block the very cells of the body from exuding only that which is real: Light. And Light is Love. And, therefore, to begin this evening and to share this message with our many friends, we would indeed speak of forgiveness.

Beloved friends, forgiveness requires a graciousness; and graciousness is but the extension through form — through the body, through the emotions, through your touch, through your smile, through the glimmer in your eyes — of that which is the Grace *already* given unto *you*.

It is always wise, then, to remember that if you would know Grace, give grace. And each moment, then, as you walk through your world, as you would cry out unto me and to many of my friends,

Teach me what my purpose is, what is my function? What is my unique and special role?

And your mind would teach you that it must be some form of service outside of your own being. I say unto you, your purpose and your function is the same as was, and is mine: To be that one through whom the Grace of a loving God is given unto those who yet dream the vicious and dark and awful dream of separation. For in that dream there cannot be anything but a deep inner anguish. And one who dreams thus acts in such a way that almost every thought and every action becomes a cry for help and healing—a cry that falls on the deaf ears of the world, for the world believes in judgment and not forgiveness, in condemnation and not healing.

Therefore, know well the power that dwells within *you*, for you have already awakened to your call. You have already begun to lift your eyes up from the dream of separation, and have begun to behold a great Light shining forever, that seems to shine forth from some place, from some source so far removed from all that you've known and all that you think you are. And yet the Light that you behold is *your* light, placed within you by God himself from the moment you first began to dream your own unique version of the dream of separation.

How, then, will you know that Light? Not by seeking it, but by allowing it. Therefore, as you walk through this world, when you cry out wondering what your purpose is, bring your attention back to the simple fact that *you are here to bless the world through the Forgiveness of Christ*. Look, therefore, gently upon all that you see. Learn to return the mind, the emotions and, as long as it lasts, even the body, to peace — that the graciousness of Christ can flow forth through you unimpeded, unlimited, *shining in its joy*. And let that Light fall upon whomever you see, whatever you see: a blade of grass, a leaf falling from a tree, a wisp of cloud passing through the sky, a snowflake that falls. Bless these things, for they too have arisen from within *your* Holy Mind. And they are pervaded by that self-same Light that gives *you* your existence.

The world cries out for forgiveness, and the soul cries out for union with God, and seeks in a thousand convoluted ways and technologies to find a way to merge created and creator, beloved and lover. For, indeed, you are the lovers of God, and in truth cannot help but be that. For God does not create that which opposes Himself. Because you are a great Ray of Light shining in that one mind, while you are the created, *you are the lover of God*. And your peace and fulfillment will come to you fully when you have retrained the mind to settle for *no other thought* than that which expresses the joyful, heart-centered devotion to your Creator — not as a stern master apart from you, but as the presence of Love itself, that ignites the very creative process whereby you have come into being. Not to suffer the things of the world, not to dream the dream of separation — it was never necessary, it was just a momentary choice — but, rather, to extend all that God *is*.

Therefore, if you would know your freedom and peace, use each moment to bring the attention of the mind back to the graciousness and the blessing of forgiveness. For, as you forgive, you will learn that you have already been forgiven. And as you bless the world, you will know how blessed you truly are. And the day will come when you no longer fear the unlimited blessing of your Father, for you will know that all things are created for *you*, out of Love — that you never need to limit yourself in any moment, within your consciousness, whatever world you might be playing and dancing within. Take, then, upon your shoulders my cloak. Take upon your head my crown of Light. For it is given unto you to be the embodiment of all that Christ is.

And, in truth, because only Christ is the creation of God, it is the only thing that you can be in Reality. Now that means that if there is even one moment in your day when the thought in your mind would pull you to the perception that you are *other* than what you are created to be, it means that you, in that moment, have chosen to become identified with pure and utter insanity. Hm!

I have said often that there is a choice between but two emotions, Love and fear. And two other words that could be used would be sanity and insanity. There is no gray area. You're either in one or the other. You might fool yourself and say,

Well, I'm really moving toward Love, but I have to get through these certain things first and then I might get there.

You are either home, or you're away from home. You are either One with God, or you are dreaming the dream of separation. One brings the reality of Peace, one brings what seems to be insane to this upside-down world of yours: the recognition that you are as you're created to be. And in *this* moment you hold all power under Heaven and Earth to *choose* for peace. To *extend* only love. To *forgive* instead of judge. To be *open* instead of contracted.

The Blessing of Forgiveness

The way, then, is easy and without effort. It requires only that you make a deliberate choice: to surrender the perceptions and ideas you've ever held about anyone or anything (including yourself) that is anything other than the preciousness of the Reality of Christ. And to allow the Holy Spirit, then, to bring forth those circumstances that can show you where you had once failed and chosen insanity, so that you can simply correct it.

And that is why, as you dance through your many incarnations, you keep bumping into the same folks. And the energies that each soul presents to you will continue to be presented ad nauseum until you have embraced that energy and owned it within your own being; and then through the reflection or the mirror of forgiving that energy, you begin the process of dismantling or dissolving that energy in your own being. For they are one and the same. You have never truly looked upon another at all. Your eyes would show you bodies that seem not to reside in the same place that your body does, but that's an illusion, because *you* don't have a body. There are *bodies*, but *you* do not have one. You do not dwell within it; it dwells within the holy expansiveness of the One Mind, the One Mind that is incarnate upon your earth. Forgiveness is the bridge to healing.

Two thousand years ago, as you understand time, I came with a very simple message. And the message *was* the message of forgiveness. I have come yet again in many ways giving the same simple technology, *for it alone works*. And yet the mind would have you believe that you must constantly make it more difficult.

Surely there is something else to acquire, some great power, some great mystical experience. If only I could get all my outer affairs in order, then *I'll remember to forgive the world because I'll be comfortable.*

Rest assured that what you want to see reflected in the world around you is influenced by — is an extension of — the quality of awareness that *you* allow within your consciousness, moment to moment. And if you seem, then, to know struggle, there is some corner yet remaining that has not been touched by your own forgiveness. Now, are you going to be able to search out that corner? Many of you might try.

But is it not easier to simply recognize that the Holy Spirit has *already created* the exact circumstances that you need to awaken? Therefore, if you would seek your path, open your eyes. Notice the place where you seem to be, physically upon this earth. Notice who you seem to be with. Take a very deep breath, and remember that all things are perfect, that that is your golden doorway, your eye of the needle. And if you would make the choice to simply be the Presence of Christ and extend the gracious blessing of forgiveness, you will feel your restlessness begin to dissolve.

And as it dissolves in the depths of your beingness, through your deliberate choice to use the power of your mind (which is all that you have) to extend forgiveness and thereby the dissolve patterns of perception within the depth of your mind, you will then come to see the world around you differently. And miracle-mindedness begins more and more to be that which carries you through this life. You meet just the right person. You get just the perfect job. And all of the rest. It rains when you want it to rain, and it's sunny when you want it to be sunny. And you will be mystified by it all.

In the end, *when the mind is completely purified* — which simply means that it's been corrected from any conflict between Love and fear, forgiveness and judgment — when the mind is

The Blessing of Forgiveness

completely purified you will know that you are *unlimited forever*. You will know that, if you are seemingly in the bodily experience—whether you're washing the dishes or taking out the garbage, whatever you're doing—you will know that you, as Christ incarnate, have deliberately chosen to allow your being this experience as yet another opportunity to bless the world with the forgiveness that it cries out for. And if the body seems to dissolve in light and you are no longer seen by other bodies in space and time, you will know that that, too, is the perfect choice of freedom.

Imagine, then . . . imagine . . . walking through this life you are living, in a world that seems to have forgotten the Reality of God, and feeling, from the crown of the head to the tips of the toes, not one trace of contraction or fear. Imagine the cells of the body feeling as spacious as the heavens. Imagine the Peace that passes all understanding to be pervading every organ of the body. A gentle smile upon the lips, barely perceptible to others. A gentleness in the area of the heart. A sense of bodily relaxation from what you call the solar plexus to the base of the spine. The mind calm and clear, missing nothing, yet holding onto nothing. Imagine being compelled by nothing, and yet not having a trace of judgment about anything arise.

Imagine walking through this life in which *nothing is unacceptable to you*, because you are so busy blessing the world with the Forgiveness of Christ, recognizing that the dream is a dream is a dream is a dream. And dreams hold *no effect* upon the dreamer when the dreamer awakens. Imagine living this life in Perfect Peace.

Is it a difficult road? No. It requires, first and foremost, the willingness *to completely embrace yourself as you are*. Even as you perceive yourself to be, though you may be perceiving insanely — you are indeed doing so if you think there's anything amiss; but that's okay — first embrace the dream, and love *yourself*. Love yourself for being right where you are, *as you are*. For there is a simple law of metaphysics, as you know this, and it is this: it is literally and always impossible to transcend and heal what is not fully embraced. And to embrace something means to *love* it to death.

Therefore, when you go through your day, ask yourself this at the end of each day for the next seven days:

> *How many times in this one 24-hour period did I stop what I was doing and love myself wholly? . . . Well, I would have gotten around to it more than once, but I was awfully busy.*

Hm. No. You were deluded. And there is a big difference. You were in insanity whenever you contracted away from love of Self. So that's the first exercise we would offer you this evening: for the next seven days, before you fall asleep at night, count how many times in that day you truly and wholly loved *yourself*.

Now, as we pause here then, what we are viewing from our level, our perspective — that has nothing at all to do with bodies; so you see, you can't really hide, there's no such thing as privacy — what we are seeing is many minds contracting with guilt at the recognition that more often than not this day they've actually *loathed* themselves. They found something to judge themselves for.

I'm too tall, I'm too short, I'm too far, I'm too thin. I don't speak well enough, I don't have enough money, and on and on and on and on goes the list. Do you know that list? That list was made by a completely insane mind—and in Reality the list does not exist.

So, remember, then, to pay attention if you notice yourself being in judgment of yourself, that is the opposite of Love. So look upon the contraction in the mind that goes,

Oh my God, I didn't think about that once today: loving myself.

Love yourself *right there and then*—*now!* And you've loved yourself. And then you can go to sleep, peacefully. Does that make sense to you?

[Audience agreement]

I've said many times that the way is easy and without effort for what comes of effort is of your world, and not of the Kingdom. I've said to you the world is diametrically opposed to the Truth of the Kingdom. The world is just the *exact opposite* of all that the Kingdom is. And if you're tightening the cells of the body and tightening the mind—fueled by fear and trying to make things happen, and they're not happening—that's a clear sign that somewhere you've forgotten to rest in the graciousness of self-love. Self-love opens the door to the spaciousness whereby you remember that *you are One with all minds everywhere.*

There is no lack. And those beings who are perfect for you at your stage of the journey will be sent to you, if you will but welcome them before they arrive. Hm. Interesting thought, isn't it? Your world will teach you: what's the point of welcoming somebody until they've rung the doorbell? Why not welcome them before you ever see them with your physical eyes? Can you imagine what would happen if you awakened in the morning, took five minutes to forgive the world and bless the world and love yourself, and then *welcomed* everyone who was going to come into your experience that day as an angel bringing you the opportunity to bless the world with forgiveness. You see, your peace would walk ahead of you. It would enter a room before your body even gets there. And before anything is said and done, you will have already created the space large enough to hold *whatever* comes into your experience. You will have *embraced* what must be embraced, and thereby the pathway to transcendence is set before you.

Hm! Now is this all getting too complicated?

[Laughter.]

Remember this: when the mind seems stymied by what is said, there are actually two things going on. First of all, the attempt is to stop the mind. Only when the mind is stopped can space come to it. If you feel blocked in trying to grasp what is being shared at all, remember that that sense of being blocked is nothing more than an old, insane pattern. It is the culprit. If you notice that you're blocked, not quite putting the pieces together, simply stop and stop striving to do so. For the Soul hears the Truth. And when we come in this manner, or in many different manners, to speak with you, we come not to speak to your earthly mind, we come not to speak to the body and your emotional field. We come to speak directly to the essence of your Soul, which already knows the truth, which *is* the Truth, and is, in fact, the *very source from which these words are coming*.

Hm... By way of levity, if that is permitted...

[Laughter.]

The Blessing of Forgiveness

… I'm never quite sure when I look at your world whether it is or whether it isn't!

[Loud laughter.]

How many times in each day do *you* vacillate? You know the pattern of laughing at the foibles of others, but taking your own very seriously?

[Laughter.]

You see, all that I do in this work with this my beloved brother, is this: I abide in a place and in a dimension where nothing is hidden, where all minds reside right where I am. And when anyone asks a question or even thinks a thought and doesn't speak it through the body, I merely am like one in what you call your racetracks — imagine me with a little green visor on the head — and when one comes and says, "Well, I wonder if I should bet on this one or this one, what is this truth or that truth?" I go, "Just a minute." And I close down the window with the little bars on it, and I race out the back door, and I run behind and I sneak up behind you and I examine your heart from behind, and I see what is written there, and I go, "Oh, yes, okay." And then I race back and come back, and open up the window, and I give you the answer!

[Laughter.]

Now, many of you — it's rather an easy process because, you see, I keep records, and many of you ask the same things over and over.

[Laughter.]

Hm. But rest assured, and understand this well: when I once said "Of myself I do nothing" —

35

I meant it. My Father does these things *through* me. That requires the willingness to learn how to be *empty of self* with every breath. So those that would see me as someone filled with all of this great cosmic wisdom, please see me differently. I am empty and spacious, resting in quiet adoration and devotion of all that my Father is, witnessing *nothing but* miracles, and that which extends and radiates the Love of God through all Creation. And if in *your* mind you see it not, it only means that you have not yet been willing to train the mind to teach only Love; to give up all of your own ideas, moment to moment, breath to breath.

I am nothing special. I am merely *your equal*, your brother and your friend—created in the very same moment you were, with all the same attributes, all the same potential, all the same reality. And I marvel, just as you will when you truly ponder this, I marvel because throughout the expanse of my existence—which has been since before the beginning of time, just as yours—I have never been able to fathom the moment of my creation. Think about that one. Do you know the moment when? you began? No. And you'll never find it. And that means there is, indeed, an unfathomable mystery that I have called Abba that is present at a place within me that is deeper than can ever be known, no matter how much the mind becomes enlightened. Knowing that, there can only be humility, devotion, appreciation, love. There can only be the fulfillment of the truly only meaningful relationship that you can ever have: Relationship with your Creator. For all of the rest of your relationships are merely reflections of you abiding with an aspect of yourself. And the only way *that relationship can reflect Holiness is from the spillover from your devotion, and the purity of your relationship with your Creator. Does that make sense to you?*

[Audience agreement.]

Creation is grand. How could you ever comprehend it all? You can't. You can *only allow it* through your beingness without fear. For fear is a contraction, which is the opposite of Love. And when you know fear you are in the world and not in the Kingdom.

And so, beloved friends, I've revealed to you something about the nature of my own being. I am not a great master, as many would have me be, wanting to project onto me all manner of skills and abilities and powers because they are afraid of embracing these things for themselves. And *projection*, what you have tried to regurgitate out of your soul and get rid of, is what *makes your perceptions*. So if those that would come into a temple to worship me as the savior of the world would only stop and understand the truth that *projection makes perception,* they would see that they are *literally creating* the savior they believe must be there out of the denial of who they are.

That is why I have often said to those of you who would choose to build an altar, to have a room of prayer, whatever you call it: why do you have all of these pictures of saints and masters from all over the world? Where is *your* picture? Rest assured, try that for one hour. Get a picture of yourself and treat it like you would — pay homage to it like you would — a picture of your favorite master. Place it upon your altar and light your candles and your incense, sprinkle it with holy water, whatever you want to do, whatever your rituals are; and then do nothing but relax and contemplate your own image. And ask yourself this one question: From where has that being come? Can you see how that would be very opposite of what the world teaches you to do?

I'm not speaking here of the danger — and there is a danger — of slipping into an egoic identification of yourself as being so great and regal and special, and everybody else a peon. That's not what we're talking about, but to move through the temptation to let the ego grasp the insight that you are as God created you to be. For while you abide in space and time, vigilance and discipline are absolutely required. And the more you awaken, the more you will need them.

In my day and age we spoke often of the temptation of Satan. The story that many of you know of my forty days and nights in the desert, in which Satan himself came to tempt me, is a symbol, of course, that shows that the more Power and Light shines through you, the ego—the egoic energy that pervades your creation at this dimension, to a lesser degree other dimensions or planes—will *always* try to find a home in your mind . . . *always*. Therefore, the more your Light shines, the more what is called these little specks of darkness want to rush in and clog up your drains. Hm. Never become lazy. Never become satisfied. Keep wanting more and more of God, selfishly *demand it*, and learn to be vigilant over what thoughts you are allowing into the mind. And be very careful. For, as you awaken, and suddenly you have a vicious and evil thought, the temptation is,

Oh, my God, I've blown it!

That is a judgment, and that is the opposite of Love. And only Love can heal. You simply notice the thought, go,

Ha, yes, I've had those before.

Self-love. Love alone heals the mind. No other technology will work. Forgiveness, self-love, the recognition that no one comes into your sphere by accident, and that in Reality each is an aspect of

The Blessing of Forgiveness

your own being, bringing treasures of gold and frankincense and myrrh, coming to see if you will *receive* those treasures and thereby recognize that each day is the Birth of Christ within you accomplished.

Each time you accept those gifts, and the way you register your acceptance of their gifts — that do indeed come in some rather interesting packages! — the way you recognize it or pay recognition to it is through your willingness to return to your reality, your purpose and function, and to bless that being, that gift-bringer, with the Forgiveness of Christ.

And that forgiveness is not from a mind that thinks it is *above* the other, but recognizes not just the commonality but the *self-same identity*. Do you see the difference? It is very important.

Well, I'll forgive you, you poor simple creature.

No.

I forgive you and bless you because you are who I am, and in Reality there is only one of us present, and together we have the power to bring Heaven to Earth through our holiness — now!

Somebody's got to extend it to the other aspect of themselves.

Why not you? What are *you* waiting for?

If only my mother would forgive me, if only my father would forgive me, and oh gosh that first wife I had and then the fourth husband, oh my goodness. If I could just get things straight with them, then I would get on with being Christ.

So. The pause that was just created seemed to be in the midst of a thought or a direction, and your second exercise is this: Abide at peace and become your own conduit for completing the direction or momentum of the thought that was given just before the pause. Does that make sense to you all? If you will give yourself to that exercise, not just once but often, and in a relaxed mode, you will find that the process takes you to deeper and deeper levels. And those of you that sincerely engage in that process will embark on a series of what you call insights or revelation. And it will assist in refining the deep energies of your own mind. So would you be willing to do that?

[Audience agreement.]

We will see. Remember, there is no privacy!

And, so, it will be appropriate to spend a short time and there will be questions asked by those who are seemingly seated here with bodies.

Therefore, in conclusion of that which has been shared with you this hour, remember: forgiveness, self-love, accepting the *perfection* of each moment in which you discover yourself—for because you have already asked for healing and awakening, the Holy Spirit already goes before you, setting straight your path. Remember, if you knew how to set your path straight, you would have been done a long time ago! So accept the fact that what is occurring is part of a pathway being set before you by an Intelligence or Wisdom that knows far better than your thinking mind how to find the way home. And the more you surrender to each moment's perfection, the more you discover that the eye of the needle is *always* before you, and it's actually a royal highway that carries you to peace.

And so, with that, if you would prepare the technology with the buttons and all of that, we can continue.

Jeshua, as we enter this very profound time of year, is there anything that you would recommend that we hold in our hearts?

A request for winning lottery numbers would be nice.

[Laughter]

Beloved friend, you asked a question that must be filled with levity, so therefore I answered the question with levity.

For listen well to your words: "as we enter this *profound time of year*." What makes it any *more* profound than any other time of year? There's nothing special about your month of December. There are symbols written in the stars that indicate a process of consciousness that's going on in you all the time.

Therefore, rather than ask what should we hold in our hearts *now* as we enter this profound time of year, ask what you can hold in your mind to create the profundity *in every moment* of your experience, until there's no difference between any day of the year — so that every day is the Mass of Christ.

Hm. Got you!
[Laughter]

Always, always! But it makes a lot of room for other people to ask their questions.

A profound sacrifice you have made.
Thank you. I love being your bull's eye.

So does that answer help with you question?

Yes, it does, of course. Thank you.

You see, the tendency of the mind that has become enamored with the thinking of the world will carry the egoic pattern of wanting to shift its frequency by making something more special than something else, even a time frame. And that attempt to create *specialness* is the attempt to create *inequality*. And inequality, as you obviously know, is the opposite of equality. *If you seek unity, give up the need for specialness.* Therefore, this Christmas season, ask not what you can do to bring a profound experience to this time, but reflect on what you must be doing in your consciousness the rest of the year to not experience the profound mystery of life.

That's a very good question. I wonder where it came from?

[Laughter]

The One of us, yes?

Indeed.

So the one of us on this side of the horse race window asked a question, and the one of us on the other side with the green visor (Hmm… I never did like the crown of thorns, I changed it for a green visor) simply raced about and plucked the answer out of the Heart that we all share and has given it to ourselves.

[Laughter]

[Inaudible, audience member speaking]
There are two forms of busyness. One is based in fear, the other

The Blessing of Forgiveness

is based in Love. Which energy is fueling your busyness?

For the one generates the extension of the Kingdom, and the other denies it. Hmm.

Hmm. I believe we have done well with that one. So, any more questions?

In regard to the land we call Shanti Christo, there are many friends coming to this area to participate, and many of us have in our hearts the desire to live more closely to each other, in sharing our growth processes, our loving each other, our understanding of your teachings, and so on. There seem to be many unanswered questions and desires of people who want to come together more closely, quickly, and I wondered if you would address this?

Beloved friend, unanswered questions are *always* a form of *doubt*. Unanswered questions reflect the quality of mind birthed not in God but in the world. The attempt to *hope* that someone else will create the energies necessary in the third dimension to allow you (not necessarily 'you' but the general you) to get what it thinks it needs, closer proximity to other bodies in space, yet being in denial of stepping into the role of what you might call leadership to bring that about. Therefore, understand well, there are many that are being called, and some seem to have answered that call a little sooner than others.

The call to Shanti Christo is the call to awaken first from every obstacle to the presence of Power and Love and Light within their being. To no longer tolerate anything in your consciousness that creates the barriers to the manifestation of the vision that seems to be calling you, and the willingness to take complete responsibility for being the one that manifests it.

For you see, that vibration is a very refined vibration. There is no room for gamesmanship. There is no room for riding on the energies of others. There is no room for denying the power of Christ within yourself. This level of purity is absolutely necessary to bring forth in the field of time, patiently, with quality, the vibrational *field* into which even more can be called, who will experience what you call spontaneous healings of mind, emotion *and* body.

For if you would view that which is a communion or a coming together of souls in the third dimension, and some are relying on others to carry the frequency, you have inequality; you have conflict; you have dissonance. Dissonance weakens the field of energy and the note that would come through the instrument does not carry the power you would wish to behold. That, then, creates resentment in the minds of those who are wanting others to *really* take responsibility, and resentment simply creates in-fighting and death. Therefore, mark these words well: Shanti Christo is the responsibility of everyone who genuinely feels called to its manifestation. Pure and simple. For it is a grand experiment to bring forth the unified field, which is the Christ Mind. Does that make sense to you?

Yes it does.

Therefore, where there is impatience or unanswered questions, help those with that type of energy to remember that they are already looking outside of themselves. They need to come back to right where they are *in the moment*, and allow the process of purification of their own consciousness through forgiveness, through accepting the great power you hold to take care of anything you think looks like a problem around you, or a limitation or a lack — and to handle that *first*. That is, to seek the Kingdom first, from which all things can be added.

That was a rather good question. And, again, we must ponder its source.

Jeshua, I'm reminded of our conversation about co-creating Christs a few months ago, and I wonder if you would extend that conversation somewhat tonight?

Yes. Get - on - with - it.

Think you could make that any clearer?

[Laughter]

No.

[Loud laughter]

All that you need is given, right here, right now. All power under Heaven and Earth resides within the depth of *your* consciousness, which is that which literally is creating what you see around you and what you feel within you. Therefore, claim that power, own it, take it into your being, and *never, never* again allow yourself to deny that you are the One, *the One* Creation of God. And unto you nothing is impossible. Does that help clarify?

[Laughing] You're wonderful!

I am only yourself. Hmm.

So, James, you have no question?

Yeah, I have a question. I'm not sure. Okay, I'll ask.

This one used to always want to take me aside and ask *privately*...

Okay, I'm wanting to ask about this 12/12 stuff. So I've already listened to all these other questions, you see, and then I decide what's the point of asking any questions? The answer is already given.

So what's the answer?

So I'm still curious, that "there's nothing special." I understand that, and yet the mind in me goes, there's this dimension that we operate on and many other dimensions, and energy coming forth in waves...

From where?

From within us.

And so then, what is this 12/12? Speak from the Truth that is within the depth of your being.

The desire for freedom to be made manifest upon the planet, that's coming forth, pouring forth, from a lot of our hearts. From the One Heart. Indeed, beloved brother, beloved friend, we'll have you spoken—for in truth, that which is being called 12/12 symbolizes an expression of the desire of the One Mind to awaken from its dream.

And have we not said that there are four Keys to the Kingdom? And is not the first Desire? Therefore, you see, you did get it, right from the very core of the deepest Truth. It is an expression of the desire of the Mind of Christ to give up the dream of the dreamer. So, you see, you knew after all.

The Blessing of Forgiveness

Mmmm.

Beloved friend, there is only a small trace left of the deep pattern or tendency you've been dissolving through many lifetimes—the pattern and tendency not to trust yourself. And that, then, causes the mind to project onto others a better connection with God than your own. Always have I loved you, and always shall I.

And the day comes quickly when you will look through the eyes of your heart upon me, and no longer see me as above you. You will see in me the shining radiance of *your perfect equality* with me. And then, indeed, the dance can begin.

Yay. Yay!

Yet another timely question. So, how are you all doing?

These (what you call) gatherings of the family will now commence; and will grow. And remember—with patience, without doubt, trusting and allowing the perfect unfoldment.

And if you think it's not unfolding perfectly, don't look outside yourself—go back to the question:

> *Did I love myself today? How many times did I express forgiveness to the world? Am I, pardon the vernacular, cleaning up my own act?*

Because remember, this world is nothing more than a grand act.

So, with that, we can bring this time to a close. For what was needed to be shared has been shared; and the questions asked are the questions also, not necessarily the same words but the same essence, that are carried in many of your brothers and sisters. And, therefore, accept my blessings as my equal. Please take the cloak from my shoulders and the crown from my head, and adorn yourself. And, then, *go and do likewise* for your brother and your sister.

Be you therefore at peace in this moment and always. Be you therefore the Light that lights this world in simplicity and grace and a gentle smile. Be you therefore awakened in this moment to the Truth of your only Reality. Be you therefore of good courage, for I have overcome the world, and in that moment *so did you*. If it is completed in me, it must be completed in you because there is only One of us here. Can you, then, accept that you've already faced Crucifixion? You don't have to repeat the process. Can you accept that the Ascension is already done? Can you be — will you be-the embodiment of the Truth that sets all things free? Can there be any other use of time?

Blessings then be upon the One who shines brightly forever in the Mind of God, who has created us we know not when or how. And *that* truth is inescapable.

My love to each and every one of you, for in you I see the reflection of myself and know the Grandeur and the Radiance and Beauty and Love that my Father is. And I praise my Father without ceasing.

Amen.

The Divine Feminine

Now, we may begin.

And indeed, it is with great joy and also with honor that I come forth in this hour to share with you, to abide with you, to remind you of all that is true within you. I come forth to abide with you on this very special occasion to speak of the heart of that which is so-called *the goddess*, to speak of the heart of that which is called *Christ*, to speak of the heart of that which is called *Divine Mother*, to speak of the heart of that which is called *Abba*, Father.

I come forth, then, in this auspicious hour as you abide together in a place that speaks of the heart through the gentleness of the waves, through the vibration that is felt on the breath of the wind, through the sweetness that pervades the air and the many beautiful flowers. I come forth to abide with you, as you have chosen to come together as seemingly a small group of women upon a tiny speck of dust hurtling itself through space, seemingly so separated from all of life.

And yet I say unto you: You have not come together by accident. You *have* come together because you have well recognized that there is a place within each and every one of you, a certain quality of vibration, a certain aspect of the soul itself that you share in common. Well does it transcend the physicality of the body that you would know as *woman*. And yet it is a vibration that is shared through all those who are currently choosing to *in*carnate—which simply means to bring into expressed form—to incarnate in the very particular and specific vibrations of the feminine body. And to embody the feminine body is indeed to participate in a certain strand or vibration of consciousness that has its own unique features.

Again, we speak here not of the body itself, for the body is merely the effect of a choice that the soul has made to *embody* a certain frequency of the soul. That frequency can be awakened, what you might called tapped into. It can be tapped into by those choosing the frequency or the strand of consciousness that brings forth the male body. But it is much more easily accessed, it is much more constant for those who have chosen in this incarnation to manifest as woman.

Why, then, is this important? For there is a dawning of a New Age in which a certain frequency begins to be again primary as it once was upon the earth plane itself. We're not speaking here of right or wrong, good or bad. We're not here to evoke your beliefs that you have been the victim of some trauma that is causing imbalance on the planet at all. For the world you see is the world of a dream. You, then, have chosen to participate within that dream. And you have chosen to come forth within your own particular culture, your own particular timeframe— in the form of 'woman'— to present yourself with the unique challenge of *overcoming an ancient perception* which currently pervades human consciousness—and that perception is merely that it is the masculine strand that holds the highest value, that must be placed in a role of primacy for decision-making, for running governments and businesses, even for running what is called the household.

And have you not come forth to discover that the power of the Divine Mother, the power of Aba, the power of the Christ, the power of the Goddess—these are just various names for the same thing—is indeed present in its fullness within the strand held deeply within the soul that expresses itself right down to the cells of the body in *the image of woman*.

The Divine Feminine

Beloved friends, I have spoken before, and I will speak again, that for Christ to truly be birthed into the world, woman — the collectivity of women — will need to step forth and declare *their commitment* to again birthing forth the Divine Mother, the Christ . . . to embodying that frequency, and not standing back in the shadows, but stepping forward with boldness and with power to *reclaim* what appears to be lost, to manifest and demonstrate that which is indeed present in *all beings*, whether they be of male or female form.

The time is at hand. The thought that I've just shared with you has already been sent out upon the cosmic air waves, so to speak, to all who are currently embodied in feminine form. It is indeed time to begin to create a more noticeable expression of the joining together of womanhood that expresses, and that is devoted to, and holds sacred the frequency of the Divine Mother, the frequency of compassion, the frequencies of service that truly impacts the planet through the extension of love, through the capacity to *feel deeply*, through the willingness to trust the wisdom of the heart, to trust the wisdom of feeling over the supremacy of *mere* logic or rationality.

Therefore, beloved friends, look around at the seemingly small group gathered in a location that represents a reflection of a time when mankind, when humankind, lived in harmony with all of the earth, the water and the clouds and the creatures thereof, and did not sense any separation between self and other, between dolphin and woman, between cloud and man. When there was a recognition that play and that laughter and that the growing of flowers, the giving of gifts, the singing of songs and the making of music, held supremacy over the organization of armies, the creation of corporations through which the consciousness that has forgotten the feminine seeks to find *dominion* over the world and over the earth.

Look, then, around your seemingly small circle, for each of you has chosen as an infinite soul to choose *this* timeframe, to choose *this* incarnation to make a decision: to take on the embodiment of the feminine form and yet not to succumb to the vibrational pattern of what you call the patriarchy.

Nothing negative here about it and you'll need to let that go through forgiveness. But simply to recognize that a neutral pair of energies has been imbalanced for a while and that a certain segment of the dream has played itself out. And that is all. No reason to make a judgment.

Is it not time, then, for each and every one of you to truly take *ownership of your womanhood* by taking *ownership of your divinity*? Is it not time to bring forth your power by creating a matrix through which women can be attracted to join with you in increasing numbers? All of them dedicated to, shall we say, no longer succumbing, no longer walking next to the patriarchal consciousness, whether it shows up in a male body or female body—but rather to begin to find ways to creatively express what you know to be true: Life is sacred; war has never brought peace; there is no need for *dominion* over the earth, but there is every need to live in *harmony* with the earth as though the human body and the blade of grass are one thing and *each* needs to be wholly respected.

Is it not time to recognize that every child upon your planet cries out to be embraced by the Divine Mother, not the patriarchal mindset that would teach fear and the need for dominion? Is it not time, beloved friends, to *arise and truly incarnate* creatively, beautifully, playfully, powerfully that which the Divine Mother is?

The Divine Feminine

Now, in truth, the Divine Mother and the Christed consciousness are one and the same, for only where wholeness has been decided for within the depth of your own heart and mind can you truly realize who Christ is and what the Divine Mother represents.

It *is* time, beloved friends, for *women* to begin to express awakened consciousness by assuming the position of *authority* upon the planet. Could that be done? Oh yes. Rest assured that if fifty million of your women went to your capitol and simply sat down and said, I'm sorry. We will no longer allow any legislation that supports the instruments of war, you would quickly be joined by another fifty million. Many of them *would be male in form* who would say,

Yes, it's about time.

The point we are seeking to make here is in this transition that *must* come upon the plane of the earth, it is through the form of womanhood that such a change will need to be made. And why? Simply because the patriarchy which has been in the ascendancy for so long is identified as being one and the same as the male form. Therefore even that male who has awakened the female and 'made the two within himself as one' is still viewed by the world as an expression of the patriarchy, and the feminine consciousness of the Christed mind is not necessarily noticed or listened to. Rest assured, then, if one of you would arise and truly begin to serve as a channel for me, it would get much more press, much more attention than the many channels who are in male form who perform this service for me.

Therefore, *look not outside yourself* for the power or the means to heal the things of time and space, to heal the things of your world. Look well into the mirror and ask yourself only this: Am

I willing as a divine spirit to accept what I have set in motion and to no longer succumb to the perception that there is an energy outside of femininity that must still be placed on the seat of primacy?

Is it not time for womanhood to claim what they know to be true — there's never been anything real but love, nothing holds a higher value than compassion and nurturance for all of life — and to begin to speak loudly, to live powerfully, and to make an impact, to begin to ask other women to join *with* you?

Is it not time to stop jabbering over the back fence and rather to take time into your hands and to impact the world by being in perfect attunement to the Divine Mother which *you* have chosen to incarnate — and to be a physical representation thereof?

Indeed, beloved friends, while, yes, you have chosen to come and gather in this most beautiful location of yours to play together, to dance together, to cry together, to laugh together, to swim together with the creatures who know you and love you, rest assured you're also called by a thought that has been sent out as a thread of light to all of womanhood — that it is time to arise, to no longer believe that you can only arise if the patriarchy *allows* you to arise, that it is no longer necessary to wait to see if someone gives you *permission* to gather and become powerful. It is indeed time for womanhood to step to the forefront of the rebirthing of the New Age.

Rest assured, by doing so there will be many in male form who will very quickly also begin to complete that process of reintegrating the feminine into their own consciousness. There are many, many what you would call men on your planet who are still waiting for "Mom" to take charge. And what does that mean? Not their earthly mother, their Divine Mother whom they know their physical mother to be a symbol of.

Therefore, I come forth in this short message to ask you to take time together, to look at the obstacles, the fear, the pervasive places in your consciousness where yet you believe that a patriarchal consciousness is *still* your authority and is *still* the authority of the world. Look not to see who sits in the seats of your government. Remember the power is not out there unless *you* give it away.

What, then, can you do in *your* communities to be the one who arises and calls womanhood to yourself? How can you begin to form those groups that can begin to make impacts in your own communities in ways that have never been done before? . . . With language filled with power that will no longer tolerate a starving child upon your streets, that will no longer tolerate what you call the weapons of destruction in the hands of a teenager, that will no longer tolerate excuses for the waste of monies on the things of war that could be used to nurture and awaken a child. Is it not time to assume responsibility for your own decision to incarnate as woman, the embodiment of the Divine Mother? Will you then stretch your hearts open wide and find ways that you can nurture and embrace creation, even as the Divine Mother embraces you?

Beloved friends, though once I came in the form of a man, understand well that I did so simply because in that timeframe, without the proper what you call 'plumbing' of the body, I would never have been listened unto. And my simple gospel that there is only Love and only Love is real, that you are one with God, would never have been heard or remembered. And the name Jeshua in some feminine form would not have survived the thirty-three years of my life. And in fact, though I would have performed many miracles even in a feminine form, I would hardly have come to have been known outside my little village. That's just the truth of the timeframe. And yet the message I brought is the message of the Divine Mother. It is the message: *Only Love holds any value.* Only life is sacred; not power, not control, and certainly not fear.

Therefore, I come to ask you if *you* are now willing to begin to look more deeply, to playfully see what you can create together, what you can create in your communities to bring forth the gentleness of the Christed consciousness through feminine form so the world — who still believes that bodies are real — can look upon you and remember,

That's the way it is supposed to be upon this gentle and beautiful earth.

Are you willing to give up the value you have placed upon patriarchal consciousness? Are *you* willing to be brazen enough to invite your sisters to join you in the highest vision possible throughout the domains of creation? Are *you* willing to do in *your* timeframe what I was willing to do in *mine* — to look into your consciousness and not allow any part of it to be shaped by ideas that pervade the air of the patriarchal culture in which you live.

Indeed, the time is at hand and the cry has gone out. Think not, then, it is by accident that you gather in a little house on one little corner of a small island. For that island represents the very fire and power of a strong feminine consciousness. Tap into that power. Drink it into yourselves. Create a ritual in which you

The Divine Feminine

open the frequencies of the soul to the Goddess of the island that has birthed the very island upon which you sit. Awaken that passion and that fire within your *own* beingness, and fear it not.

And then decide—look well within your heart and see if what I have told you is true. There is a part of you that remembers as a soul why you have taken birth in a feminine form. There is a part of you that knows that the time is at hand. Look well, then, and see for yourself if this truth is not etched in the depth of your heart and of your mind and of your soul and, verily, of the body itself. The body is but a communication device. Will you, then, declare the truth that is true always and be there for the embodiment of the Divine Mother from whom all things have come forth?

And—above all—rejoice with one another, play with one another, *love you one another*, even as the Mother has first loved you, as she has loved all of us.

And with that, beloved friends, though the message be short, rest assured, you could say there is much within the parameters of the beginning and the end. Know then that I dance with you. Know well that I swim with you. Know that I will be with you in your celebrations of this short time together. For wherever hearts have chosen to come together, to remember the truth, the celebrate the truth, the embody the truth, and to release all things unlike the truth, where any such gather in my name, I am with them. And my name is not Jeshua, as yours is not your surname. *My name is Love. And so is yours.*

Be you, therefore, at peace, beloved and holy sisters of the heart of Christ, the beloved of the Divine Mother.

Be you therefore at peace, and play well. Do what you call the pulling out of all of all the stops. And know that you are never alone and *all power under heaven and earth is with you, now.*

Go then in peace, and thank you for allowing one who once came in male form to participate in your circle. It is indeed an honor.

Amen.

The Holy Instant

Now, we begin.

And indeed, greetings unto you, beloved and holy friends. Indeed, greetings unto — *you*, the only begotten offspring of the Father, of the divine, of Love. In truth there can only be one Being present. In truth there can be only one Reality present. In truth there can only be what is true.

Remember then, always, that regardless of what the eyes of the body show you, you remain as you are created to be. Made indeed in the image of all that God is, and God is but Love. Made in the image of all that the divine is, and the divine is that which extends itself infinitely and eternally from its desire to reveal Love. This is why in each and every moment when Love is expressed through you, innocently, purely and without attachment or investment, you have always experienced a state of peace, a state of ease.

And in that moment, the Holy Instant, you have remembered the truth of who you are. You have seen beyond the body in that split second. You have seen beyond the distance between you and your brother or sister, and you have reveled in the bliss of perfect union. Your life has flowed, in that moment, effortlessly. It has flowed in that moment with absence of anxiety, for there is no thought of tomorrow. There is no memory clung to of the past. There is only this freedom, in which Love, the essence of your being, the essence of Spirit, the essence of all that Christ is — that essence has flowed through the perceptions once held in the mind, the patterns, some of which you might call karma. It has seeped through the blockages in the cells of the body, and the body itself has gestured in such a way that Love has been extended into the world.

It is in just such moments that the fullness of the spiritual journey is completed. For that journey is only completed in the act of remembrance of what you have always been, that which alone you must always be. In a very real sense then, there is no evolution, there are no strategies that can get you to God, except forgetting that you are separate from God. And that forgetting, that moment, again that Holy Instance that brings you into the fullness of your being, into that state of remembrance is *in those moments* when Love has flowed through you to the world, in any of its myriad expressions, and there has been no thought to cloud it. That thought being

> *I wonder what I will receive from this giving? How will I be able to shape the universe around me in order to extract what I believe I need by being loving?*

In those moments of pure love, there is only perfect union, perfect innocence. Forgiveness itself cannot even enter such a moment, for there has been no condemnation.

In each and every moment then, when you choose to surrender the self and allow Love to be present, you have elected to live in the Kingdom. And *you* are the one who *receives* the joy, the enjoyment of witnessing Love's effects. And where do you experience the effects of Love if not *first* in your own being?

As Love flows from Spirit through the soul, through the basics or the matrix of the persona, the personalities, as it moves through the emotional field and out through the body and into the world, you must be the first that receives it. And this is what brings us to the heart and soul of what we would seek to share with you in this hour: It is not your doing that can establish you in the Kingdom. It is not your accomplishment that evolves you into the consciousness of God. It is first and foremost in your willingness to receive the reality of the Kingdom, which is the experience of Love flowing through you.

This is what I meant when I once said, 'Seek first the Kingdom within and all these things shall be added unto you.' For in every striving that the mind enters into, based on its forgetting of who it truly is, what is sought is not money, not fame, not what you call your soulmates, not the accomplishment of great tasks; what the mind is looking for is Love. That is the only thing the mind can seek, for that is the only thing it was designed to give.

Know then, that in all tasks you choose to undertake you will be motivated by only one of two things: Love or fear. Fear can come with many masks, it can even wear a smile. Fear is born, and accesses your matrix or conduit which propels your activity, when you have forgotten to seek first the Kingdom. When you have forgotten to open and receive the Love that is forever present for you, in every moment and *under all conditions*.

As you choose then to cultivate the decision to seek first the Kingdom, the tasks that you enjoin can be flooded with the Love that would flow through you, as That Voice guides your creativity, your choices, your decisions. And yet Love colors things a little differently than does fear. And this is a very important distinction. Fear will seek the results of the task, for fear believes that by the accomplishment of the task something will be received that the egoic mind believes is lacking. Love will extend itself into the task, knowing that the true treasures are the moments of relationship that arise along the journey, that become those moments in which souls can heal through learning the practice of forgiveness—of looking with innocence, of looking the shadow in the eye and choosing Love instead.

So Love is not results-oriented, Love is Love-oriented. Fear is results-oriented. This can only mean that when you enjoin any task and you find yourself depressed, frustrated that the result has not been achieved, the mind or your awareness has slipped over into the territory of fear.

Fear is an energy that believes Love is lacking, that union with God is lacking. It is run by the beliefs such as

I must earn my union with God. Performance is what will bring it to me,

and all of the rest. What would it be like then, if you learned to look upon each of your days through new eyes? What would it be like if you looked upon each of your days as merely the opportunity to discern and distinguish which of those two camps your awareness is falling into:

Is it fear that is propelling me, or is it truly Love?

How again to know the difference? If you are feeling frustrated, anxious, depressed and all of the rest and you notice finally that the mind is fixated on the results you have decided should be achieved are not being achieved, and therefore a feeling state emerges, you know that you have entered into that task from fear.

Now, what then do you do? Well, it is very, very simple. You get one of those whips and you take off the shirt and then you beat yourself with it. You take out an ad in your newspapers with your picture, saying,

Behold, an unworthy one!

You have all taken out those ads in your papers, you know.

In truth, because Love does not condemn, and because Love makes all things new, even as what would be birthed from fear is arising, all you need do is stop and seek first the Kingdom and abide there until you feel restored — until you are sober, you are in your right Mind, you have received Love for yourself for no other reason than that it is good to do so. And then, as you bring your mind to the task, simply ask that Love guide the way. That Love restore your mind and awareness to the reality that the great jewels that will be presented is not so much in the result that the mind would picture, but the moments of relationship in which Love can change a pattern of perception that has been running that mind: yours, or your brother's or sister's.

Those moments are referred to as Holy Instances, and they are the crown jewel of creation. For only in such moments — and they always occur in relationship — in those moments does the reality of Love come to be more solidly established as the basis of your consciousness. And this can be nothing more than a return to what is true.

The message then, that we would seek to share with you in this hour, is a message that can transform your life. Even if it is flowing beautifully, it can flow more deeply, for there can be no limit or bottom to the depth of God. Paradoxically then, because you are the created and not the Creator, you — just like I once had the opportunity when I walked your planet as a man — you have the opportunity to translate how you see time, what you perceive its value is and utilize it to deepen your direct remembrance of the Presence of God . . . by cultivating the choice for Love, the remembrance of Love, the dedication to Love, the surrender to Love, by learning to seek first the Kingdom and allowing each of your tasks to *flow* from that choice.

When you awaken in the morning, there is a task before you. You are going to have to lift the head from the pillow, you are going to have to put your feet on your floor and you are going to have to decide which direction those feet are going to carry the body. Is that not true? And yet, how often have you awakened in the morning and immediately the mind has gotten busy with all of your to-do lists and unbeknown to you, at times the voice for fear has been the main magnet that lifts your head from the pillow, puts your feet on the floor and you're off, running scared. Hm.

> *If I don't get this done, what will they think? Oh my God, what about that? Oh!*

And it goes on and on and on.

Once, many years ago, I spoke to this, my beloved brother, that one of the greatest things he could ever learn to do was to 'wait on the Lord', which means to seek first the Kingdom before the eyes opened fully. Just in that moment when you know you have awakened from your slumber, something is going to be activating the body — a thought, an impulse — and in that moment, before the eyes open, to remember God. To choose Love. To cultivate feeling it as it penetrates your soul, your mind, your emotions, your personality, and even the tissues and cells of the body. To make sure you are not bringing with you anything that you took to sleep with you, that is a judgment of a brother or a sister. To make sure that what is going to move the body that day will not be fear but Love.

Now that sounds rather simple, doesn't it? Hm. I would then challenge you to keep a list, a calendar by your bed and when you have gotten up in the morning, and you have taken your shower or done whatever you have done, or made your coffee, or made your fourteen phone calls before you eat — before you leave the house, pause and ask yourself,

> *Did I remember to abide in Love before I opened my eyes this morning?*

Keep track! It will be most humbling, for this simple act is the most difficult to achieve. To learn to choose for Love at the most subtle moment, as consciousness is beginning to focus into the physical domain every morning. To remember Love *then*, is indeed a difficult task and yet the mind can be trained more and more to make that choice.

Would you be willing to enjoin such a challenge? Remember, we will be watching!

{Audience laughter}

And always, beloved friends, without judgment, without condemnation.

The mind that has awakened comes to each moment anew. The mind that has been fully established in the remembrance of the Truth that is true always, comes to each moment fresh and anew. It is not possible for such a mind to lose patience with a brother or a sister, for lack of patience can only arise from fear. From a mind that has forgotten the Kingdom and therefore is keeping score, adding up the past, it has the results about what it thinks the future should be, and this other one obviously isn't fitting in quite right.

But Love looks with innocence upon each created being, for Love sees that they look not upon another but upon themselves. This can only mean that you are your brother and sister's keeper because you *are* your brother and your sister. This is why I have often said that your greatest saviors are those that really push your buttons. For do they not call you to the task of patience? Do they not call you to the task to uncover more deeply within what must be preventing Love from showing up? For Love also provides you the wisdom to know what to do with each moment. Luckily, and by grace, it is not given you to know what your brother or sister needs. Luckily, by grace, it is not given for you to be the *caretaker* of another but the *keeper* of another. And what could that mean?

To *keep* another means to hold in your consciousness the image and remembrance of them as the perfection of the truth that they truly are. And within each soul is the spark of Light, which is the Christ Mind, which is that Mind, whole and complete, made in the image of God. To keep another is to be the *friend* of that one. And a friend indeed is one who sees the other as Christ in the journey of remembering Christ and holds them in that Light until they can hold it for themselves.

The Holy Instant

A friend is one who does not condemn or judge. Therefore, the greatest state of consciousness is to be a friend to the world. But because it is not given to you to know what your brother or sister needs, you are released from the burden of believing that *you* must know. And in any moment, as you cultivate the ability to remember first the Kingdom, to receive Love, to abide in that place, where Grace can speak to you, the Holy Spirit—that part of the mind that remains perfectly united with God and is heard when all the other dimension of your being are at peace (and peace requires non- attachment to the world)—in that moment, the Holy Spirit will guide your words, your gestures, your choices and decisions. You might find yourself speaking, you might find yourself being silent. There is no handbook, you would say, for each moment arises fresh and pure.

Seek then, seek within your own consciousness to desire the Kingdom more than anything else. More than any result you have ever imagined. More than any richness or fame or what have you. Above all created things, seek to nurture within yourself the passionate desire to have released from your consciousness anything that impedes it from being entrained to seek first the Kingdom.

So that more and more and more with each moment, even as you live in this physical dimension and the body moves about on your planet, and decisions and bills to pay and all the rest arises, but the mind goes

Oh, I think I'll just receive Love. I'll just receive Love. I think I'll just abide in the remembrance that only Love is real.

Ah, drink that sweet, sweet, clear water, if you will, and *then* enjoin the task before you. For in that way you'll begin to access more and more clearly the guidance and wisdom of the Holy Spirit.

But what might arise in the mind that could prevent it from wanting the Holy Spirit to hold authority over the mind? Fear. Fear. For the guidance of the Holy Spirit is not circumvented by the rules of the world. It is not contained in the guidelines that you have learned from the world. In this sense then, *wisdom is radically free*. To be guided then by the Holy Spirit is to grow into a state of being, which could be called 'radical freedom', in which no part of the mind is caught up in fearing what the perceptions of the world might be. The body-mind itself, the personality, the soul itself, becomes fully the servant of something invisible, something quiet, and yet something which in its wisdom knows how Love can serve this moment, whatever that moment may be.

To embody such a state of consciousness is the true goal that you are all seeking. It is the true result that the soul wants. It is the result for which the fearful mind creates substitutes or idols, by translating the results of its plans, its endeavours, forgetting that only Love is real.

That the very purpose of time and creation is but the creation of contexts in which Holy Instances can arise and Love can be remembered and restored to the minds and hearts of friends.

Peace then comes into your life and into your relationships, into your nations, and eventually into the world when only friendship exists — true friendship — whether it be between political leader and one casting a ballot, whether it be between husband and wife, man-man, woman-woman, man-dog, cat-dog, it doesn't really matter, all forms of relationships — when they are established in friendship — *then is peace restored. Then can Heaven come to earth.*

The Holy Instant

As you learn then to want Love alone to be your guide, as you learn then to recognize that it is only in those moments, when Love has successfully (shall we say) out-shouted the voice of fear—and you know you have had thousands of those moments, in which Love has been enacted through you and you are left with the sweetest, most sublime feeling of fulfillment—when you want more and more those moments, until those moments are established as the ocean from which the waves of your life emerge, you become the gift to this world that can transform this world and *is* transforming it. Rest assured, indeed, beloved friends, each and every one of you in those moments, when through your desire, your cultivation, your practice, if you will, you have remembered Love—you have already begun to transform this world. You have taken up the cross of crucifixion, which is a symbol of the burdens of this world, and you have demonstrated that there is another way. You have literally become the embodiment that models to each brother and sister that behold, we don't need to spin in the same circles. There *is* another way and that way is Love.

Take a moment then—and I would indeed ask this of all who would hear these words now—to take this moment and turn your awareness within and imagine that you are speaking to yourself, to your very soul. Pause right now, and give yourself deep appreciation, deep gratitude, honor yourself for every single moment when only Love has led your way, when only Love has been extended. And then ask of yourself this simple question,

Would I desire more of such moments or fewer of such moments?

If the answer is 'more', simply say, "Yes," to that desire. Invite the Holy Spirit to become increasingly the authority of your consciousness. Ask It to become the magnet that pulls your attention to It before each decision. For the Holy Spirit can only come to you to the degree that you invite It in.

Your are beginning to near a certain time upon your calendar, called the Christmas Season. As I have shared with you many times before, rest assured it was not the month of my birth into the world, but it became a symbol, a symbol for the birth of Light into the world, even as my life has become the most universal symbol in the human psyche for what *must* occur within each created mind. For that which alone can truly fulfil the journey of the soul, the remembrance that only the truth can be true, the recognition that Christ — which is simply a word for the purity of consciousness untainted by fear, resting in the remembrance that only Love is real — the symbol, then, of my life, celebrated at this time of Christmas should be enjoined with prayer, with silence, with celebration with true friends of the Heart, those who would be willing to join with you in celebration of every loving thought that the two of you, or the four of you, or the hundred of you, have experienced in your lives.

Imagine a Christmas celebration in which you tell stories, one to the other, of the moments in which you knew that Love had acted through you. You have in your phrase, where you are living here on this speck of earth, the 'talking of the story' — 'talk story'? What wonder stories those would be! If you would come together at that time of Christmas and listen to each other share the moments in which they know in their heart and soul that God, Who is but Love, moved through them and spoke or gestured out into the world. Would that not be a Christmas to enjoy? Would it not be a time of great celebration as you honor the great courage of each and every one of you in that group, to have chosen the courageous act of enacting Love instead of the products of fear? In which you set aside all remembrance or trace of thought of the moments in which you think you failed and did only one thing, to celebrate those moments of Love — for in those moments, you were enacting the incarnation of Christ. You were literally living what the symbol of my life is all about. The moment in which Christ came to earth, to the body and to the mind, and was birthed into the world. For each Holy Instant is Christmas.

Would you be willing to have such a gathering? Does it not create within you a tickle of excitement and enjoyment? What indeed if you wrapped your presents of your gifts to one another and placed only in them a piece of paper, or several pages, in which you write to the other all the moments you can remember in which you were the recipient of love through that other? Hm. Would that not be to give a precious gift? — to help remind your brother and sister that they have indeed succeeded, probably far often than they even know.

Would you be willing to do that? Does that sound as like it would be a good gift to give to another? What could you possibly give from the material plane that could possibly create such a permanent gifting? What could possibly match the gift to another's consciousness that *you have experienced the gift of Love through them*? What could inspire that soul to know the truth of who they really are, to be inspired, to cultivate even more moments in which they have been the birther of Christ?

Therefore, we would leave it up to you, everyone hearing these words, to set about, to take what you call the initiative, to experiment with this whole new approach to your Christmas Season. Rest assured, it will not look good on your gross national product but is it not time for the national product to cease being so gross?

{Laughter}

Is it not time for it to shine with the brilliance that can heal the wounds and the fears, the distrust, the judgments? Is it not time for Christ to be birthed into the world? To truly celebrate, to be celebrated, to be praised? And how can you praise Christ? Certainly not by attending your functions in which all attention is put on me. But rather that you create those functions in which the attention and praise of Love is offered to the brothers and sisters through which Love has touched your soul. This is to truly honor the Christ that must come cosmically.

I am indeed one who looks forward to the day when the life of Jeshua ben Joseph has been entirely forgotten by everyone, for they are too busy *being* that one, celebrating the living Presence of the Christ Mind amongst themselves. So that if my name comes up, someone says,

> Oh yes, that was a brother. I think he was here a long time ago. Let's get back on with what we are doing.

That would be different indeed.

I have looked upon that which is called the religion based in my name. And rest assured, it has brought sadness to my heart and soul, *for my message has not been heard and received.* They have projected their praise onto the messenger and not the message.

In your Christmas Season, when so many gather in their buildings to remember *me*, to turn their attention to a historical event that occurred so long ago, what I see occurring in their souls is the attempt of fear to project the Christ Mind *outside of themselves*, to keep it at a safe distance; and when they leave those buildings, no transformation has occurred. If you would remember me on that day, please remember me only as a friend of the world, a brother equal to each and everyone of you and not above you in any way. If you would honor me in any way whatsoever, please remind your brothers and sisters of the times in which they have been the bearers and gifters of Christ to you, the times that your soul has been uplifted and inspired, the times that you have healed and transformed in their presence as they took the courageous act to let Love be given through them. In this way, my heart will indeed be gladdened. This is the transformation that must come to your planet and to your human consciousness.

Only fear projects the essence of truth outside of you and keeps it at an arm's length. There is not anything that this world has to offer that you need. There is no material thing that can fulfill you. Indeed there is no relationship that can fulfill you. There is nothing that can fulfill you. You are already fulfilled in your perfect union with God. Your only task is to cultivate more and more the remembrance of that, for it is again in those moments, when Love has flowed through you, that you have experienced your deepest peace, your greatest joy, and your deepest certainty of who you are. That is the sublime state, that is the sublime drug that you are seeking with every results-based picture, dream, endeavor. Does that make sense for you?

Christmas, the mass of the Christ. Why not be a mass of Christs, celebrating each other? Hm? And then some day a critical mass will be reached and no more criticism will be necessary.

Indeed beloved friends, there are times when many of us would wish indeed, to merely find the way that we could blow what you call the veils of ignorance, or forgetting, away from you. We see when you suffer, we feel when you suffer, because we are one with you, because you are an aspect of the Christ Mind, the one and Holy Son or offspring of God. And yet in your sovereignty, there is no one who can remove those veils for you. They remain in place only because you choose them. Look well then to see, with great innocence, what must be at work when you choose to move from fear and not Love. For everything that arises, arises only within the sovereignty of your own awareness. And you can only see outside, what you have chosen to see inside. And you can only place a judgment on what is outside because you have already placed it on yourself.

When you experience impatience with a brother or a sister, it is because there is a place within you that has been impatient with yourself. There is a place within you that is calling for your own forgiveness and love. And as you find that place within and bring it to Light within, and extend that Love to that part of you, you will suddenly find yourself feeling only patience with another. Any time you look upon anyone or anything with judgment it can only be a projection of that reflection within *you*, that you have judged.

When you perceive lack in the world, it is because in that moment, you have chosen a perception that lack lives within *you*. What then restores consciousness to holy sight? By now you should know — the decision to choose for the Kingdom, to simply stop and to remember.

To drink that Love for yourself, to drink it well into yourself and then, as you open your eyes again, suddenly, the world you see has changed. For Love indeed does change and heal all things. And this is the *one and only purpose that time and space can have*. There is nothing here to be accomplished, save this: The restoration of the memory of God in the seat of the soul, so that it becomes perfectly centred as the conduit through which Love creates.

The Holy Instant

Then indeed, as you enjoin your plans, you know that you are merely creating contexts in which Holy Instances can arise. Reasons to celebrate! Reasons to dance! Reason to give praise! Reason to give thankfulness! You are looking for moments as excuses to have a party. You are not solving world hunger. You are not ending child abuse. You are looking in all the contexts you enter into for the moments of relationship in which Love is restored to the minds of those, in that moment of relationship. And of course, *that* is what ends world hunger, that is what ends child abuse, that is what ends everything that is not Love.

Look then, in all of your endeavors, not to achieve a result that *you* have decided, but rather allow Love to be the stream that carries you and energizes you for that journey within that context. And be vigilant for the moments of connection with another, playing with you in that context, in which the remembrance of Love can occur.

We would end then this simple message with one more exercise, if you will. When you rest your head upon your pillow at night, and you notice that the body's tiredness is beginning to call your attention to fuzziness—as indeed the soul begins to retract its focus on the physical domain and journey into other dimensions while the body sleeps—in just that transition time, just before you drift off to sleep, ask yourself this,

> *How many Holy Instances did I give myself permission to experience this day?*

Rest assured there will be times when a big fat zero is the answer. Know you those days? Doesn't it look then like the world is very bleak? {Jeshua chuckles} You can only see on the outside what you have seen already within.

That indeed is a very, very powerful exercise and I do not give it lightly for, hear me well, that very question was given to me by one of my Essene teachers when I was but fourteen years of age. And it was given to me, to my fourteen-year-old mind, *every day* for two years! "Have you remembered, last night when you went to sleep, young Jeshua ben Joseph, you who think you know all the answers? Did you remember to count the moments of your Holy Instances?" And as you well know at fourteen, there are often many zeros and many 'No, I forgot again!'

And yet, as finally I began to taste the transformative power of that remembrance, I began to realize the wisdom of my teacher and more and more, each evening, I *relished* that time, just before consciousness slips away, the remembrance of the Holy Instances I had experienced that day. Those moments became the sweetest of candies, they became the most valuable moments in my consciousness. And from about the time of fifteen and a half or so onward, it became the foundation of my purpose for rising from my sleep each morning. To cultivate contexts in which Holy Instances could arise. That is what fueled my entire ministry, as it has been called, that is what fueled my entire field of desire until it was so established, so deeply established, that I couldn't shake it off. And everything in my field of consciousness, the sovereignty of my own soul, just as you have your own field of sovereignty, became fully enjoined, aligned with, dedicated to, committed to one thing — the taste of the Holy Instant. Everything in my mind, everything in my gesturing became willingly transformed to serve the experience of the Holy Instant.

Let me give you a little proof of that. Have you ever wondered why I have ceaselessly sought to join with minds, such as this my beloved brother, in order to find contexts in which I might communicate with and join with my brothers and sisters? Is it because I see you as, shall we say, deluded? In need of fixing? Hardly! The impetus of all the work that I do to reach into the field of human consciousness is born of the taste and the knowledge that the Holy Instant is as a pearl beyond all price.

For in the Holy Instant is the perfect remembrance of God.

So now the cat is out of the bag!

Imagine this... Imagine that you are walking this earth of yours, associated with a bag of molecules you call the body, for the last time. And everything in you is oriented only to the creation of contexts in which the Holy Instant can be experienced between yourself and your brothers and sisters—that is the only thing that lifts your head from your pillow each morning. What would such a life be like? Hm. Something worth pondering, is it not? And it is perfectly okay that you have had occasional moments when you wanted something else. {Jeshua chuckles} Proof of your guilt, proof of your depravity, proof of your failure, proof that the world really is a bad place—and all of the rest. Those are just movies in a theatre—you know, those theatres you have, where you go and watch the movie and there are ten or twelve different screens and you get to select which images are going to vibrate in your nervous system? All of those choices in the mind are just movies. Just movies. Just movies. Sooner or later you get tired of looking at the screen and you put down the popcorn thing that you have been eating out of. You dump your napkin on the floor and you leave the theatre and you go outside, back to Reality.

And Reality is the Presence of Love. The great joy of relationship. Those moments in which two have come together—and this is of course the great, great height of possibilities you have—when any two or more have come together in my Name. What did that mean? In the vibration of recognizing that only the Holy Instant could possibly hold any value at all, as a means to justify celebration and praise. The reality of the Presence of God.

Between the time of now and the day of Christmas, you have a certain number of days, in which you are going to be lifting your head from the pillow and placing it on your pillow again that night. What if you were to dedicate the time between now and that day of Christmas to enjoin the practices I have suggested for you in this hour, in which you learn to relish and desire with great passion the cultivation of attention on the making of Holy Instances with your brothers and sisters. Might it not carry you into a celebration of Christmas unlike any other, in which you will be able to relish the degree of wisdom and the depth of joy that you have allowed to grow within your consciousness, as you have trained it to not settle for movies?

This then in truth completes the message that I would seek to extend to you, those of you that are here present, and those of you that will be present when you hear these spoken words.

Christmas is indeed a precious gift—if it is held in the right frame of mind. If it is utilized for its right purpose: the Mass of Christ. To join with brothers and sisters in celebration of every Holy Instant that has shined through you into the darkness of this insane world. For remember, the world was birthed in the desire to try to create something that is opposite of the Kingdom. And from that very moment Love has worked to transform that dream, to restore reality.

Celebrate your successes, celebrate your Holy Instances, by celebrating each other's loving thoughts, loving gestures, the moments in which each of you has birthed and expressed Christ.

And so to those of you who are present in this hour, how are all of you doing?

Good.

Hm. Hm. Good!
Would any of you then be willing to commit publicly to becoming an addict of Holy Instances? You can have what you call your support groups.

{Laughter.}

And who would want recovery? See how much more addicted you can support each other to become! Indeed.

And with that, actually, a suggestion has been given you not by accident, though it sounded a bit 'tongue in cheek', I believe you say. This is only a phrase I can use; I have neither tongue nor cheek.

What would it be like to transform the purpose of your friendships, your relationships, so that the primary goal was to support one another in remembering to cultivate Holy Instances? Hm. Would that transform your business meetings? For this is truly the power and the gift of your relationships and your friendships. To find and seek out, to attract to yourself and to settle for nothing less than relationships based in the holy desire to cultivate the ability to remember Love, so that Holy Instances can be increasingly experienced in the moments of your coming together. Would that be a worthy goal?

{Audience agreement}

Well, it's up to you! It's up to you!

Heed well, then, what was just said. That you would seek out, that you would desire to attract to yourself, and that you would be willing to settle no longer for less than relationships based in that commitment.

Well, there goes my grandfather.

It does not mean that you reject another. It means you look wisely at where you place your time and energy. Which relationships that you know in your life now really begin to (what you call) fit that bill? Which ones could fit that bill if only you extended yourself a little bit and set up a 'business meeting' for the business of talking about how your relationship can be transformed and cultivated into one that helps grow each other's capacity for experiencing Holy Instances. Rest assured, if you let your attention even now begin to sift through all the relationships you have, you'll see right away which ones perhaps you should be giving less time and energy to, and those that could indeed bear much good fruit with just a little bit of exertion on your part. Would you be willing to do that?

And so, there are a few among you who have questions being held in the mind. In fact, a few of those questions have been held so much in the mind that what was being shared at times was bouncing off the questions. {Jeshua chuckles.}

Which of you would then would like to ask a question that can be explored? Hm. Not going to ask it then, huh? Hm. And is it not because there is a part of you that knows the answer has already been given? This can only mean that there is really never a time that the questions being held in your mind are really 'private'.

Did you know that when something is going on in your life and you have a question turning over in your mind and you walk into a room of a party, everybody instantly already knows what's going on in your consciousness? Now, through social training, they will pretend they don't. There is no such thing as privacy, for all minds are but fragments of one Mind. There is nothing unknown by everyone. Ha!... Hardly then worth the effort trying to hide.

Indeed...

So, how are all of you doing? Has it been worth your time to be gathered together for this hour?

{Audience agreement}

I am afraid that I must report to you that it has not been worth mine — I have none! I can only hope that it has been worth my brother's time for allowing me to use both mind and body.

Know then, as we bring this brief time to a close, please know this: I love you. I love you in a preciousness and to a depth that it is not possible to understand until your consciousness is so fully established in the desire for Holy Instances, that those moments are woven together like beads tightly on a string, so much so that time itself dissolves and there is only one continuous Holy Instant. For in that moment you will have become so fully established in the Christ Mind that you will know me perfectly, for you will have known yourself; and together we will have known the Father and we will have been known of the Father; and our journey into dreams will have been transformed into the celebration of the Kingdom of Heaven, knowing neither birth nor death nor limitation.

I am but your friend and your brother and rest assured, please, I am *not* apart from where you are. And in the quiet of your heart and mind you can join with me whenever you want, for you will have no difficulty in convincing me to utilize relationship for creating the Holy Instant. I am always willing to play!

This can only mean that it is not possible for you to be alone. It is not possible for you to have nowhere to go in which you are not seen and heard and recognized and restored to the gift and power of Love. Please, then, remember that I am but friend and brother to the world, calling all that would but listen to the glorious celebration of the Mass of Christ.

And with that then indeed, merry Christmas to each and everyone of you.

Amen.

The Holy Spirit

Now we begin.

Indeed, greetings unto you yet once again, beloved and holy children of Light divine. For in Truth you are created before time is and indeed even now you abide in that which is timeless and eternal, has never been born and will never taste death.

I know that's confusing to the mind of the world; but indeed if you would know Truth, you must in a sense turn the back of your awareness on all perceptions and ideas that the world has sought to teach you. For the world is nothing but the reflection of the limited perception that the holy and only child of God can indeed be separate from all that our Father is. And from that belief the world that you have experienced many times has been born.

Therefore, if you would know the Truth of the Kingdom, turn the back of your consciousness to every perception the world has taught you. It is indeed the meaning of "turning the other cheek."

It does not mean that if one would slap you on the left side, to let them slap you on the right, but rather to see and understand how the perceptions of the world have created for you—and you all know what I mean by this—the experience of being slapped on the left cheek.

You know what I mean—a bit of suffering here and there, a bit of disappointment, expectations not achieved—and some of you are well aware of how many times you have gathered together the molecules of dust to form a body only to find that it has not kept you safe and, therefore, it has gone back to the dust of the ground again.

Would you be willing, would you in Truth be willing to turn the other cheek? That is, to turn away for just a moment from the perceptions born of the world and to ask that Truth be restored to you? For indeed a primary perception your world would have you learn and hold is that you already know what Truth is.

That it can be measured, it can be tasted. That it is like a box that contains many other beliefs about birth and life and death, the meaning of special relationships, the hope that in the body you can find freedom. *That you are here to be "the creators of your own reality" is utter nonsense.* Utter and complete nonsense.

Let no one say unto you that you are here to create your reality, for you are here but to allow the expression, unimpeded, of the only reality that could ever be: The reality of the perfect and holy union of Father and child, of God and child, of Love and the extension of love.

There is no effort in this. Effort comes from resistance to the simplicity of the only Truth that can ever be: that you are but Love and that is all. And your function and your purpose rest solely in the extension of the Love you are. For indeed, as you give that love away, you will know that you have received it.

How can you create a reality that is the basis of your eternal being? You cannot. It is given unto you freely. For though you can be one with God, you have not created God. But God has

The Holy Spirit

created you, for the Son is the offspring of that Light of Love divine, and you find your purpose and your function and your fulfillment every time you turn the cheek away from the world, so that the head and the eyes of the heart turn with it and you behold a different Voice, a Voice that speaks softly, speaks gently, without fear, without longing, without anxiety. A Voice that does not tell you in the future you will find the peace you seek, but a Voice that whispers so gently: *You are already the peace you seek.*

The world cannot bring it to you and this world cannot take it from you. And yet, it is in the giving of it that you will know that you possess it eternally.

Now, what does that mean in practical terms?

It means this—and if you would contemplate this one thought daily, it will bring many shifts to your perceptions, healing to the perception. The thought is simply this: there cannot be at any time, at any place, in any dimension of this drama—this dream that some of you think is real—*there cannot be a single set of circumstances that hold the power to destroy your right to choose peace.* Nothing.

Not the birth and death of a child. Not the loss of a relationship. Not a bankruptcy. Not major cataclysms upon this Earth. Not a steak that has been cooked too long. Hmm. Not one thing can steal from you the freedom of the choice given unto you that rests in the essence of your mind and your heart to choose peace. Nothing. And if that is true—and I assure you that it is—it also means this: there can be no special circumstances you need to achieve before you can choose to be the peace that you seek.

Shucks. But, Jeshua, that takes the whole game away. It brings a stop to the world.

Good. Good. For in Truth, when the world is stopped — which means the mind stops spinning in its attempt to create its reality that it thinks will bring it peace, and allows itself to become as a servant of the heart, in which stillness abides and in which peace has never been lost, and through which the Love of God seeks to be extended through you like great rays of Light that would caress and enfold the whole of creation — indeed, when the mind is set at rest and it becomes the servant of the heart, then everything vanishes right before your eyes. Hardly.

And yet, it does, doesn't it? Because what you see is an act of *perception,* and it could well be said that all you ever see and all that you ever experience is your reaction to what you choose to perceive is in front of you. And what you perceive is directly related to what you choose to believe. What you *choose* to believe.

You do not believe something because the data of the physical senses prove that it exists. Rather, the data of the physical senses reflect to you the belief you have chosen.

I cannot walk upon hot coals.

Nonsense.

I cannot possibly walk on water.

That is nonsense, too, unless of course you believe it — in which case it would be rather wise to use a boat.

I cannot survive in this world unless I find someone to give me a job.

The Holy Spirit

Do you know what it is like to be in a plane, as you would perceive it, removed from this physical plane, and to look into your culture and see these buildings that you have? For every day countless thousands of people line up to sign their name on some kind of a form so that some authority sends them a few shekels of golden coins — and you call it unemployment.

No one is unemployed save by their total free choice to be in that experience. Why? Not because there are not enough jobs to go around, but because nobody needs a job unless they believe they do. Within you there is great creativity because within you the Kingdom of Heaven lies, and there is no one on the face of this planet who cannot allow that creativity to spring forth, to break through the limitations that you have held onto for so long, and indeed find a way to contribute — to extend your love into this world — in a way that provides you with a roof over your head and food for the belly. No one.

But those who believe that there is an authority outside themselves with a greater power, will hold the belief that reality means that you find a job and you go to it from nine to five until somebody tells you that you can go home. It is just a belief, and that is all it is. And that belief creates a limitation within your own consciousness, and everything you do and experience becomes somehow enmeshed with the limitations of that one simple belief.

Does that make sense to you?

And yet, what takes place and has already occurred in several of you:

> *If what Jeshua is saying to me now is true, and I happen to be one who works nine to five, knowing full well here in the secrecy of my mind, I don't really like it,*

What comes up if what I am saying is true? Is it not fear?

> *The set of circumstances, I see, have become limiting to me. I chose them at a time when I didn't know that another choice was available to me. Now I am beginning to learn. Now I am beginning to awaken. Oh my goodness, could I possibly let go of the belief that another must give me a job so that I can sustain myself?*

The question I would ask you is simply this: *what do you want?*

Seems simple enough doesn't it? What do you want? For what you want you *will* experience. That is the golden rule of how consciousness works and you are consciousness. You have wanted a job as much as you have wanted a physical body. As much as you have wanted special relationships. As much as you wanted to believe that you must eat a certain food three times a day every day of your life in order to sustain your health; you can't dare change it. It all comes from a want because the perception has told you that what you are perceiving and believing can make you safe and keep you safe.

There is only one problem: the soul you are knows that it is unlimited forever, and you can deny what the soul knows only so long. True, you could deny it for lifetimes but sooner or later a movement begins, for the soul cannot be denied forever. And it will begin to press out against every belief and perception you have ever carried, and it will make you question everything you have held to be true and valuable—and yes, that will bring up the experience you call fear. But on just the other side of that narrow ring of fear there is a perception that would see it as a blessing—as a blessing that comes directly from God. For the soul presses you to examine the beliefs you have carried that have created the world of your experience, but not your reality. And the soul asks you,

The Holy Spirit

Allow my wisdom into the small part of the mind that clings to the belief, and if you would but trust my guidance, I will show you how to walk through that ring of fear.

For indeed within each and every one of you lies equally what is also within me.

I am not a savior above anyone in this room, much less anyone on this planet. And if I could learn how to return and listen to that one Voice and trust It and It alone, so can you. That is why I ask you: *What is it that you want?*

For notice that I have never said there is something wrong with having a job. It's a matter of the belief you carry that creates that situation for you. Are you happy? Are you contributing all that you want to contribute? Not what somebody tells you could contribute, but what you want to contribute? It is the only place you can find freedom. The only place you can access the door to freedom is in your heart, not in your mind that is full of perceptions based on limitations and separation from God.

You are already all that I am. You are unlimited forever. There are no boundaries to what can be done through you. None at all, because that bag of dust that you call yourself is just that — it's a bag of dust called the body — and you have used the infinite power given to the Son by the Father to create body after body into shapes so that it does certain things for you. Unfortunately, it always seems to break down. Within you, within *you* lies the very power to perform miracles. Ultimately, the greatest of miracles is to allow the Voice of the Holy Spirit to be your Guide in all things. Now, the Holy Spirit resides as fully within you as it does the one who sits next to you, as much as that one Teacher resides within and with me.

And as you learn to turn every decision over to that Voice, to trust It without analyzing It, you will come to be nothing less but the perfect manifestation of the Holy Spirit. The perfect manifestation of the Holy Spirit. Here you realize that you are one with God and therefore, one with all of creation. There is no place else that you can understand that. You can *think about* it in your mind, but until you *live it* through your heart you don't really understand what it means to be one with God. Indeed.

Those of you that feel there are limitations in your life, first ask of yourself,

> *What has this given to me? Why did I seek it out?*

Not out of a sense of blame. That has nothing at all to do with it. For you have attracted unto yourself experiences for no other reason than you wanted to — you wanted to. There is no other reason. You have even chosen to be born into a world of uncertainty, of things that change, of things that seem to be chaotic, because you wanted the experience of uncertainty and chaos and madness.

And in that place within you in which you chose to create not reality but an experience called "this world" — in that place alone can you choose anew by choosing to relinquish the world you have created in error, and ask the one Teacher to release from you every limitation and block to the presence of God's Love that dwells within you. To begin to see, to allow that one Teacher to teach you that you are unlimited forever and that indeed never once have you ever existed within a body.

Whew. My goodness, such a statement.

> *But, Jeshua, I know I am in this body. I can tell.*

The Holy Spirit

You are experiencing the effect of a perception you have chosen to believe in, and that is all. And that means you are free to choose anew, to come to see that you exist outside of the body, that the body in a sense arises within you and not the other way around; and that you animate and activate this bag of dust with every thought you think and every perception that you have held dear to yourself, so dear and so long that you have forgotten what they were.

And if that is true—and I assure you most assuredly that it is true—it means that even now you can begin to choose anew. Indeed, to look out upon all that you have experienced and to acknowledge for yourself that you have never known what any of it was really for. Yes, you tried to use relationships for this; it didn't work. You tried to use careers for that; it didn't work.

It takes great humility to totally accept that if you are experiencing limitation in your life, it means the perceptions you have held so dear have failed you. And because they are not you, you are free to discard them at any time, to realize that perhaps after all you haven't been your own best teacher. And you have learned perceptions without looking at the life lived by those that would teach you, and you have not seen *their* pain and *their* limitation and *their* confusion, and therefore you have bought the things they have sought to teach you.

Why not discard all of them and start over? Why not be willing, just for the heck of it, to trust a Voice that is wholly unseen and the hearing of which may come softly and gently as a nudge in the heart? Only after much listening does it begin to take on the shape of a voice that you can have complete conversations with. Why not? Give it a try.

What would it mean if tomorrow morning when you woke up, you looked around yourself and said,

I don't know what a single thing is for and I am no longer under the sway of the habits of my perceptions. Holy Spirit, unseen — and I don't even know if I really believe in You, but what the heck — what is the best thing that I can do in this moment?

Some of you will end up sitting in bed all day waiting to hear, and yet when that happens it's because you have not acknowledged that you have heard. *For every time you ask the question of the Holy Spirit, an answer is immediately given.* Immediately. It requires only your willingness to hear with different ears.

It is much like turning off the stereos in your house, asking the children to sit and be quiet, waiting for the cars that are going by to complete their journey, closing the windows so no noise enters, and when all is quiet and you have released even your need or your fear or your expectations over what the answer will be, when you become and come to that place of quiet, the Voice of the Holy One rings loud and clear, like notes struck from a crystal glass.

Those of you in this room that have been putting that into practice in your own way know what I mean, because there is a resonance as the answer is given, and you know, not in the mind but in the heart. You might find that you need to get up, take a shower, get dressed and go to work. But you might just find that you need to go and find a meadow of flowers, to lie beneath the rays of the sun, to dig your fingers into the soil of this beloved and holy Earth and just say to God,

   I give it all up.

Maybe.

I cannot possibly come to you as a brother and as a friend

The Holy Spirit

if I come with a prescription and a set of proscriptions about what is real, what is true and what you have to do. That would mean that the power is not in you—and I assure you that it is. If you are made in the image of God, it means that you *are* the reflection of perfect freedom.

Does that make sense to you?

And that is why, no matter what you have ever chosen to dream, the One I have called Abba has never interfered with your dream; because if He did He would be acknowledging that your dream is real. That would be a mistaken perception and I can assure you that our Father does not have mistaken perceptions.

Therefore, He sits gently, perceiving only the purity of your being, the unlimitedness and the radiance of the Light within you, and He waits while you utilize your freedom to dream dreams of limitation and separation from God. And that means that there is no such thing as what you call (some of you) karma:

> *Well, I'm just here because of the result of everything I've thought and done, and I'm going to have to live through this in order to balance the scales.*

If you decree it, it will be so.

It means that every single moment, and closer to you than your own breath, the fullness of the Kingdom of Heaven resides. It does not need to be earned. It needs only to be allowed. Accept it and receive.

Now, how can that happen?

If you cling to your baseline perception and belief that you are a separate entity, that you are just this little being that has been born and will die, if you believe you are guilty of any sin whatsoever, if you believe that you really are not in union with God, then when you seek to reach for the Kingdom, you only push it away.

Therefore, to allow and to accept and to receive — and therefore to manifest the Kingdom of Heaven on Earth as it is in Heaven — requires that you begin with the perception which is indeed now translated into knowledge that you are right here and right now the holy and only child of God, that you rest in perfect union with your Father forever, that you are not the body, and that space and time is not your home. You cannot earn it because it is given freely. Only when you begin with that acknowledgement can true change come to your life. And why?

Because if you have built a world in error on the perception that you are separate from God, it means that everything you have experienced in some sense reflects or is the residue or the effect of that belief, and as you choose to take a deep swallow and walk through the ring of fear and leap into the infinite pool of union with God, the water is quite fine, the temperature is always perfect and no one cares if you wear a suit or not — how would you put a bathing suit on an infinite Light? When you choose to do that, it means that something begins to move through you called Light and it must necessarily transform every aspect of what you call your experience. So, you see, those of you that have houses and cars, if you will allow this to happen tomorrow, does it all mean they are all going to be gone and you are going to be living in a cave in the Himalayas?

Not at all. It means that the Holy Spirit will change your perception of everything you think you see and understand. And what is it translated into?

The Holy Spirit

No longer objects, whether they be relationships, careers or automobiles or what have you that can somehow *bring* pleasure or fulfillment to you, but rather they become nothing more than tools that serve the holy Son of God as he allows love to be extended through him or her and to be given to the world, until the great ray of Light within you shines so brightly that it envelops the whole of creation. And *you* are the one who brings it back gently and lovingly and lays it in the lap of God. *You* are the saviors and the salvation of all worlds.

The question remains, are you willing to allow every limiting perception to be released? Are you willing to allow that fear that really only comes from a very small part of the mind that I have described like a gnat shouting at the vastness of space, that you have unwittingly allowed yourself to believe is the real you? That is the only place fear comes up—in the mind of the gnat trying to resist the vastness of space that is filled with God's wonder and love. Why not let the little gnat be fearful but continue to make a new choice?

You cannot rid yourself of fear and then walk on. Acknowledge that the fear is there. See what small part it plays. Acknowledge the grander reality of who you are—and *then* walk on. It is how one walks on water, upon hot coals. It is how you walk through the need to communicate with another when something is not going right. It is how you walk through having a limitation of golden coins. It is the key to everything. Everything.

I once said unto you that there are four very precious keys— keys to the Kingdom— and they are but simply this: desire, intention, allowance and surrender. Those keys are found as the foundation for every experience that you have ever drawn to yourself. Somewhere you have wanted it.

You have held the intention of experiencing it. You have opened yourself to allow the molecules of this physical dimension to form themselves into that which will be the messengers of the experience you want, and then you have given yourself to it as a bride to a bridegroom. Unfortunately, sometimes you say,

Why did I marry you?

[Laughter]

Desire... Do not seek to be without it but seek to understand its source. Desire is absolutely critical. Without it, there is no creation. *You* are the offspring of desire, the offspring of Love, which is our Father, to extend Itself infinitely. That is what has created the rays of Light called the Sons of God, and you are a ray of Light. Nothing more and nothing less. Desire, then, is always the first factor in awakening or changing anything.

Intention... Only when there is uncompromising intention can you begin to draw the resources to you that can begin to carry you from where you are to where you would be, whether you are talking about getting a new job or awakening to your oneness with God.

Many of you have mastered those two keys. Some of you are just beginning to see how the use of those two keys wittingly or unwittingly has always formed your experience.

But the transformation begins with the use and the subsequent mastery of the third key of *allowing*. When your desire has been for nothing less than the unlimitedness that comes from your acknowledgement of your union with God —

The Holy Spirit

total and complete remembrance of who you are in reality—and when your intention is for nothing but that, the whole of your life begins to serve as the means that will carry you through each illusion that has been blocking you.

And when your choice to become vulnerable—for indeed your safety can only be found in your choice to *be* vulnerable—to be innocent of heart, to acknowledge you have never known what a single thing is for, when you begin to allow that unseen Intelligence that I have called the Holy Spirit to reshape everything in your experience so that it becomes the means for your awakening, then miracles begin. Some of you know what I am talking about. Suddenly resources come to you. Masters come to your life who are well to be heeded, and indeed you don't even know how it happened, and yet it has been the direct effect of your desire and your intention and your willingness to allow a different Teacher to teach you. And as you begin to rest in the mastery of that key of allowing, something rather magical happens that can in no way be explained completely in the languages of your world.

For *allowance* itself slips gently into *surrender*. It is nothing you have done; but out of your choice to allow, the one Teacher given of the Father takes the final step for you. And allowance becomes surrender, and in surrender the peace you are becomes manifested in every moment of your experience. Others begin to see it and feel it and are attracted to you, and when they ask you,

>*How did you get to where you are?*

you just shrug your shoulders and go,

Hmm, I'm not too sure. Somebody must have done it for me, because of myself I can do nothing; but I have learned that through me, my Father can do all things.

Surrender... Surrender is the state that everyone in this world truly desires above everything else but they have forgotten what it is, where it comes from, and what it would mean. For only in surrender can peace come to be known fully.

What, then, begins to change? You will look into the mirror and you will not see yourself any longer. You will not even say "my body." You might say "a body."

I suppose I should put some clothing on the body since there are some in this world who still actually think that to look upon a body without clothing is an embarrassing and sinful thing.

Have you ever been embarrassed by looking at the dust of the ground? Hmm. Odd perceptions.

But if somebody looks at the real me without my clothing on...

No one can look at the "real" you save one who Is awakened to the Christ that dwells within them, who will look well past the body anyway.

Indeed, precious friends, something quite magical happens. It is something felt and known cognitively. That is, your perception has wholly been changed and though the body seems to move about much as it always has — or perhaps not move about, it really doesn't matter much — there is a new intelligence if you will, an awakening that is infusing the use of that body.

The Holy Spirit

It no longer becomes used as something that you seek to draw power or pleasure to yourself through. It no longer becomes something that you think can keep you safe. You no longer seek to beautify it just so others will smile, so you feel you've been accepted—called self-worth. The body becomes nothing but a bag of dust formed by the Mind of Christ into a tool for the extension of love—not to *receive* love, to *extend* love—and only because the world in which you find yourself is totally wrapped up in believing in the reality of bodies. That is obvious.

Love can never be received through the body. Never. It can be *extended* through the body so that another who believes they are a body can understand or feel the reflection of that love.

But truly, love can only be received through an open heart and a quiet mind. And it will not be received from the objects of your world . . . it is received by the descent of grace into your heart.

For ultimately, the only relationship that is real is the holy relationship between the Son and His Father—or between the Daughter and the Goddess, if you will. I really don't care what words you use, and I'll let you in on a secret: my Father doesn't care either.

Is all of this making sense to you?

It means that every time that you are not at peace, every time you know doubt, every time you taste loneliness, it is because a part of you is choosing to withhold your love. It is the only thing that is causing it. And you are choosing to listen to the little gnat shouting at space,

I can't be happy until this person,

singled out of the whole of creation,

> *comes and bows down before me and says, "I love you." Then I might choose to be happy.*

While all around you there are hearts and minds crying out for you, the arisen Christ, to extend your love.

Some of you well know that in the moment you choose to set aside all your worries and concerns and be busy extending your love, suddenly all the problems go away.

> *Where did they go? I still have to make that mortgage payment.*

It's still there, but the reaction to it is not there. It will be taken care of as long as you are busy never allowing yourself to restrict the extension of your love. For the lack you are experience in your life is the effect and the direct result of the choices you have made previously to withhold your love.

I'm sorry, but that is the simplicity and Truth of it all. There is no other answer. It is not because of your parents. It is not because of your upbringing. It is not because you were born black in a white man's world. It's not because you were born a man in a woman's world.

Jeshua, I'd like a specific example.

Of what?

Jeshua, I need some sort of concrete example here. If I am in a place where I have grown to be something that I have looked at and said, "Oh, I don't want this." Right at that point am I to turn away from it and start extending love?

The Holy Spirit

There are two things here. First, you have created a vast generalization.

Yeah, I was trying not to be too wordy.

But, by so doing, you have overlooked the simple fact that what you experience is right in front of you. Do not make the logical mistake of extending to generalizations.

Now, that's the first thing. By turning away—and I use the analogy or metaphor of turning the cheek from the world—I am talking about turning your consciousness from the perceptions you have chosen to believe in. It does not mean that if you are driving your car and there is someone in the wrong lane coming at you, and you say,

> *I don't want this,*

that all you need do is turn the other cheek. Do you see? Obviously you need to take action to correct that. In the sense of lack you are never without knowingness about the road you are headed in. Does that make sense to you?

Yes.

Therefore, to look and see the car that's coming down the lane at you and to take corrective action means already you have turned your attention from the perceptions you have held that had begun to draw that experience to you. It may be, for instance, that money is the root of all evil, therefore I'll live in lack because that is more spiritual.

> *Well, yes, it would be nice to turn the heat on in the middle of winter, but after all that would take money and money is evil.*

Very well, have fun shivering.

I am speaking, precious friend, of looking at the *perceptions* from which your world of experience has been built. To look at it honestly and openly, not by beating yourself and saying,

> *Oh, my God, what have I done? What a jerk I have been. Oh, gees, I'll never get this straight.*

Not at all. Look at it with the innocence of a child. When a child in a sandbox begins to build a castle — and if you've seen one — they sit back and they look at it and they go,

> *Not right, [motion of knocking it down}*

and they start over. They don't beat themselves. They don't go in and say,

> *Father, whip me for I have sinned.*

They just start over.

I get confused, I think, when it comes to relationships.

You are not the only one.

[Laughter]

I know. I know. We all have lots of trouble with relationships, but you have been teaching us especially strongly the last couple of weeks that relationships are the avenue of the greatest growth and understanding, and today I have reason to believe that someone I love very much,

The Holy Spirit

one of my children, has stolen from me. And things like that have happened in the past but I thought they were long past. And driving over here I was really upset for quite a few miles. It's a good thing I have a long way to drive.

Anyway, I was really upset for quite a few miles and then I suddenly realized that I didn't have to do this. I didn't have to make myself upset because I didn't decide to do the thing.

Someone else decided to do the thing. I felt like what I needed to do was just let it go. But then I get confused because I feel hurt because it is someone who is my child and who I raised and loved. And I don't want to judge him and say he is a horrible person and he will always be a horrible person, but I do feel like I need to move out of the way of this kind of treatment. I can do that without being judgmental, can't I?

Can you?

Well, I seem to have a hard time knowing when exactly to do that — to let it go and not feel heartbroken that my son would do this to me, his mother. I want to let all that go.

Now you are beginning to get to it. Listen to what you said and say it again. What you just said.

I want to let go of this being hurt.

No, that's not quite it. The sentence with the words "son" and "mother" ...

Well, I have this feeling. I feel so badly that my son has done this to me, his mother, who loved him so.

Is that perception not the source of your hurt?

Yes. But is he not my son? Is that just my perception?

Yes. It has been said in many forms and ways that your children are never your children. They are your equal. They are a soul. They happen to have a bag of dust for a while. Within this world, ones that come from your womb, you feed and clothe them, you nurture them. They are never yours.

That's the first mistake of perception: to use the word "my" ... It is a word of possessiveness. You cannot possess a soul. You cannot possess the body.

Is there no special bond? More special than any other bond?

When you seek a specialness of a bond in one relationship over others, you will have already decreed that you believe in separation from God and that you are in need of something that only a certain other can bring to you.

Right. That's right.

Yes, it is. Now that doesn't mean—I am not drawing the conclusion therefore—that you go callously in the world. Of course not. But everyone in this room has been your mother, your brother, your sister, your father, your grandparent. You name the relationship. You have all enacted them a million times.

The point here, beloved friend, is exactly the whole point of our theme tonight.

Are you willing to release every perception you have learned of the world and to allow the one Teacher to re-teach you? Your pain comes always and only as a result of how you react to your perception of what you think you see.

The Holy Spirit

Does that make sense to you?

Yes.

Let me give you a concrete example. I would be willing to bet that if I asked everyone in this room and everyone on the planet, if an angry or fearful or judgmental thought or perhaps a victimhood thought like, "Why me?" — if I were to ask them if such thoughts were to arise if one of your own friends kissed you on the cheek as a way of identifying them to your government, and then the government took you and tied you to a cross and then pounded nails through your hands and feet... In that experience would such thoughts arise?

Yes.

Had there been a trace of identification in my mind to the perceptions that the world would believe in — that such a thing is barbaric, that it ought not be done, that it is a cruel thing and how could they do this to me, anyway? All I wanted to do was pat them on the back and love them — if one iota of such a thought would have entered my mind, *the whole demonstration would have failed miserably and I would have died a death like anyone else.* There would have been no resurrection, no ascension and I might not even be here to blend with this mind to communicate with you. That is how powerful your perceptions are. And your pain can come only from the soil of the perceptions you have believed are true because you believe they would bring you something that you are lacking.

There are many, many in your world who actually believe that if they come together and create a baby, that somehow the relationship will become happy. Hmm?

Yes.

It usually doesn't work!

Now, precious friend, do you see how essential this is? What you are bringing up is not just yours. The dilemma, if you will, of every single mind that has bought into this little spinning vortex called your world and gotten caught up in it—which is only to get caught up with believing certain perceptions—the relationship of a son to a mother will never, under any circumstances, hold the key to the mother's fulfillment or peace. And we can also say it is the same for the father, of course.

The one who has stolen is not your son, but is our Father's son.

And that act is a cry for help. For in Truth an awakened, healed, sane mind knows it need never take anything. Hmm?

Yes.

That is the act in itself. The hurt you are experiencing must always come from the perception that you've described.

> *How could my son do this to me, his loving mother that has done so much?*

And you have.

But, precious friend, though it may seem a little confronting, I don't mean it that way. Let me ask you this. How could you begin to hold the perception that because you have sought to extend love to another, they must repay that by behaving in a way *you* would conclude is an inappropriate expression of love toward you? Do you see?

The Holy Spirit

I don't think it is so much that as my question to myself is: Why would he hurt me? It's like a deliberate hurt, as opposed to ignoring me or just going off and doing his own thing. I have not felt like I've held on to the children who were born through me, like I was clutching them to me.

Precious friend, clutching has nothing to do ultimately with the emotions or with the physical hands. It has to do with your perception. And the clearest indication that you have clutched is the very description you used:

Why would my son do this to his loving mother?

The hurt does not come from the act. It comes from your perception of what the act means. Do you see?

How can I let it go?

By choosing to do so. To begin to see — and this is why I have talked about vigilance — to see that when an action takes place in your experience, to notice your reaction and to see that it must come from your perception of it.

Let me give you an example. Two people are asked to stand before a crowd of ten thousand and to give a speech on the meaning of love. The first walks on — and they don't have time to prepare, by the way — the first walks onto the stage and looks out and does what you would call the wetting of the pants... [Laughter]

...and has to literally be carried off the stage, stiff as a board, barely breathing. The second comes and stands on the stage and looks out on all those sea of faces and goes,

They are just like me.

Then says to the ten thousand,

I love you. That's the meaning.

and walks off skipping and singing, and everyone stands and gives him an ovation.

Nothing has been different except their perception. Nothing at all. The situation is the same. Nobody did anything to change anything except the infinite power of one mind chose a different perception. And you have a saying in your world: "That made all the difference in the world." The perception of separation and fear has created a lot of differences in your world.

And you are being asked now to choose a different way of seeing, a way that doesn't ignore what's taking place but sees through it and beyond it, to choose only peace no matter what, to understand that none of your perceptions have ever been wholly true, and that is why you need in each situation to ask the Holy Spirit to teach you the meaning of your experience. He will not keep it from you whenever you are willing first to acknowledge that you are reacting not to what happened but to your perception of what happened, and to ask it to be replaced. There is something for you to see in this experience, something you would be asked to do in this experience for the soul — who is actually crying for help and doesn't even know it, who lives in a state of consciousness of the virtual lack of self-worth, lack of power, is totally confused, sees the world as threatening and overwhelming; and because of his perceived powerlessness, believes that he must secretly take what he thinks will bring some pleasure. Totally insane perception. The act is a cry for help. Nothing more, nothing less. And your son has not hurt you, because your son cannot fulfill you.

The Holy Spirit

The questions that you have asked and asked often, if you were to go through and lay them out one after the other since first we began to communicate, you would find that there has been a progression, a movement to subtler and subtler levels of the same question. And in this moment, beloved friend, you are getting about as close to the hub of the wheel as you can. You are just beginning to touch the place of truly seeing — that's not thinking, that's a seeing that involves the wholeness of your being — that your perceptions have created everything you have experienced, and your perceptions are the only thing that have been creating limitation in your life, and that *you* are *not* your perceptions. That is the great point of freedom. And you have come to understand that you are not, never have been, the thoughts of the world. You just got a little entranced with them, that's all, and you are free even now to choose anew.

Guidance will be given in how to deal with that situation, for turning of the cheek doesn't mean that you let the car hit you head on. It never meant that. It means that you choose to listen to another Voice rather than the reactivity of your perceptions to know how to deal with it effectively.

Sometimes dealing with it effectively means you have to turn the tables of the money-changers over rather than asking them to reconsider.

And indeed, you may be asked to confront wholly this other soul who is not "your son" and to say,

> *I'm sorry. That's enough. If you choose to be in a disrespectful relationship to me, you therefore cannot be in relationship to me, because I am a child of God and I am to be honored as such.*

That would create a little shockwave in that one's mind.

> *Are you trying to tell me...? But you're my mother. You are supposed to always be here, no matter what I do.*

Why? Who said that was true? Do you see?

Yes, but what is the price to pay? That was coming to me just before I drove up here.

Now, do you know why it was beginning to come to you?

Yes. No. Why?

Because, as you stated earlier, you began to shift, did you not?

Right.

And that shift brought you into a place of openness where a friend of yours could begin to whisper and indeed said unto you,

> *You know, this would be a very good thing to bring up tonight. It will help a lot more than just yourself.*

You know, I didn't hear that part.

[Laughter]

Right.

Are you okay with all of that so far?

Yes. Fine really, thank you.

There are a lot of others in this room that are thanking you for bringing it up.

The Holy Spirit

You know, I think a lot of us have read or heard that children that come to us—and significant relationships with the opposite sex—that we might have had relationships with in past lives and we need to work out whatever problems it is that keep bringing us back together, which has always tended to stop me from saying, "Okay, that's it. Enough is enough." Because I felt like if I didn't resolve whatever it was in this life, it would come haunt me in another one.

How do you resolve anything?

Forgive it? Somehow, reach some understanding that, is this an appropriate behavior and we just don't do this to each other? I don't know.

Stop right there. It is very important.

The statement you just made comes out of at least a loosely held perception indeed that resolution must require an agreement reached by two infinitely free minds; and that only when an agreement is reached that precipitates a change can there be a resolution.

That already is to create a limitation. What if you resolve within yourself to not participate in that energy any longer? For indeed, that which you call the drawing back of souls to keep playing the same old circles of dramas over and over—and some of you know what that's like even in this life, you keep drawing to yourselves relationships and somehow they all have the same flavor to them—it is because something in you believes that you are supposed to draw that to you. Which means to say that you want it because you are unwilling to accept that you are worthy of the fullness of the Kingdom.

What if you were to resolve that simple perceptual error? And to understand that if that other mind wants to continue they are going to have to find somebody else to play with, because you are in a sense taking a quantum leap and only choose to allow those who resonate in the understanding of what it means to extend love—that those are the only beings you want in your life? That is not a selfish thing. That is called wisdom.

Do you see the difference there?

That's really mind-boggling.

I hope so. For when the mind is boggled, the wisdom of the heart can begin to seep through its cracks, finally.

You mean, that nowhere is it written or said by God that we have to resolve all issues together? We can resolve them in our own mind and that's enough?

It could be said that the only place *you* can resolve it is in your own mind. And because all minds are joined, as you heal your misperceptions you have already enlightened the weight of *all* minds.

And you have made it easier for other minds that, in the moment it may appear that you are walking away from and they have to find somebody else to play their games with, you have given them something that they witness. And what is it? The freedom to make a different choice. And the seed becomes planted, and guess Who comes along to start watering it? So that eventually that seed will also break through the soil of the mind and begin to flower, and that mind will begin to make new choices. You may not physically see the effect of the new choices, but you will feel it at the level of the soul.

The Holy Spirit

When I have said that relationships are the grandest and most significant of things you have, it is because they will reflect to you every perception you have ever held. And when you are willing to extend love to embrace the one in front of you unconditionally, without need or expectation of any kind, then you have used the very soil that you created in error—that is, bodies floating about in space—you have allowed it to become translated into the means through which you manifest the power of a new choice and therefore experience the healing of your own mind.

It takes great courage initially to begin to see that sometimes in letting go and walking away you have done the grandest thing you could do for yourself and for another. God has never etched into stone that you have to pound on each others' heads for lifetimes. Your purpose and function is to extend love, to allow yourself to receive love.

Therefore, look well at your life—and do this honestly, of course, so that you are not falling into the trap of trying to please the gnat, but be very honest—to see:

Where am I not allowing myself to receive the beauty of God's love and where am I withholding it?

If that means that the picture surrounding you has to be shaken up and changed, if you are moving toward love at the guidance of the Holy Spirit, you can rest assured that the changes that come serve the highest and best for everyone. I almost said "everyone concerned" but then you would think it's just those limited minds involved in that one situation, and that is not the Truth. All minds that exist are affected by everything you think and do.

Hmm... What a responsibility. And it seems like it until you understand that all you are asked to do is to live as though you are not an ego. And the only other choice is to understand that you are just a — to use your popular word — channel for God's love and that there is one Teacher that knows and will guide you, and Whose guidance is certain.

Fair enough?

Yes, very fair.

Does all of that help?

Yes. A lot to chew on.

Rather, just embrace it a lot. The mind likes to chew; the heart likes to swallow.

[Laughter]

No bad. So, how are we all doing?

Great.

Look, then, around yourself. Now, just take a moment. Allow your eyes to rest with the eyes of another.

If that means that three of you need to do that, that's fine. Allow, truly allow yourself to let the bag of dust relax. Stop holding it as an armor that would separate you from your brother or sister. Block not the angel of air; it is the presence of the Holy Spirit.

It doesn't require any talking.

The Holy Spirit

Who is before you? What you are looking at is not a body. It is not a body. Allow your heart to see through your eyes and through the eyes of the one in front of you. Look deeper and deeper still. Look beyond the body. Look beyond the personality that you think is attached to that body. Look beyond any imagined or known history associated with that being, that body, that mind, that personality.

And if you would allow yourself, you can begin to see the reflection of rays of Light. Allow those rays of Light to shine ever more brightly and let the attention of your seeing be only on those rays. And if thoughts arise in the mind, they are just clouds passing through the sky. They don't mean anything.

Look deeper still. Look without fear. Look without expectation. Look without a perception of any kind that you would cling to. And in your own way in this moment ask your Father to show you the reality of the one before you.

Is it not Love that waits to be recognized in the one before you? Is it not the Love in you that waits to be unleashed, to recognize the Love in the one in front of you?

In your vulnerability is your only safety. Let Love rejoice in the perception of Itself given wholly as a ray of Light seeded into each soul since before time is.

You are that Light and you are that Love, and from Its power you can see the Truth in everyone and everything. And, right now, know that as you allow yourself to see the love in the one in front of you, you are providing healing for them because they can rest in the vulnerability required to see you as you choose to see them. And in seeing them as the holy ray of Light that is the Father's Son, you have finally seen yourself.

> *Love alone is the essence of all that is real. Choose, then, love. And abandon perceptions born of fear.*

Are you your brother's keeper? Oh yes, because you are the one you see. Love them as your Father has first loved you and *you* are the Light that lights this world and returns the whole of creation into the hands of the One Who has sent us forth. The Kingdom of Heaven is no further from you than your choice to see your brother through the eyes of Christ.

Now, indeed because the Holy Spirit translates everything you have ever created in error, it means that even the body has already been translated. Would you not then reach out and place your hand upon the heart of the one in front of you? Indeed.

And who said miracles can't come through you? The hand, look at the hand you think is yours. Look at it. It's not yours. It's made of dust. It's nothing more than a means of communicating the Love you are. Allow, then, that infinite Love to be transmitted through your hand. Let that Light penetrate the heart of the one in front of you.

Embrace the Heart of Christ . . . with the Love that *is* Christ. Let it go. Let the perceptions of separation go. Let the veil of the world go. Reclaim your innocence.

Reclaim your union. We are infinite and unlimited. We are the Thought of Love in form. The world can bind us no longer, for we choose to see with different eyes, the eyes of an awakened heart that rests in vulnerability; and through us the Father does all things.

The Holy Spirit

And to you who sit in front of me, you are the presence of my Redeemer and I give the fullness of my Love to you in gratitude for your beauty, your wisdom, your strength, your courage. I see you as healed and I see you as perfect and I am with you always. For though bodies can be moved from place to place, minds that join in Love cannot taste separation.

And now all things are made new again and our union is restored on Earth as it is already in Heaven, and therefore *we* bring Heaven to Earth with our choice to extend and teach only Love.

Indeed. Some of you are feeling some heat and warmth in the area of the heart, to put it mildly. Those of you that know how to open the inner eyes and see not just physical bodies, the room is full—helpers, guides, teachers, call them what you will; masters indeed. For wherever two or more are gathered in my name, there I am in the midst of them, and therefore we come and we will give you our strength until yours is as certain as ours. It is called friendship.

There. Now there *is* Light. And there is really nothing left to do except to give one another a big hug.

Now, I have a favor to ask all of you. And the favor is simply this: you need not make it public, but some of you had some rather interesting experiences just then.

As you return home this evening please don't make the mistake of saying to yourself or to another,

Oh, what Jeshua did tonight . . .

But rather say unto yourself,

Oh, what I, the holy Son of God, have allowed tonight.

For healing can only come when you use the power given unto you, even as power was given unto me, to choose to be the fountain which spreads the healing grace of Love into this world. To see no one as above you ever again, for right where you are—and this is the Truth of reality—you are not in the body. You are as much with me above this world as any master has ever been. You are as much with me now as this my beloved brother is when he allows himself to let go of the limitations of mind and therefore sees me and feels me and sits down on the bench with me. You, too, are there now.

And the only barrier—the only barrier—between you and the fullness of the miracles that would be manifested through you into this world, the only barriers are the obstacles called perceptions that you have not learned in the Kingdom but in the world.

A very good exercise to do is to sit down with a piece of paper and just begin to let yourself, allow yourself, to list perceptions you have been taught and have believed. Look at them and ask yourself,

Is that limiting?

And if the answer is yes, rest assured the Holy Spirit did not teach it to you.

And then on the other side of the page draw a line and write the belief or perception that would be the antithesis of the limited belief. Not a new exercise by any means, but a very powerful one. And if it speaks to you of unlimitedness, if you allow the cells of the body to feel joy, rest assured you've been listening to a new Teacher.

The Holy Spirit

You are already everything I ever represented to anyone, and in reality you are but a brother, a sister, a friend who comes to everyone you see in your life as a messenger from God. And God is but Love and therefore has but one message to deliver. Never limit what I can do through you, for if you would but choose to join with me—and I am but a manifestation of the Holy Spirit—understand well that there are no limitations to what I can do through you when you are willing to be the witness of miracles in your life. And when you have seen those miracles, you must then acknowledge that they have been done unto you.

No one comes save but to answer their own call to awaken. You have come unto this hour, some of you many times, some of you for the first time, but understand well the level of the soul: you have come to answer your own call, and you have chosen me to be the brother and the friend through whom you will be finally willing to receive the reflection of the Truth that lies in you. Because in a part of you, you know that there is safety in abiding with me and you have not yet extended that sense of safety to abiding with yourself.

And that is why I have said that in all things—and I give this as my promise unto you—I will give you the fullness of my strength until yours is as certain as mine. And then indeed we walk together. And where two of us have gathered together the power of Christ becomes unlimited forever.

Walk with me then with every breath, every thought, and I shall not leave you until together every mind and every heart has reawakened to the presence of Christ that dwells within us all.

Remember that miracles shorten the need for time. Think not then that together miracles cannot bring an end to the need for time itself.

And when you have chosen with me to embrace the whole of creation as your very body; when you have seen that this planet is not outside of the need of your love; when you see that your brother or sister or your sons or daughters are but aspects of your own self and need to be embraced with the Love of Christ that dwells with you, and you are the only one that can bring it to them; when you join with me in embracing the whole of all worlds that have ever arisen; then indeed together we will translate those worlds into the reflections of the Kingdom of Heaven—and time will be no more. Suffering will have been forgotten. Birth and death shall be no more.

And for a brief moment that is wholly out of time, all things will rejoice and reflect the Light of the perfection of God's Love for His creation. And His creations will have reflected what He intended when He brought you into being, and then the purpose of creation itself will have been fulfilled and there will be naught but the Light, and Light eternal: that which is, that which was, and that which forever shall be. Heaven waits on your choice to believe it, to acknowledge it and to live it. The only barrier between your world and the Kingdom of Heaven is the choice to hold on to perceptions created not in Heaven but in the world.

And your brothers and sisters wait for you to arise from sleep and to never tolerate error in yourself again, so that *you* become that one who walks through this world as the presence of Love and thereby extends to everyone you see an opportunity to make a new choice. For if you would have your brother and sister awaken from the chains that bind them, you must release your own first. You are your brother's salvation, as he is yours.

The Holy Spirit

Join with me, then, on the park bench, and indeed I will come and I will talk with you whenever you want. Isn't that right? And indeed, through you, if you are willing, we will awaken every mind of our brothers whom we love. Hmm. Why not? You've tried everything else.

[Laughter]

Wherever you are, wherever you are, the fullness of the Kingdom is present. All power is given unto you in that moment to be the Light that lights the world. You may think you will have to be a little crazy at first. Perfectly okay.

It may feel like you are dreaming just a little bit. When you have been asleep dreaming this long, waking from the dream *seems* like a dream. Don't let it stop you. Don't say,

> *Oh, I've got to get my feet back on the ground. Only angels can fly.*

Hmm. That's just a perception. The angels know better.

Precious friends, let there in this evening then be no more questions that need to arise, for all questions have already been answered.

And if you have come here with a question, ask it of yourself and then touch the place provided for you by the glance of your brother's eyes and his or her hand upon your heart, and go to that place; and there the one Teacher Who also taught me is waiting for you, and there you will find the answers that you seek.

And yet, when all questions have been asked and they have all been answered, there is still but one choice left to make:

Since I am in Truth the holy child of God Himself, will I choose to live it?

I have said elsewhere that there is only one question you need ask of yourself: what do you really and truly want? When you are clear about that, everything else falls into place. What do you truly want?

Some of you know that in this evening you have already experienced or had reconfirmed for you the answer that you have always known. And when I said to those of my old buddies that some have called "disciples" — what a term of specialness that is —

Ah, yes, the grand apostles. Boy, they were chosen by God. Did you know that? Whew, maybe if I hadn't sinned so much in my last life, God would have chosen me, too.

Saint this and Saint that. Why not Saint Judith? Why not Saint Edith? Why not Saint Marilyn? Why not Saint Hank? Why not? You are already saintly in the eyes of your Creator. You might as well live it.

What do you truly want? That is the question that requires an answer, and from it every other question and every other answer will be but servants that bring into manifestation, in and through you, the fulfillment of your heart's desire.

Be at peace in all things, for I am with you. And the promise that I gave you then in the drama of time has never changed. I am with you always. All you have to do is open the shutters and look through the window of your perceptions and you will see me sitting on that bench—legs crossed, palms open, smiling—and you will notice that there is space on it for you. All I have ever asked is that you allow me to be a friend. No false piety is required. No great chants and no great cathedrals. You are the temple of Christ. And because I love you—because I love you—I abide in unlimitedness so that I can be with you always. I can be with all of you always, as you can be with me always. And nothing—*nothing*—is impossible to minds that have joined in love.

My peace I give unto you. My blessings I would shower upon you, and do. Some of you like to deflect it a little bit. That's okay. Somebody else will pick up the spray. But I do want you to know that no matter what choice you make, I will never stop the shower of that love upon you.

Sooner or later you will give up the game of the ego and accept it, and then all things shall be made new. No longer a journey to the Kingdom, but the glory of a journey within it.

Carry, then, peace in your hearts—and give it away, for in your giving you will receive. Love the world as yourself and you will have manifested the knowledge of what it means to live as though you were not an ego. Indeed.

Peace to the precious and holy and only begotten offspring of Light divine, the One that I call Abba, because that Love is so personally yours as it is mine.

Peace to the great rays of Light that shine forever and touch every corner of creation. That is who you are, nothing more and certainly nothing less.

Be, therefore, who you are and your Light will light this world, and together you will know that there has never been an order of difficulty in miracles.

Amen.

The Light that You are

Now, we begin.

I have come unto you many times. I have sought to express unto you my deep and unfathomable and, in Truth, eternal love for all that you are. I have spoken unto you that I see not so much the body but I see the great ray of Light that seemingly animates the body and cries out to be allowed to express itself in its fullness through the guise of the body. Not in order to prove itself, not in order to gain Heaven, but out of compassion to be allowed by the small part of the mind that you have thought you are, to be allowed from the base of compassion to bring itself and give itself unto the world; to allow every moment and every thought and every deed and every vision and every dream — every moment of existence — to be imbued with a clarity of thought, a clarity of purpose, knowledge, and no longer false perceptions; to be imbued with the presence of the Love that God is; to joyously be expressed and to be given.

That Light is who you are. And that Light is the Light that I see. That Light is the Light to which I have come for a thousand lifetimes. I have knocked upon the door of that Light and said,

> *Yes, it is okay. Just press a little harder. Eventually they will let you in.*

And indeed that small part of the mind that you have restricted yourself to, must eventually be dissolved. And how? By your willingness. Your willingness to ask the Holy Spirit that the

Bridge between you as the Holy Son of God and God Himself open that window, open that door and allow that Light to flood your being, to bring Light into every dark corner and every shadow that you have tried to hold back, so that you can keep yourself believing that you are unworthy of being the presence of Love and living above all fear and all limitation and all doubt.

And I have watched you through a thousand lifetimes come unto the threshold of the Kingdom, so close, so close, only to allow one thought to again steal across the mind:

> *No, no, no. I can't possibly be the Son of God. That was left up to Jeshua. Somehow I know, no matter what is said, no matter what is done or how many miracles come into my life, no matter how often I feel the descent of grace upon me, I know there is yet some place within me that is guilty of some sort of unpardonable sin, and therefore I must hold back a small part of myself and become identified with it.*

And so you oscillate constantly between your dreams and your prayers of opening and your fear of that opening, which leads you to constrict into but a small point of the Light you truly are. And all the angels of Heaven, if you would well receive it, feel a tinge of sadness. The Earth feels the sadness and, if you would well receive it, the brothers and sisters who even now are with you also feel the tinge of sadness, because they need you as much as you have ever needed them. They need you to be the one who says,

> *No longer will I lie down in the bed of crucifixion, but I choose in this hour to stand in the resurrection.*

Do you know what it means to exist? It means to stand up out of nothingness. Out of nothingness. To stand up and say,

> *Okay. I might as well be here. And where am I if I am not in the Holy Mind of God, embraced by a warm and fuzzy blanket called Love? What am I if I am not choosing to be the presence of Love? What is the purpose and function of my being if I am not allowing myself to open to unfathomable vision? To serve the rebirth of Light upon this plane? To bring Heaven to Earth?*

Not to escape the Earth. Not to find some magical means by which you can flit about, become so light that you ascend the body and laugh at everybody left behind. But to choose to see that indeed you walk in a very magical kingdom. You walk in a kingdom that is a construct made from the energy of thought itself, and you are sharing in this great construct with your brothers and sisters who have created it with you. And your only purpose and function is to be happy.

To realize that where you are is not in the body at all. But where you are has *never* tasted birth and cannot know death. That the body is exactly that: it is the body. Not *my* body, not *your* body — *the* body. And through you, through the body, through its personality, a great Light can shine forth at any time you decide to allow it.

I have come unto you for so long now and said, I'm sorry, but there are no magical techniques. There is only a simple choice to be made: To sit down in the quietness of your own beingness, your own existence, and to realize the simplicity of the Truth that must be:

> *I and my Father are one. I have never been who I thought I was. I'm not this body at all. The small part of my mind that has thrown up the smokescreens of fear, in Truth, has no part in me.*

I have come unto you. I have cried out unto you as you stood at the threshold of the Kingdom and reached out my hand in a million ways—not just through this communication, but in your dreams, while you drive your automobiles, in the midst of your relationships. In every moment you can conceive I have extended my hand to you and said:

Come. Come to where I am. It's not far. It's not far at all.

Heaven must exist right here in this room or it exists nowhere. It is where I abide, and the whole gist of my Gospel has been eternally that it is where *you* abide also— even when you believe you don't. That, you see, is the great trick. That is the paradox that brings illumination back to the mind. When you are willing to concede your needless sense of struggle, when you are ready to embrace the Truth that where you are now, Heaven is, because you are the one who chooses to be awake, now, in whatever moment the world throws at you:

I choose to be awake. Therefore, I will teach only Love because that is what I am. I will not choose to look upon strife. I will not draw it to myself.

And that does not mean that while you are in the world you never see strife. It just means that you don't identify with it.

And I will choose to walk this world a little lighter because I am Light. And I will allow the Holy Spirit to use each moment of my life as a way through which there can be communicated the remembrance of Truth.

What if . . . What if you were willing to acknowledge that there is absolutely nothing for you to do save to allow Love to be extended through you? What if you were to accept that there is absolutely nowhere to go, nothing to achieve save to be willing to join with me in serving the atonement, the awakening of the mind of the Son of God? What if right now — *right now* — as you look upon your life, you were to acknowledge that it has been fueled by a kind of searching, a searching that has become so habitual that you have convinced yourself that surely Heaven must be just around the corner.

> *And when I have squeezed out every last piece of emotional baggage of my being, then God will smile on me.*

What if you were to acknowledge that the Truth about you cannot be dimmed by the body, by space and time, by any trauma you have ever experienced? And that indeed to stand at the threshold of the Kingdom of Heaven — which is merely the remembrance of where you are always — requires only that you abandon fear and choose love?

To stand up, to exist, means to acknowledge that somebody on this plane has to stand up for a new vision and to live it. To be willing to be the presence of Love and to never need to cower before anyone. To look even a perfect stranger — and we all know that there is no such thing — in the eyes, and when they complain, when they lament, when they say,

> *No, it's impossible. I can't change my life's conditions. I'm too weak. I'm too poor.*

— there's this excuse and that excuse — look them in the eye and say,

> *That's a bunch of nonsense.*

Not because you are judging them, but because you see the

Light of Christ that is just behind the limited set of beliefs that they have chosen to be identified with. And if you have to nudge them just a little bit and perhaps they hate you for it, so what?

Would you conform yourself so that an illusion can love you, or would you choose to love the Light of Christ that lies just behind every appearance of lack and incapability and doubt?

I have said to you a thousand times that what you teach will teach you. And if you choose to be a miracle-worker, miracles will necessarily transform your life. That means you don't have to get there before you begin. That by choosing to begin now, in this day and in every hour, to be the presence of Christ, you will learn what it means to be that presence. There is no other way. There is absolutely no other way that works. There is not a single set of skills you can master that will ever enlighten you. But you can bring your Light to whatever skills the Holy Spirit would ask you to learn and use in this world by acknowledging first,

> *I and my Father are One.*

And the perception of struggle, the perception of doubt, indeed the experience of fear is wholly unreal and touches not the Holy Son of God.

Now, I know that that brings up fear. Does it not? Can you feel it?

> *Gulp. If I accept what Jeshua is saying, I have no choice but to give up the game of separation and acknowledge right here, in front of God and everybody, that I am awake, that I simply will not tolerate error in myself again.*

That is the eye of the needle. That is the crack between two worlds. That is the quantum leap that brings you home again. That is the simple choice that takes you from just on that side of the threshold of Heaven and brings you fully into the midst of the Kingdom, and you realize you haven't had to fix a thing. But you have indeed become humble because the holy Son of God *always knows* — and listen to this carefully — the holy Son of God *always knows* that of himself he does nothing, but the Father through him, does all these things.

Gone is the dream of the dreamer. Gone the hope of being the doer. All things are given back to God, and in the place of the dreamer there arises the perfect servant of Love and of Light. It doesn't even really know how it all happens. It is just willing to be the presence of Love and to become available. You never know what you might find yourself doing once you have truly made that choice.

Are you willing to risk it? Is that not what it's really all about?

Are you willing to risk truly releasing every last trace of your hold, your grip on the ego, which *is* the thought of separation from God?

> *Oh, my God, what would happen in my life if I were to sit down, look at myself in the mirror and say "I am awake?" I couldn't possibly be anything but awake. And if I am awake, I know that all minds are joined in love. And because I love Jeshua, I can certainly talk to him without having to borrow Marc's "carcass."*

. . . but you can join with me to celebrate the Truth.

So, I know that was a rather interesting greeting. Good evening to you. But there were some who desperately needed just to get the little laser shot of Truth because, you see, the mind — the ego — constantly wants to play games. Constantly. That's what the ego is — it *is* a game. It's like turning on your television set and instead of watching a comedy, you watch a drama with sickness and disease and death and fear and egos beating up on one another because they believe they live in lack and if they give all they have received, they won't have anything:

So I'd better hoard it and store it all up.

When just the opposite is true.

And, indeed, if you do not find avenues through which you can give the grace and love that you have received, if you cannot choose to find the avenues and find the ways to give away all you have received, what you have is taken from you. Not by an evil God that sits outside of you and goes, "Tsk, tsk." But you relinquish it. And the tree of life within you withers and dies, and the mind will project the cause of that outside of itself — outside of itself.

Surely it was a set of circumstances. If only my maid hadn't left me. It was inflation; that's what did it. Why did they let those Democrats get in again?

Hmm. There's always something, isn't there? Another excuse to delay existing. Think about it. There's always an excuse to delay existing. And the only way to exist is to be real. And the only way to be real is to accept that you are the holy Son of God, here and now, and everything else is a fantasy, a delusion, based on a habit of fear. Everything.

All power is given unto you to attract to yourself the means whereby you can extend the Love of God into the world. They are all around you in every moment. And that is the turning about in the seat of the soul. The Greeks used to call it "metanoia." That is, the turning about that has to be chosen, simply chosen:

I choose to be awake.

And that is what will make all the difference in the world — because you and you and you and all of you, and me, together, choose to be awake. That's all. Then, you see, what happens is that I no longer have to walk with you, trying to shout in your ear. We can lock arms and skip down the path together.

Ah, love, sweet love. Love! Indeed, it rides on every breath you breathe and desires to be heard with every spoken word. Love is indeed the alpha and omega of all things. Love is the essence of all that is real, and the only thing that is real is you. Therefore, you are that Love that was there in the beginning with me, is now and ever shall be, a Love that wholly outshines the body and the frailties of this wholly insane world, that cries out to see the demonstration, the demonstration that it is possible to do things in a different way.

One of the habits of the ego is to turn a deaf ear toward the cries of your brothers and sisters. Yes, the cries when they are hungry physically, the cries when they feel abused and rejected; yes, all of those levels of insanity. But the cry that I am addressing here is the cry that comes up in every soul and is constantly going on. It's like a siren, and it's been going on for so long you become a little deaf to it. It's the cry that says,

Will somebody please tell me it's okay to be awake? Will somebody tell me it's okay to feel safe? Will somebody teach me that only by being vulnerable, by choosing to be the presence of Love, can I find my safety?

I've said unto you that I need to hire you, in a way. You see, so many of your brothers and sisters have been so programmed to believe that only the body is real and what is outside its boundaries must not exist. And so I come to them and oh, my God, how I come to them. I come to them in their dreams. I whisper to them. If you want to know the Truth of it—and I haven't shared this with you yet—I have materialized a form in which to talk to someone more times that you could possibly ever count if you sat down for a hundred years and did nothing but count. I have come to so many, and they have seen visions of me and in the very next moment they said,

> *No, it had to be my imagination.*

Some of you know what that's like.

So, I've taken out a classified ad and I said,

> *Wanted: Servants of Light. Those who have become willing to be my eyes. To be my hands. To be my heart. To be my physical appearance in this world.*

And I have asked only one thing:

> *Just be willing to join with me and to trust me. I know what your brother and sister needs all the time.*

And I have explained to you how I know that. It's not because I'm smart. It's because I finally figured out two thousand years ago that if I go to the Holy Spirit and ask, the Holy Spirit will tell me. And I have said to you, rather metaphorically and jokingly— but it's much closer to the Truth than you know— when I ask what someone needs, the Holy Spirit races around and sneaks in the back door of their heart, pulls out what they need and brings it back to me; and then I show it to them. And they go,

Oh Jeshua, what a miracle. What a miracle. How did you know that?

And the Truth is, I didn't until it was asked.

Now, if the Holy Spirit can do that for me, it can certainly do it for you. I indeed need you to answer my classified ad and to come to work — which is really play, by the way — and to sit down with me and to look out upon all of this world, indeed to look out upon every world you have ever constructed and tried to wrap around yourself, to look upon all of them and go,

Oh, that's just a harmless sideshow going on. What was I ever frightened of?

Even the body isn't real. It's a hologram. It doesn't even have existence apart from the value you place upon it. And yet, for a little while, because it has been constructed out of infinite possibility, I can indeed teach you how to use the body anew so that it becomes the perfect means through which love is extended and taught — and therefore received by the mind and heart that is willing to be re-taught.

It is so simple. So incredibly simple. And, of course, that's what makes it difficult. Because the world believes in struggle. Because the world teaches you — and the part of the mind called the ego *is* the world mind — teaches you that it must take effort and it must be complex. It must be very difficult indeed to ever become so purified that the grace of God would descend upon you like a dove and a voice from Heaven would shout, "This is my beloved Son in whom I am eternally well pleased."

> *Boy, that may happen to very special beings, but it will never happen to me.*

So what happens is this: your Father's been shouting that through all of eternity as He looks at you and the Holy Spirit says,

> *Dad, this one isn't quite willing to get it yet. What should we do?*

And the Father knows the answer and tells the Holy Spirit,

> *Weave a tapestry with everything that they create — every thought, every action, every deed. Let them pretend that they are running around getting somewhere in all of their seeking, in all of their striving, in all of their lamenting; and secretly weave a tapestry out of everything they construct so that without their even knowing it they will be brought back to the Holy of Holies, the place of peace within, in which they can again relearn that the only choice that must be made is the choice between Love and fear.*

And, rest assured, when the tapestry has been woven, when the Holy Spirit has brought you back face to face with God, He will take the last step for you. You don't even have to do that — He will do it for you.

Now listen very carefully. I have said unto you that time is given unto you so that you might use it constructively. And the only constructive use of time is the practice of being the presence of one who is awake to their reality as Love. That means that from the moment you realize you are awake until the moment you think you've fallen asleep — only the body does that, by the way — every single tick of your clock is the greatest of blessings you could ever receive. And why? Time

The Light that You are

has been constructed as a device to separate you from eternity but it has been translated for you into the tapestry that returns you to all that *is* eternal. And when you really get that, when you really truly get it, something wells up within you called gratitude. Do you know that feeling?

I know what it means to feel gratitude when you have enough golden coins to pay the bills. I know what it means to feel gratitude: I see it happening in your minds when the weather is just right. I know what it means for you to be willing to feel gratitude when you get the date you've always wanted. There are a thousand other times, special times, when you've allowed yourself to touch gratitude.

When you really understand the blessing of time—that it is not a prison at all—then every breath you breathe comes forth from an incredible gratitude because you've finally gotten it. It's just a game.

> *All I'm asked to do is practice being the presence of Love. To be unlimited. To realize that I can't be limited. All I have to do is say, "Holy Spirit, what do you want me to do today?" And then set about to do it.*

And if a vision begins to be born in you, "Pack up your bags and move to this other place", why not go? Fear of loss?

> *What will I lose if I leave these things behind me, these roots that I believe have kept me safe?*

You will lose nothing.

> *Leave my friends? You mean, venture out into the big world? What will I lose?*

A limitation. A friend of the heart is never lost.

I learned that if I gave up the body, I wouldn't lose anything either. And, after all, is not the body the one thing that you continue to insist upon identifying with?

Has it ever kept you safe?

Has the body ever, ever, ever, ever brought you the perfect intimacy of a Holy Instant?

Have you ever experienced through the senses, through the use of the body, what we will call here eternal satisfaction?

Have you ever fed the body so that it's no longer hungry? Darn thing, you have to keep feeding it.

Has any adornment upon the body ever truly won the overwhelming approval of everyone you share this planet with?

Has the making of a muscle so that it is bigger than it was a year ago, has that ever given you the acceptance you would like?

You rise in the morning, you pamper it. You feed it. You clothe it. You construct an entire world around it, and then you busy yourself from nine to five, five days a week—and sometimes longer—so that you can feed it, clothe it, and house it and pamper it a little bit. Has the body ever presented you with the gift of grace?

They might be questions worth asking.

Now, of course, therefore, the conclusion is this: hate the body. Despise it. Beat it. Flog it. Some of you have done that before. Whip it into shape and keep hating it. Always see it as imperfect, so work on it a little harder. No, that's not the conclusion, but it is the conclusion some minds reach.

Since I'm not the body I'll just ignore the darned thing. Great error.

The great error in all of your spiritual traditions has been this: That the whole goal is to somehow find a means whereby you can escape the body; for the body is the symbol of the ego, it is the symbol of time itself. *The point is not to ascend; the point is to realize that ascension has already been completed, because the holy Son of God has never left the Kingdom of Heaven.*

The whole point of the game is **descension**. To descend, to bring the Light and the Love that you are and to utilize the body as a means through which you communicate Light and Love. And that requires that you embrace the body just for what it is and not for anything else: as a means given unto you for a very short time whereby you can relearn how to radiate Light and Love into this world that believes that bodies are the final definition of reality. And if you shine enough Light and enough Love through it, other minds can begin to get the message that there is life after the body. There is life beyond the body even now. And there can then be a process of awakening.

The point I am trying to make right now is this: I have sought to find a thousand ways to get the idea across that you cannot transcend what you do not embrace and love. That does not mean that you try to add inches of muscle to body — unless, of course, you enjoy that. It means that you allow your perceptions of the body and of what the world is for to be corrected, and that requires your willingness to take all of your perceptions, lay them on a tray and give them back to the Holy Spirit, and just say,

> *You know, I haven't figured it out yet. Maybe I should read the directions.*

And indeed correction does come and you begin to look upon the body — *the* body, not *my* body — the body, and you sit back from a perspective in which you realize you are Light. You go,

> *Oh, what an interesting toy this is. If I press this button and do that, I can activate Light in the cells and they can actually shine from the body. If I do this and do that and do this, I can radiate so much Light through my eyes that people will actually stop and wonder what on earth hit them. Oooh, this sounds like fun.*

And the body begins to be something that no longer is seen as a prison, something that limits you.

And you can look at what it means to be in this world as if you have just come to a costume party. You see that everybody else seems to be playing the game of believing that the body is real, and you can look and see that so many minds are enshrouded with seriousness. They actually believe that life requires struggle and strain and lack and all of the rest of the things that represent limitation. And you can become so outrageous because you've thrown away all of your own perceptions and you are beginning to be re-taught. You can begin to be the one who lives just the opposite of the way the world would try to teach you to live.

The Light that You are

You can become one who joins the ranks of those who have chosen to exist. And to exist does not mean to just get by. It means to be the radiant presence of outflowing Love and joy and dance and laughter and play and vision and contribution and service. Love, Love, Love.

That's what the world is waiting for. Gone is the time—and please hear what I am about to say—very quickly gone will be the time for me to come even in this way, because if I do not go away, the Comforter cannot come unto you. Therefore, cling not unto me for you do not know the day and the hour in which my Father will say unto me, "That's enough now. Either they live it or they don't."

Whew! But Jeshua, I thought you said that you would be with me always?

Well, of course I will. But *you* are going to have to come to *where I am* to realize it. So now is as good a time as any. Right now. Right now. Are you willing right now just to take ten of your precious seconds and acknowledge in your own mind,

I am that one in whom my Father is eternally well pleased, and all things are possible for me, because I am not the doer at all?

Now that means that, from this moment forward, you can never go to a single workshop unless you do so from the perspective, now healed, that you are the holy Son of God, and obviously the Holy Spirit wants you to be there or you wouldn't be there; and all you are there for is to polish up a few skills so that you can become like a laser and bring the Light of Christ and give it to the world—never again out of a perception that there is something you lack. And never again to believe, whether the friend you are with is me or some other teacher, that they are somehow other than who you are. And to honor them for being willing to play the role of teacher so that you get to play the role of what seems to be the student. And the whole purpose of teaching is that the student becomes as the teacher is. Otherwise, there is no point; there's just no point.

The time comes quickly now when this world is going to cry out for masters, not seekers. The time will indeed also come and I am certainly not coming from fear when I say this — the time is also coming when this Earth, the vibration of it, simply won't be such that anything but masters will be able to be here at all.

So. I need you to answer my classified ad. Will you? Hmm. The great truth is that in accepting the job on faith, all things come to you.

Jeshua, I need a new job.

Why?

Because I've outgrown the one I've had.

If you have outgrown the one you have had, why does that mean you _need_ another one?

I think I'd _like_ another one.

Ah. What would you do with it?

Play.

That would be different than the last job.

For sure.

Would it then be a job?

I guess not, in the traditional sense of a job.

Hmm. What if the traditional sense was a wholly insane one?

Oh, I know that.

Indeed. We are talking about perception. The mind believes it must have a job in order to survive — that is, to keep the body in survival — so it accepts or receives impressions that says,

> *A job is a place of imprisonment. I can't possibly be happy here so I'll run and get another one.*

But, of course, you just take the same perceptions with you and nothing really changes.

Therefore, beloved friend, remember that what you decree is. Do not say that you *need* another job. But instead ask that the means might be brought to you so that you might be a servant of the atonement. Now, that doesn't mean a lot of serious stuff. It means indeed play — that you can allow yourself to, shall we say, abide in a different frequency than in the past, recognizing that while it pays the bills and all of that, your real purpose is to practice being the presence of Love, to nudge other minds to begin to think in an unlimited way. To be the one through whom the Holy Spirit brings gentle correction to your brothers and sisters, to their minds.

Say not that you need *another* job because that implies it must be like the one you had before — which means it implies the quality of beingness that you carried within the mind while you were there. Ask instead for a field in which you can play at a higher frequency, if you will, with minds that are resonating with greater freedom within themselves. Do you see?

That sounds really inviting. Higher frequencies.

Indeed. Be careful how you wrap up the package of your desire.

This constant vigilance is kind of exhausting, you know?

Only because you bring effort into it. There is no need for effort. All that it requires is that,

> *This day I will be the witness of my thoughts. How am I thinking my thoughts? What words am I choosing when I speak?*

The word is very powerful indeed.

To be vigilant does not require effort as much as it asks the *relinquishment* of effort. It requires only that you watch. It's actually the easiest thing you could possibly do. But you've taught the mind to be sidetracked, and it becomes sidetracked — please listen to this very carefully — the mind becomes sidetracked every time you let yourself believe that what is occurring out there on the screen of your life is something that is real and independent of your own mind. Do you see?

It doesn't matter what the event is around you. What matters is, are you aware of how you are choosing to think about it? And when you come to see that there is nothing outside of *you*, that it really is all in your head — except that the mind is not in the head — then great power begins to be reborn in you; and you begin to realize that by reconstructing the foundation within the mind, what is projected out here must necessarily change. And when there are enough awakened minds that are doing just that, the world that you have been taught is real out there, the real world will be different.

If the mind can construct a world that reflects separation, it can indeed construct that which reflects union with God. Your philosophers call that being an idealist. Well, I should certainly hope so, since everything is the reflection of an idea. You might as well just admit it and begin indeed to turn the attention of the world from trying to conquer outer space, and turn it so that it begins to understand the power of mind itself. The further your scientists go out, the more they are returned to what is within. Your physicists in this century have indeed learned that the more they try to plumb the depths of matter, the more they run right into their own mind. Hmm. Talk about chasing your own tail!

Now, if it is true for the greatest minds within your realms of science, it is obviously true for you, too. You never see anything save that which you construct in your mind. The day comes when you begin to realize just how staggering a Truth that is because it includes the body itself. And to use time constructively is to be vigilant in observing how you are allowing the mind to work, to begin to see the patterns that create limitation and lack and fear and hurt and judgment and all of the rest, and begin to interrupt them at their inception and make other choices.

If I am feeling hurt, the correction is to extend love.

If I am feeling lack, the correction is to extend love.

If I am feeling rejected, the correction is to extend love.

Because to do so you must return to your right-mindedness in which you remember,

> *I am the holy Son of God. I cannot indeed be hurt. I cannot know pain and I cannot taste death. I am the Thought of Love in form and I am held perfect and safe now.*

Love indeed heals all things. Nothing else works. It's the cosmic salve.

And each time hurt seems to continue, you are only experiencing the choice you have made in the mind to insist that it continue. There is no other Truth. That's it. Your mind is perfectly healthy at all times—perfectly healthy. You may choose to use it in an unhealthy way but the power of choice is never taken from anyone at any time.

Does that make sense to you?

Yes, it does, But Jeshua, when I am vigilant and I see the pattern of negativity that I have allowed to run my life, it seems as though throughout my entire day I am constantly calling myself up short because I've gone back to that old habit, and I am saying to myself, "No, you don't need to think that way any more." And sometimes at the end of a day when I've had to do that a lot, I am really whipped. It's physically exhausting to me, and you sounds as though I can do it more quietly or something, and I am not quite getting that.

Now, let's take a look at what you just said since what the Son decrees, the Son experiences. You have stated and therefore created a perception that when you are vigilant and you notice you've been allowing some negative perspective, some limited perspective to, in a sense, guide you, to own you—

that when you notice it you are then constantly calling yourself up short. That is, you are berating and judging yourself, are you not?

Yes.

There is the source of the error. When you see whatever it is you happen to see in your perception, your perspective, that is limiting you, a strand of negativity — however you want to label that it doesn't matter — when you see it, there is only one cure: laugh your buns off at it.

[Laughter.]

Because it is not part of the reality of who you are. You will never kill the ego. You will only love it to death, by withdrawing the value you place upon it.

Oh, my God, there I go again. What a jerk I am.

Oh, that's me.

No, that's not you.

Or, that has been me.

No, that has not been you.

Okay. It just doesn't exist.

You are the presence of the Thought of Love in form. You are unbounded and eternal. There has never been a time that you have not existed as the Thought held lovingly in the Mind of God. Your reality knows no boundaries. It knows neither beginning nor end, and therefore you have never tasted birth or death. You cannot possibly have ever sinned against God. You are indeed loved wholly, and the Light shines in you as completely in this moment as it has ever shined in me. That Light you are. And to be vigilant means that in each moment when you watch the movie and the ego seems to creep in to the mind, you simply retrain the mind to notice that that's not a part of you and you have a very good laugh because the drama has become a comedy; and then you choose anew.

Don't make a transition by thinking you have to *beat yourself* into love. Just be love. The constructive use of time—which is the only use there is of it—is to choose to be the presence of Love. Each time the thought comes into the mind that

> *There I go again. I've blown it. What a jerk I am,*

that is part of the same voice that has created the strand of negativity trying to seduce you, trying to say,

> *No, no, don't let me die. I've been in control of you for so long.*

And all you need do is withdraw your value from it and choose anew. And have a good laugh while you are doing it.

Jeshua, that really helps a lot. Thank you very much.

I will send you a bill.

Okay. More bills.

Do you know what the bill will look like?

[Laughter.]

The bill will have the names of brothers and sisters you may not have even met yet, and they will be sent to you so that *you* can be their teacher. For as you learn and as that awakening process deepens, your ability to be responsible also broadens, and then the Holy Spirit sends unto you those who need to receive what you have learned. And if you do not give all that has been given unto you, even that begins to be withdrawn because it dries up within you. And if you do not give all that you have received, you cannot know that your Redeemer lives, and that Redeemer is the face of Christ that dwells within you now. And that is why in giving, you receive; and to give all means that you receive all.

The only difference between us is that two thousand years ago I figured that one out:

If I give all that my Father has given me, I will receive it eternally.

It's like—liking chocolate ice cream so much that you want to have it all the time. And you finally peer behind the scenes and realize that the way the universe works is that you keep giving it away and that's how more gets delivered to your door. Do you see? You give away a pint and they bring you a gallon. Your Father's going,

Oh, thank you so much for giving that away. Here, take more, because now I know you know what to do with it. You are finally understanding what it means, what you are supposed to be doing with love and with intelligence and with vision, with inspiration, with compassion. Oh, indeed, with all the power of Heaven and Earth. You are finally getting it. So here you are; I am going to give you more of it.

And you turn around and you go,

Oh my goodness. Here comes more. What do I do with it? Oops, I'm not going to keep it. I am going to go give it away. Oops, here comes even more. Wow, what a fun game this is. The more I give away, the more I receive.

You could call it, in your culture, being addicted to love. What do you think?

I think it's a great idea...

Just a moment. Now that's a very good word. It is an idea because *you* are an idea. Ideas are extended as you choose to receive them and be identified with them. *The only way to be awake is to choose to identify your self as one who is awake and no longer tolerates error within yourself. By choosing to draw the idea of being awake to yourself and identifying with it, you become the presence of that idea.*

It has well been said that everything in this dimension is channeled. It's a representation of an idea. So, you see, you can go to one of your malls tomorrow and just walk up to people and say,

What idea are you being today?

Now, that sounds a little light-hearted, and it is because the heart is filled with Light. But it's also the Truth.

What idea am I being now? Am I being a Thought of Love in form or am I being a scum-bucket?

Hmm. I do love that term. I don't know where my beloved brother found it. Beloved friend — and the rest of you know that obviously these questions asked are your very own — eventually then the last trace of ego vanishes from the mind.

You don't even feel when that last trace leaves. You simply notice that it has been absent for a while and the Holy Spirit has crept into your dreams and stolen the cobwebs of shadows outgrown, and there is naught but the presence of a mind that is wholly corrected and a heart that rests at peace. And each time a thought seems to press against you,

> *Oh, gosh, the body is so beat. How am I ever going to get all these things done?*

without any effort at all you remember,

> *Oh, I'm not even in this world. I'm just the presence of Love. If I choose to take the day off, it'll be done tomorrow. And I'll take the day off because I've learned to ask the Holy Spirit's guidance in all things. And if I hear the thought, "Take the day off; go fishing," you will find me fishing.*

That is what it means when I said that the wind blows as it does and you cannot know where it comes from or where it's going; and so is everyone born of the Spirit, because they no longer mistrust the gentle voice of guidance given unto everyone wholly and without measure.

It feels rather nice just to be awake because nothing any longer obstructs your perception, and you look out upon a world that is indeed wholly safe; and you know that because the world is harmless you can live the fullness of the Light and Love that is longing to descend through you into the world. Gone are every last traces of fear. Gone, every doubt. Replaced by a perfect certainty and a constant state of laughter. Because the whole thing has taken but a moment, and you have become that mind that I once demonstrated to the world. You have learned what my old friend, Paul, learned when he tried to tell his friends,

Just let that mind be in you that was in our Lord, Christ Jesus.

That's all. Let the whole-mindedness of Christ be in you — and that is all. And then indeed you walk much lighter in this world and you smile a lot, and even when you notice you are not smiling, a little bit of laughter comes up because you are just watching a little game called the ego and you are not even identified with it anymore. And you look upon your brothers and sisters and they sense a softness in you. They sense an acceptance. *They sense that there is nothing they have to do to earn your love.* You just accept them as they are because you see the Light that shines in them. And that is the Light that you embrace. That is the Light you talk to, though they think you are talking to their mind, their lower mind. That is the Light that you worship and give thanks for. That is the Light that you dance with. And they will know it, for they will walk around the corner and see you and something makes them turn and look at you twice.

I don't even know what it is, but something . . .

The soul has recognized a reflection of its own Truth. And without raising a hand you will have brought the miracle of grace because you have chosen to throw off the shackles of the world and to be the living demonstration of one who is awake.

Does that require standing on a soapbox? There are no brass bands that have to play, because only the ego needs those things. There is just the presence of Love right where you thought *you* were. Indeed.

Now, in the last few moments have you not felt a peace descending upon you? Have some of you felt that? Seems to happen every time the Holy Spirit whispers to me,

The Light that You are

> *Go and use the mind of your ancient friend and brother, and speak the Truth.*

And the peace comes not because I bring it, but because that part of you that knows the Truth recognizes it and acknowledges it within yourself. That is what brings peace to the world. And that is what it means to be gathered in my name.

You are the Thought of Love in form. You, right where you are. You are free to change your lifestyle anytime you want. Free to give up struggle. Free to create unlimitedness if you want. Free to join with higher frequencies — if you want to use that kind of terminology — that are now descending into the minds of mankind. Free at anytime to take up your cross and follow me; and as you know, my cross is made of Light and it brings joy to the world.

Question: Jeshua, I have a problem, which I want to ask you for a little help with. There are three of us that go to a prison and there is a man there who keeps writing me these letters, and he evidently is projecting a lot onto me. I can't quite get it through to this man that we are just friends. I love him as a friend and I don't want to hurt him. How can I deal with this? Can you help me?

No, but you can help yourself. Now, precious friend, can you see how this situation is mirroring what has been rather much a lifelong pattern? That is, when an energy is projected upon you, not just in this specific way, but in which other minds would perceive that there is something that they need from you, that it has always brought up within you the sense that you are responsible for somehow finding a way to fulfill what they need, and if you cannot, or if you feel that you cannot, it brings up within you a sense of guilt or failure?

Yes.

Well, that was a good guess.

Now, if that is true — and we both know it is — it means that this situation is also your blessing, to look at that pattern of perception. You need not try to find its source in some ancient childhood experience in which you were punished for eating your Cheerios with your left hand. But rather, in seeing that you are being presented with an opportunity to put into practice the Truth that when you abide in your integrity and in your Truth, you cannot possibly harm anyone. That you are not responsible for being the one who fulfills the needs projected upon you by fearful minds, by confused minds.

We are striking to the core here, aren't we?

Yes, we are.

That is what I meant when I said you can help yourself. I can't wave a magic wand and make that one disappear, and I wouldn't want to because it is really good for you. But you can stand in the integrity of your Truth and communicate to this one very, very clearly — and, quite frankly, I would suggest a bit strongly — that this is the way it is and this ceases *now*. Do you see?

Yes.

Now, does that not bring up a little "gulp?"

Yes.

And yet, do you realize just behind that old pattern lies a power waiting to be born in you?

To claim responsibility for your right in time to draw the boundaries, so that your Light can be like a laser and not be dissipated by the thought or perception that somehow you are responsible for being the salve on everybody's perceptions of wounds? Sometimes the greatest of gifts you can give to someone is to insist on absolute responsibility within them for what they think, what they feel, and what they do. That your friendship and love is never in question, but the form it takes requires impeccable integrity on that one's part because, you see, that has been part of that one's problem: this constant projection of fantasy that blurs the lines. Quite frankly, that's why that one is where that one is. Hmm?

Therefore, can you see then how every time an event takes place that confronts you with the need to grow, to be the strength of the one who is awake and realizes their own worthiness, what you teach also teaches your brother or your sister; and everything serves the awakening of the Sonship. It's healing. You are being given a grand, grand gift. Hold it in your hand. Don't lose this precious moment.

I am going to ask you indeed to write to this one in no uncertain terms, and when you do it, really let the feeling come up within you, not of anger — of power. Power of certainty and integrity.

> *This is who I am. This is what I offer you. Do not step on it because that will only show me that you are not willing to assume responsibility for true friendship and holy relationship, and therefore I will have no choice but to withdraw it and give it to somebody else.*

Let that one knows that you are totally worthy of being absolutely respected at all times and in all ways, and that this is the last time that these words will need to be spoken. What do you think?

That sounds right. It sounds good in my heart.

Do you see how it will also heal what your culture would call part of a wounded little girl?

Yes, I think I do.

So, flex the muscles of the heart. With gratitude, by the way. Put PS: Thank you for being my teacher.

Now, once again, precious friend, you asked me a question and I raced over to the window and said, "Holy Spirit, you are not going off duty yet, are you?" He said, "No, no. I'll hang around if you want me to." I said, "Would you mind?" "No problem. I've got it." Out through the back door of the office, a little army crawl through the grasses, sneaking into the back door of your heart. "Ah, this is what she needs to do." Pulls it back out. Fills it out on a piece of paper and said, "Here's the prescription." So I took it and said, "Well, okay." And I spoke to this my beloved brother who, by the way, when we do this is, shall we say, elsewhere than where you might think he is. Because, you see, all that I do I always use as a teaching tool for him — that is, the mind, the Light that is him — so that he can someday learn to do these things on his own. I said, "Look, this is the prescription the Holy Spirit has given to me. Now, I am just going to kick some ideas loose in that mind-field of yours, create a few sentences so that I can deliver the prescription to our friend."

That is why it strikes the chord deeply. The answer came from within you. And the only difference is that you already knew the answer but a part of you was fearful of receiving it and acting upon it. Is that not true?

That's right. I had a dear friend share the same thing with me and . . . but I just really needed to have you share with me.

I am your friend and I am your brother and I am your servant, as was your dear friend who told you basically the same thing. So happy letter-writing.

Thank you so much.

Question: I really need to ask you something for my son and his girlfriend. I told him I would do it if there was an opportunity tonight. It seems that there is a little soul who insists on coming to them whether they are ready for it or not. And they've really been in an uproar for the last week or two.

And I told them what you said about their souls have an agreement before they are ever born, that their own souls agreed to have this child even if they don't remember it consciously, their souls agreed. And that even though this seems like the most inconvenient time, it's going to turn out to be a real blessing. And, Jeshua, even though sometimes they raise their eyebrows because I come here and I listen to you and I read the transcripts, they see that I am getting happier and lighter, and so even though they're still a little skeptical . . . I did laugh tonight because they asked me if I would ask you about this.

First, do you see how this represents what I prophesied for you?

The teacher part?

Yes. And you are beginning to see how it works?

Yes.

As you become lighter, other souls begin to be attracted, though they may go kicking and screaming, they still find themselves drawn to asking you, in this case, to be one who goes and gets the message. Eventually they'll ask you for the message.

Oh boy.

Now, you will know that of yourself you can do nothing, and you'll slide over to the window and ask the Holy Spirit the way I do it. And then the student becomes the teacher. He who drinks from my mouth becomes as I am, and I become that one — a blending so deep. And why? Because the identification with the ego is relinquished and only the Mind of Christ shines.

That is what it is all about. I am not here to perpetuate the perception of separation between you or anyone and myself. I am here to eradicate it.

Now, about that little one. All souls are the same size.

[Laughter.]

And yet the soul has no dimensions. It doesn't take up space at all. It cannot be measured. Now, the only thing within them that feels like this is the worst possible time is the part of them unwilling to acknowledge the Truth of who they are: that all power to deal with whatever situations may arise must necessarily be within them. They are just not yet at a point where they are really truly ready to own up to the fact of reality that nothing happens by accident, and everything brings a blessing and a teaching.

This, then, seeks to be made manifest because a part of them has been asking for something that will push them beyond the limits that they have become identified with. You could say an experience that is going to ask them to — how do you put it? — either you do, or you get off the pot.

It is not coming by accident. Now, they can lament. They can believe they are weak. They can believe they cannot find solutions. They can believe they cannot rise to the occasion. That doesn't change the Truth one iota. Tell them to stop lamenting and start celebrating. Time to start realizing that the power is in them. They have attracted it to themselves and, therefore, this "little soul" comes as a grand teacher.

> *What, you mean we have to heal our perceptions and become the powerful beings we were created to be?*

Powerful, responsible, loving, kind, efficient.

> *You mean we have to grow up?*

Oh. They're not going to like that!

Of course not. But that can't be helped. *I am not here to pamper egos. I am here to help everyone see that all power under Heaven and Earth is given to everyone, and there is no problem that is given to anyone without also the ability to find the solution.*

And that process is the process whereby each soul comes to realize the infinite strength and power that lies within it. *All problems are gifts* — when they are accepted and embraced. And I get the added pleasure of being a grandma. Thank you very much, Jeshua.

Now, please do say unto them: I know they have all that they need because the Light and the Love with which the Father has created them are still within them.

Please let them know that if only they choose to look upon this as a great blessing, if they only choose to look upon it as an opportunity to relinquish their fears and judgments of themselves, so much healing will come to each of them that even in a year's time they will look back and not even recognize who they think they are now.

Please tell them. Please tell them. That for the sake of that grand One Who loves them beyond all of creation, to seize this opportunity and awaken from the guilt and the self-judgment that has been the only thing that seems to be keeping a damper upon them. I know that the Light is in them and I long to see them accept it within themselves. Fair enough?

Fair enough.

Question: I've got a little knot in my stomach of fear of even asking a question so I think I've got to do it to get over the whole step of feeling fear and inadequacy, because in listening to you and what you say, I know that there is no question that I can ask you that I don't know the answer to myself. So perhaps in formulating a question to put forth to you, it is just going to help me understand my own way of what's going on.

I realize from what you say that the dilemmas that are created in our lives are there to be blessed and to be thanked and to learn from, and I have in my living environment created such a perplexing, trying reality. I think this is part of what's pushed me off of the . . . I'll call it the diving board of the quantum leap, and I feel like I am staggering to the end and to where my soul wants to head first, go into that quantum dive totally trusting of Spirit. I kind of feel like I am slipping off feet first, and I've got a lot of fear and a lot of reservations of making that fall or making that jump.

And a lot of it is concerned with the ego issue of making sure that as I am coming into awareness, that I am the living expression of the Love that I am. And I wondered if perhaps you could just share forth to me some things that might help me to understand that?

Please understand that everyone awakens to their own call. You are indeed awakening to that call. Beyond intellectual ideas, beyond the use of words and concepts there is a part of you that some months ago began to shift into a willingness to live the experience that the concepts point to. You are now undergoing what could be called a crucifixion. It's kind of fun, isn't it? Just kidding.

Now, you have described it rather well: a bit of slipping and sliding. You feel that if you could just dive head first, it would go much more gently, but something in you wants to throw your feet in the way. Now, please receive this then:

> *As you have made the belief that you are separate from God, so, too, have you constructed the drama, if you will, by which you will choose awakening.*

Each soul does that. I cannot relieve that process from you but I can assure you that on just this side of the experience you are now undergoing — it need not last long — there lies the peace that passes all understanding and the rebirth of a strength carried by one who is well on his way to being nothing but a teacher of God.

You had a certain experience a very long time ago, and the experience was really an initiation and a test, if you will. But it got you. And there arose a sense of doubt and a feeling of guilt and of failure, and it began to turn you away.

It began to turn you inside out a bit. And you have carried the weight of that perception for a while. And what you are undergoing now represents certain kinds of energies that were present in that experience where you made a mistaken choice.

Therefore, the way to complete the dive is to continue to hold all things that are unfolding with deep gratitude and — and this is very, very important — recognize that the choice you made a long time ago, in a sense is being presented to you as situations so that you can choose anew. And the choice requires your willingness to trust wholly that, indeed, all things could be taken from you, and all that does is free you. It will return you to the path that you were on once upon a time. For your mission and your purpose is indeed to be a teacher of God.

I ask you to trust the eye of the needle that is before you now. And if you are willing to step or to dive, to trust each day as it unfolds by remembering only to return love, to be at peace.

And I can assure you that something quite beautiful will begin to blossom on just the other side of the eye of that needle.

Beloved friend, as I say this unto you, there is yet a bit of resistance within you at wholly accepting the profundity of what I am sharing. What you are undergoing is not unlike crucifixion. And if you are willing to look upon all things through the eyes of Love, and if you are willing indeed, just be willing to relinquish everything you have ever thought, believed or possessed, every friend you have ever thought you've had — if you are willing to relinquish the whole of the world, on just the other side of that choice is the completion of the dive.

Okay, so they'll only give you a three. So what? Let the dive be completed.

Just the other side of that begins the rebirth of the purpose for which you have indeed chosen rebirth in this world. The time of your firing and of your final — shall we call it — purification is upon you. You cannot solve it. You cannot change it. You cannot fix it. You can only allow it. I know that it feels like the allowing of death to occur — and it is. But it is the death of everything that you have carried because of an ancient perception that somehow you had failed and, therefore, carried guilt upon yourself.

Which I still feel very much from that past incarnation. And I know at least to love it, but yet there still is that fear that arises within that jump — because I felt like I let you down once before.

I know.

But it still comes up.

Precious friend, rest assured, if you had let me down, I couldn't be here now. I understand that. It's how I feel right this moment.

I know. And what I'm sharing with you is that dive requires that you *allow the fear to be there while you make a different choice.*

> *I am loved wholly and I have not sinned. There has been no judgment or condemnation. I have not failed my ancient friend.*

If you try to get rid of the fear first, the dive will not be completed. Dive into the midst of it and carry with you the jewel of Truth: I am with you always and, the appearances of your experiences notwithstanding, there can be no separation between us.

Thank you.

And if you think your strength is waning at any moment, remember what I taught you then: all you have to do is raise your hand and say,

Give me about a pound of your strength.

And I will deliver it to you gift-wrapped. And indeed, precious friend, I love you. I am with you always and I will give you my strength until yours is once again as certain as mine. I have long waited for just this hour. Kind of like I had to say to the Holy Spirit, "Look, I know you're a good tapestry weaver but let's get on with it here."

Thank you, brother.

Question: Jeshua, I've gone through a lot of changes lately and I am really grateful for them, most of them . . . but I can't seem to feel the Holy Spirit or anything. I feel sort of . . . I don't know, I don't know if it's resistance even. I know that things are going to be taken care of, I know that I am growing, but I can't _feel_ the Holy Spirit. Do you know what I mean? I don't know if I should do something or if I'm resisting, or what it is that's going on. Does that make any sense?

Well, you've just been a bad girl and you are being punished by being sent to your room without dinner. And I'm afraid we are going to have to leave your glass empty for quite some time until you learn better! Beloved friend, what would it feel like to feel the presence of the Holy Spirit?

It feels just perfect. I know where I am. I'm balanced. I know it just feels perfect. I don't know how to explain it more than that. Are you willing to acknowledge that right here in this moment you *are* balanced and you are whole and you are perfectly safe?

The Light that You are

Yes.

How does that feel?

I'm sort of trying to feel it.

There is the problem.

Trying?

Beloved friend, do you not feel the volatility that is going on in the body right now?

Yes.

Do you notice how the breath has itself become a bit chaotic?

Uh-huh.

Breathe.

I can't.

If you don't choose to breathe, you die. So you might as well breathe.

I feel like a part of me is dying.

Good. Breathe anyway. Do you feel that welling-up that seems to be beginning about in the area of the solar plexus up through the chest?

Uh-huh.

It is a very ancient fear. I am with you and I am with you now. Do not think that because you look upon this physical form and you hear certain words coming out of it that I am somehow limited to it. I am just pulling the strings. I am with you and I am beside you, now. And I want you to be my breath. Give that body to me by breathing breath for me. You notice how the thought arises, "I can't?"

Uh-huh.

But is it not lessening?

Yes, it is.

Breathe, beloved friend. I need your breath. Breathe life for me. Feel that breath like a ray of Light. It gently begins to descend down the center of the body through the solar plexus. See it like a gentle ray of light that comes to dissolve the mists of the morning. Let the breath rise within you that its Light might descend through a very ancient fear.

Breathe for me. Be my breath. Let the body soften.

Precious friend, as you breathe, without needing to know the source of that ancient wound, give it to me. Within yourself just relinquish it. Give it to me. I love you and I need you. Breathe for me. Let the breath come now even more deeply and a little faster, as if you could just drink it in. And as you exhale, begin to create a little vibration as if you were just sighing within yourself. Hmmmm. Breathe for me. Hmmmmm. Hmmmmm.

Precious friend, as you breathe, without needing to know the source of that ancient wound, give it to me. Within yourself, just relinquish it. Give it to me.

The Light that You are

I love you, and I need you. Breathe for me. Let the breath come now even more deeply and a little faster, as if you could just drink it in. And as you exhale begin to create a little vibration as if you were just sighing within yourself. Hmmmmmm. Breathe for me. Hmmmmmm.

And as the thought arises,

I don't know how to give this to you,

remember that you don't have to know how. Just be willing to give it to me. I have a few friends who know how to take it from you. Hmmmmmm. You are loved so deeply. You are loved so deeply. I have not left you, and I will not. Please be my breath. Those around you now are indeed your friends and there is not a thought of persecution, not a trace of judgment. Indeed. It is safe now to simply be loved.

There, do you feel that starting to change? Indeed. Trust the tears. Trust them and allow them. Each tear is a thousand ancient hurts, just welling up to be released from the place you've stored them. Breathe for me. Your breath gives me life, and I need you as much as you have ever needed me.

Radiant and beautiful soul, the past is taken from you and its weight need not accompany you any longer. Oh, indeed, you are so loved by those who surround you now, there is no place for hurt to enter in. There will not be persecution as you choose to live the Light and the power and the love that you are. The experiences of persecution are over now. Breathe. Hmmmmm.

Each evening and each morning give yourself just five minutes in which you breathe in that way. And I meant what I said:

You are breathing for me and giving me life.

Feel that Light descend to the very depth and core of your being and as you do so, remember you are loved wholly.

Your heart's desires are worthy of being manifested and lived, and by so doing, a thousand minds are going to be touched and healed. And I will never be further than the width of a thought away, because I love you as deeply as I know you have always loved me. Hmmmmm. Yes.

Tears are an extremely sweet blessing. Think not that your willingness to allow them has not also touched and healed and uplifted every mind, every brother and sister who is with you now. Nothing takes greater strength than to allow an old hurt to be released. And each time you choose to breathe and to remember how loved you are, you uplift the whole of the Sonship. And I give unto you my thanks for your willingness to breathe.

Though it seems a simple thing, rest assured, I speak not just to hear a voice with words. Each time that you do that, you *are* healing the Sonship. You are making it easier for your brother to complete his three-point dive. Indeed.

You have loved me for a long time, haven't you?

Forever, I think.

Know precious friend, forever you *know*.

This world no longer holds the power to ever create a veil between us. Rest assured that in this hour you have lifted your hand and our fingertips have touched. And mine are coated with a certain kind of glue and once you're stuck, you're stuck. Indeed.

There. There. If you can, tomorrow, be very gentle with yourself. The mind is going to tend to say,

Well, I have this to do and that to do.

At least through a majority of the day, unto at least the early afternoon, as much as you can, just do nothing. Save breathe, of course. Just be gentle. Nurture yourself. A bit of a rest after . . . what you call, post-surgery. Indeed. Thank you for your courage. Quite frankly, right now, there are a lot of others who would like to say thank you, too. It's okay.

Thank you, Jeshua from my heart.

Some minds dream of what they think are grand and glorious things. A long time ago I learned there is no greater job than just to be a messenger of the Heart and to deliver my Father's Love to my friends. To some, well . . . it doesn't pay well. The hours are long and eternal, but the rewards are priceless — because you are priceless.

Love, sweet Love. The Love that heals all things cannot be created, it can only be allowed. Therefore, indeed, with allowance are all worlds transcended and all ancient hurts released. With Love, freedom is reborn. With Love, joy returns. With Love are all things made new again. With Love do you become indeed the Light that lights this world.

Oh, beloved and holy friends, in whom our Father has always remained eternally well pleased, you are His only creation. You *are* the Thought of Love in form.

Be you therefore, at peace in all things, and remember always you are the ones who are indeed allowing the things of Heaven to be wed with the things of Earth, that the Light of Christ might be extended as far as from the East to the West. Be you, therefore, the completion of the atonement and you are the Light that lights all worlds.

Amen.

Walk with Me

And once again, greetings unto you, beloved and holy friends, those that have journeyed with me since before time is and those who will *remain* with me after the purpose of time has been completed, and the things of space and time are needed no longer and dissolve away into the Source from which they have arisen, and the Holy Child of God remains eternally One with Its Creator. This cannot be described in the languages of your world and yet, by faith and with vision, the heart can see and sense and know that surely Creation holds a purpose, surely it will know an end... an end to the things that reflect Creation in time, but not an end to Creation itself.

For Creation is but the unlimited extension of the Love of God, in perfect union with God's only Creation, His beloved Child you, the one Heart of Christ, shared by all, beyond the body, beyond personality, beyond your dreams of a history that you think still is carried with you, for these things have been taken from you and you remain as you are created to be.

And yet within the dream of time and of space, even as you have known birth into this world, so too did I come and took birth within time itself. And I came as *you* have come. I came not as one who was already a master far above you.
I came to *be as you are*.

I came forth, therefore, from the womb of a woman. I came forth and, legend notwithstanding, indeed I screamed and cried, as every newborn babe does. I came to learn hunger and cold.

I came to learn to feel the subtle energies of those around me. I came to wonder at the way a bird flies through the sky. I came to marvel at the way the sunlight dances across the waters. I came to marvel at the gift of song, and of dancing and of celebration that would seem to well up through the souls of those that I saw around me.

I became troubled, as I looked upon many and saw veils of pain, and of doubt and of guilt and wondered,

> *Where have these things arisen from?*

For indeed I came forth and chose, even as you have chosen, to be birthed into a timeframe, into a culture upon this Earth, in which the simple truth was always taught:

God is but One and God is Love.

And yet the kernel of this simple message seemed to be veiled and veiled and veiled and veiled, complexity upon complexity upon complexity. Some would say that "The Lord thy God is a jealous God," and I could not understand this, for when I journeyed and sat beside the calm waters and watched the sunlight dancing across them, when I heard the song of a bird, when I heard the voice of my mother, I could not comprehend that God was jealous, that God could want anything but the expression of the Love that He is. And I looked upon my own people and indeed I was troubled. But he that searches *does* find, and when you find you will be troubled, and that troubling creates an opening in which you ask more deeply than ever before,

> *Father, show me Thy Face, teach me Thy Truth, that Thy Will might be done through me, that Creation might be restored to you.*

Therefore in this hour I come to share gently with you the simplicity of the truth that you are as I am and have been, even in the field of time. I have felt the things that you have felt. I have questioned the things that you have questioned. I looked upon the political structures of my age and wondered,

> *Why this feeling of insanity? Why this fear, why the attraction of power that can never satisfy? Is it not enough to feed those who are hungry and to embrace those who are alone?*

Therefore, and because I chose birth into a family fully dedicated to discovering and expressing the Love of God, I was given many teachers and as a child I was taken to many teachers. There were many factions in the Jewish community of that day. One such group was what you would know as the Essenes and, unlike what many of your current scholars would say, the Essenes were not just merely a sect that separated themselves from the main population.

Yes indeed, they had their monasteries, they had their communities apart—but there were many Essenes who lived *within* the Jewish population of that time, who lived in the cities and were carpenters and fishermen, who were merchants and teachers and yes, even rabbis.

For the Essenes simply represented a core or an essence of a teaching that sought to restore the Jewish family to an ancient knowledge: that man is one with the Earth and that it is by honoring that connection that the soul reawakens to the truth of its dependence, not just on the Earth and things of time but on God as the Source and the Creator of all.

The Essenes, therefore, taught me how to find attunement with the body itself, how to heal the body, how to balance the body, how to listen to its subtle messages, how to utilize the gifts of fasting and of prayer and of meditation to correct the subtle imbalances that come only truly from the mind, and from its fears and doubts.

By the age of five, I was already being taken to certain teachers, both within the monastic tradition of the Essenes and also to teachers that lived in Judaea and also in Jerusalem. One such teacher is one known as Joseph of Arimathea. This one also was a distant uncle, a part of my own family. He'd achieved what you would call great wealth in the merchant trades but was also a man of high standing within the Jewish community. Often I would spend time with him, my parents would simply leave me with him, and even at that age, he would begin to chant to me the heart and essence of Judaism:

> *God is but Love and you are fully dependent upon that Source of Creation. Therefore, render every decision unto Him, trusting that Love will guide you.*

Even as a child, these thoughts began to plant their seeds within me. At the age of seven, I made my first journey with my mother, and the one who had come to be as my father, and my uncle. Because of his wealth, he arranged to take us by boat and we journeyed forth to that which you would now know as England. We went to study with certain groups, to begin to reveal to me the perceptions of various groups and their attempts to understand the Mystery of Creation, and their attempt to relink themselves with the Source of Creation — to study their ways, to feel their perceptions if you will, to *learn*.

Therefore, indeed, we journeyed forth and in my first experience in that land I was introduced to the priestly caste — you have heard of the term "the Druids." This energy, this basic strand of approaching the Creator and Creation goes back a very very long ways. As I spent time with them, having already learned to rest in innocence, making no judgment, but feeling and listening and learning through empathy, I came to see that there seemed to be a fundamental energy that pervaded their entire approach to the Mystery of God. They sought to align themselves with the energies of the Earth and yet, while this is perfectly okay, I began to detect that there was a subtle hope in gaining mastery or power *over* the subtle sources of energy in this creation. And as I began to feel that, I questioned more deeply,

Holy Spirit — given unto me of God — bring wisdom, that I might understand what I am feeling.

And I began to sense and to see and to know that, while the intention of this strand had indeed been good at one time, the mind of man, the ego of man, can take anything and turn it for its own devices and therefore there was a subtle intention of seeking power *over* nature, accessing certain powers in order to gain power or control over others. It was not an overt or an evil thing, only in this perception. I stayed with them upon that journey for a period of nine months and then we journeyed back to Judaea. I brought with me many questions and the memories of all that had been shared with me.

I was guided then to spend much time journeying into the desert, to begin to learn the practice of resting in prayer and meditation — *alone*. And if any of you have ever tried it, you know that fear comes up when there you sit in the midst of a grand darkness, the things seen with the eyes by day have disappeared and certain sounds seem to come, and even the wind brings fear within you. And I was taught that these are but as demons, but you would not call them that today—psychological fears—arising within me that needed to be transmuted and healed, *to trust the Voice for God in all circumstances.*

So even as a child, I was guided to begin this practice of leaving the roar and the din of the world, to seek a place of solitude, to re-establish my knowing connection with the Source of all of Creation that I came to call as Abba, Father. And Abba doesn't mean just "Father." It evokes and carries a sense that the Source of Creation holds an intimate and direct relationship with every aspect of Creation, that God was not just an abstract energy but a personal Being, through which there could be communication in the depth of the soul.

I studied much with the Essenes and learned much from them, but also I felt that often there was a subtle underlying energy of fear. There would be a tendency to make judgment of the Sadducees and the Pharisees, and indeed a subtle hatred of those that had come to our land: the Romans. And I could not reconcile this subtle underlying energy with the simplicity of the Truth that I found when I read the Torah:
God is but Love!

Therefore, I asked to seek further, and going then to my uncle once again—who was very much like a spiritual preceptor for me—as he began to see that my questioning was maturing, that I *needed* to seek out and understand, he made arrangements. And I went with, again, my family, my parents, to what you know as Egypt, and there were then at that time also groups, collectives of Essenes, who were aware of me (even though I was not aware that they were aware), that I had a mission to fulfill in this life, I was growing and evolving *into* that mission.

And so we journeyed forth, and there I was introduced to the priesthood at that time. And I asked them questions, and I watched their rites, and I listened to them, and I spoke deep into the night with their "philosophers" if you will, and here again—and even to a greater degree—I found what we'll call here a dependence on "magic." For the rites that had been passed from generation to generation in that strand, that culture, had come again to hold the greater power: that the rites themselves, the rituals themselves, held the power and that it was through the correct… hmmm behavioral methods that you could unlock the powers, whether it be in stones and crystals or staffs or chants. This did not feel appropriate for me. And yet, now that I was at the age of about eleven, as I questioned the priests, they would become greatly troubled and they went unto my uncle and said, "Take this one from us. This one is not quite ready to learn what *we* have to teach!"

My uncle smiled. "We will journey back to our home." He knew that I was troubled on the journey, as still my mind and my heart sought to understand,

Why is there this difficulty? My Father is but Love!

I was quiet and sullen on the journey home, and when I was received back at home I went back to my father's shop, the little carpentry shop. I was never a very good carpenter, by the way… I was somewhat preoccupied with other things and my father, unlike the tradition of that time, did not insist that I remain with him in the shop, and when he felt that I was being pulled to journey into the hills to meditate, to pray, to walk, to go and to speak with others, he would just let me go. And many of his friends would come to him and say, "That son of yours is never going to be a good carpenter. Discipline him a bit more."

And he would smile and say, "He is called by a different Voice." There were some that understood that and supported me, but there were many who were greatly troubled by what they perceived to be my rebelliousness, my lack of discipline, my lack of a sense of duty to tradition.

I journeyed back, first to Egypt, and then back to Judaea, where I set about seeking out those who would support me and walk with me. You have known these as disciples; I prefer to call them friends. The abilities had been awakened within me and here we would speak for a moment of what many of you call chakras or subtle abilities, and as these energy centers open the mind, the heart can indeed access levels of knowingness that seem to have been previously veiled. As I sat in prayer, what you would call meditation, I merely asked,

Holy Spirit, what would you have me do this day?

And a picture would come and I would see one standing by the shores of the lake, a simple fisherman, and I knew immediately I was to make contact with that one. And so I arose, and I journeyed forth. It was a several hour walk through the heat of the day. And I arrived at the shores of what you would know as the Sea of Galilee, and there indeed was a fisherman: not a fisherman completely unknown to me, but one who was indeed a part of my family, a cousin. This one's name was John. And he arose from his work with his nets and he looked at me. He had not seen me since I had made my long journey. And yet as he looked into my eyes, he knew that much had changed and in our gaze, there was what you would call a communication in the depth of the soul, and he knew that the time was at hand. Something compelled him then to look upon me and say, "Well, what do we do now?" And I said, "Follow me."

Now in time, and to keep this story short, a certain group was gathered around me. You've been told that there were twelve disciples. Fundamentally this is true, but there were actually much closer to a few hundred and the vast majority of those numbers were women, not men, because it was through the feminine that the simplicity of the Gospel that I was to restore could be heard and understood and felt through the feminine nature; because my Gospel was the simplicity of Love, the simplicity that God and His Creation remain as One and that *each simple act of Love is sacred*—for it is through the feminine, the woman that can understand what it means to prepare the simplicity of a meal and give it with love, without asking anything in return.

The men would often spend much time quibbling over the theological meaning of a simple parable, a simple story, while the women would smile and nod their heads and say, "Ah, this one's journey to ancient lands, to that which is called India, has served this young Jeshua well. His heart is opened, he feels the simplicity of the Truth." And yet they too knew that in that culture what they would teach would not be received.

Therefore, the simplicity of the Gospel of the Heart must yet come through a male form, a male teacher, one taught and raised within their rabbinic traditions, one looked upon as having some sense of authority and understanding of the sacred texts. Therefore, the women seemed to be in the background and yet in actuality held a very important role. Often it was to them that I would send my male disciples and simply asked, "Return to me when your heart is corrected and restored to the simplicity of Love, and you've given up questions, and because the heart is open you long only to give Love."

I was a man, born into a culture, like every other. I was a man who asked the questions you have asked. I was a soul who found the answers because I learned to *seek first the Kingdom of Heaven* and all things were restored to me. I came to see that I was as my Father had created me to be: that I was unlimited forever, that I was truly Spirit and not just body and that therefore the body itself could become but a vehicle for Love's expression and extension. I walked from village to village and simply taught, "God is Love, and you are with Him now." I taught the heart to celebrate. I taught my people to set aside the seriousness of the priestly caste and to spend their time playing, to set aside times of celebration and of dancing and of joy, not as a way to invoke the powers of God but to celebrate the Reality of God's presence: "I and my Father are One!" And indeed we danced often, we celebrated often.

Indeed, precious friends, there arose a bit of dissension: "Who is this one that teaches that the soul needs not intercession, that needs not the priestly vows, that need not come to the leaders of the Jewish culture at that time, but need only retire into the quiet of the Heart to be restored into the Love of God and then to seek out those to whom they can give service? For this one teaches even the farmers and the villagers that they have no need to pay homage to the tradition in which they are born but to honor that tradition by being the presence only of Love. This one makes great waves; what will we do about it?" Not all, only some in positions of power. And they went unto the political leaders, sent from Rome, and convinced them that I could cause much damage, create much dissension and because there had been the hope and the prayer for a Messiah—and many thought that that Messiah would come as a political leader to overthrow the enemies—I began to be feared as a political enemy. Even though I had participated in the healing of many,

I came to be seen as one stirring up the pot. It was only then as I neared the latter days of my ministry that the full revelation returned to my soul that I had chosen to create a demonstration, a teaching of which could not be denied by anyone, that it is possible to suffer the slings and arrows of this world and overcome anything. I would teach that death is *unreal* and need not be feared.

I journeyed forth one last time into the desert, there to pray and, yes, to cry, and to feel the last vestiges of fear, of a moment's doubt and to give these things over to my Father and ask only that His Will be demonstrated through me. His Will is only Love.

There were at those times many travelers that would come from the East and in one such journey of certain teachers that came from what you know as India, they came and spent much time with a group of the Essenes that were living quite apart from the rest of society, and my uncle and my mother journeyed with me and went to this place in the desert, alone and isolated. And I sat at the feet of these strange men who spoke in a different language that seemed to hold a melody, that seemed to hold a resonance, as you would call it, deep within my soul and evoked the sense of peace that I felt when I myself read in my native language of Aramaic—as if they were sister tongues, singing the same notes from the same song.

I became greatly compelled to dive deeper into the philosophical strand that these teachers brought from this distant land. My uncle never once said, "You need to go here now." He waited for me to ask. And so early in my, what you would know as, teenage years, I went unto him and said, "I am called to go to their land. I need to understand their perceptions, their techniques; I need to study with them." And he said, "My friend, if you go, you may not return. It is a great distance and there is much to learn. Are you willing then to leave family and home?" Without hesitation, being young, I simply said, "Well, of course!"

And he said, "Very well, we will make the journey, but first we will return to Egypt for a short while, to rest, spend time with friends, and then I will send you on with some of those who will journey with you."

Leaving then, Egypt, I traveled with a group of about seven that had been given unto me to protect me, to guide me, who had also been to this land. I did not know it then, but they knew where they were taking me. They seemed to know already who I was to meet, who I was to spend time with. And so we journeyed to what you call India, a very strange land indeed.
And yet there seemed to be a pervasive knowledge, a knowledge of the eternality of God's presence. But there were many sects and many creeds even then, and some seemed very much to be attracted to "magic" — the attempt to invoke the Will of God, to attain power over it, to be seen with favour of God. This always troubled me, but I was taken into what you would know as northern India, and from there we journeyed to what you would call your Himalayan mountain ranges.

Here I began to meet certain teachers who emanated a peace that I had seen but rarely, a peace that called to me and immediately brought my mind and emotions to silence. Here I knew there was a knowingness. I spent many, many months with a group of teachers at the foot of the Himalayas and I learned what you call commonly the ways of Yoga. I learned the way of the breath; I learned the way of the body: I learned to fast the body and to get by on very, very little. I was told that this was important. Only later did I know that it was simply a device for taming the restlessness of my adolescent mind that helped me think I was doing some arduous path. It was my entertainment.

As I spent time with these teachers, they taught me of the depths of consciousness, revealing to me—bit by bit, day by day—that the Heart and the Source of Creation was not outside me at all, but that the feeling I had had as a young child was accurate: that *God is but Love* and can be known by many names, and that which brings the mind to silence and allows the heart to freely and safely be opened by whatever means. This was a true path, a true teaching, a true gift that could be given to anyone.

I learned the subtle art of *listening*, of abiding with another in relationship, thinking not that I knew what my brother or sister needed, but learned to attune ever more deeply to the realization that there is the presence of one teacher that I have called the Holy Spirit, the Comforter, with me at all times, that would whisper unto me the simplicity of what was needed in each moment.

I learned that the path of awakening was not one of gaining but of losing, not a path of striving but of allowing, not a path of the intellect but a path of the heart. And my practice became the simplicity of remembering,

God is with me now and the only time that exists is this moment.

And there in that land of very high mountains, yes, I experienced the cold of the snows, I experienced journeying into caves to be alone for weeks at a time. But in time, I saw through the limitations of these techniques.

And of my own accord, I left those mountains and journeyed back down into the valleys and I found my teachers and simply said to them, "I think I'm getting it." And they smiled and then said, "It is time for you to leave, but before you do so, there is something that must be shared." Unbeknownst to me, they had already known that I was coming to the completion of all my learning that I could gain from them and had sent message. Had they had telephones it would have been much easier! My uncle, my father, returned for me and as I came down to meet with my group of teachers, I was surprised to find that they were with me.

And there in a circle, my father shared with me that there was a purpose that awaited me, that there was the need to be like a light piercing the darkness of the culture in which I had been born; and that I was being asked to give, indeed, of my life — to minister unto my own Jewish family, to help remind them of the simplicity of the Truth that there need not be an intermediary between anyone and God … that the priestly caste, the rabbis, the temples, all of the complexities that had been created over a great period of time, were not truly necessary and yet could still be utilized to honor and celebrate the simplicity that "I and my Father are One." I did not know at that time that the plan for my life's mission would involve a rather unique demonstration. Therefore, indeed, I *allowed* the drama to unfold. It was not so much that I directed it; it was already set in motion. I simply allowed it.

And when I was asked, "Are you king of the Jews?" I simply replied, "Some say that I am." "Are you the Son of God?" "Do you say that I am?" And I answered every question with a question. For these things mattered not. This began to create much turbulence in my own followers, my friends, for they, just like you, knew their own fears.

Some had become dependent upon me, some indeed hoped that I was the Messiah, the political Messiah that would come and overthrow the Romans through force. Some had come to doubt me and to begin to move away. There were many who loved me and they could not understand what was about to unfold, even though I taught them, "In three days I will raise this temple again. Therefore, be of good cheer." And they were puzzled, "What does he mean? The temple took many years to build! Who is going to cast it down, who could put the stone upon stone in three days? What does he speak of?" And some of them began to understand that I spoke of the temple of the body.

Therefore, understand well that those that were with me were just like you. They were human beings struggling to understand within their own culture how to be at peace with God, how to extend Love, what does it mean to awaken? And in that day and in that hour that I was given over to the authorities, communication between me and my followers was broken, even though I had said unto them, "I am with you always."

Let no one say unto you that the crucifixion never occurred. If that is true, then my own experience was surely an illusion and perhaps I had gone mad. The body was crucified, dead and buried. And my followers and friends were scattered. Many of them took upon themselves a great sense of guilt and pain. They abandoned my mother, except for a few, and they fled to hide.

Some stayed to be close to the action, but not too close, because they did not want to be identified. All of you know the feeling of guilt that comes if you feel you have abandoned someone. The guilt is always an illusion.

Understand well then, that upon the third day, the stone was rolled away and those that had been closest unto me — the women, who understood and were in communication with me — came forth to discover that something grand was happening.

And I indeed appeared unto many.

For when you understand that you are not the body, and when you want only Love and therefore see nothing else, you too will learn that you are Spirit, that you are Light Divine. You will come to understand that *in this very moment,* the only reason the body that seems to be yours is with you, is because you are choosing from the depth of your *compassion* to be present in this robe, and yet the truth of who you are has never changed. You remain Spirit and this alone. You are creating a façade through which you can extend Love into a world that needs it.

Precious friends, my journeys were not unlike your own. You too have traveled to distant cultures. You have studied every spiritual technique there is and has ever been created. You know the pathway of hoping for magic. You know the pathway of doing certain ritual acts to appease God, as if God has ever judged you. Each of you is awakening to the simplicity of the Truth that I too as a man learned,

> *I and my Father are One. Here and now, all power of Love can move through me by simply relinquishing every perception I have ever held, acknowledging only that Love is real and that what is real can never be threatened and what is unreal exists not.*

This Truth is diametrically opposed to everything the world would teach you but as you choose to practice it in *each moment,* correction comes to the depth of the mind and the heart opens.

Laughter returns to the soul, for appearances no longer have the power to master *you*, for you see only Love and you have remembered that death, in all of its forms, is unreal. You remain as you are created to be and there *is no separation* between minds that are joined in Love.

Please understand, then, what is at hand, for you come to demonstrate in your own lives that there need no longer be reliance upon magical means to invoke the Power of God. *You are the presence of that Power!* Understand well, I come to *any heart* that prepares a place for me. This does not require lifetimes of purification, because guilt is *not* in you; perfection is the nature of your being. And the simplicity of abiding with me rests only in your willingness to relinquish the weight of the world, to turn from the roar and the din of what we have called now the voice of ego, which is the collective chaos of the worldly mind, and to abide in a simple acknowledgement:

> *I am as God created me to be. Because all minds are joined, I choose to rest in the presence of an ancient friend who has never left me.*

Only, of course, if you want to! It is not a requirement for awakening. Teach then this world, that I come only as a brother and a friend.

As a man, I completed my part in the Atonement and by teaching that death is unreal, I *learned it*. "What? Jeshua's saying that when he went to the cross, perhaps there was a doubt?" Oh yes. But if it was true that one receives what one gives, and that as one teaches one learns, because I knew what I wanted was unlimitedness forever, I allowed the demonstration to be *my* final lesson as well — to learn that it *is* true: *death is unreal*. And where death is unreal, there can be no thought of sacrifice and nothing can be lost. There is only all to be gained through remembrance,

I am indeed here to be truly helpful, wherever "here" is.

For me it seems to be without a body, because it is not the Will of the Creator that I assume physical form, and you are coming in your own way to rest into that innocent simplicity of the meek that will come to inherit the earth:

Father, what would you have me do this day? Oh, take a nap? Okay!

It's very, very simple.

What can I do? How can I serve?

By being the presence of Love! And your gifts will be activated through you, for there is one Teacher that knows how to weave the awakening of this world and is already actively involved in it. Hmm. Therefore seek not to be the supervisor, but the supervised, trusting the Voice for God, as I too learned to hear *only that Voice*.

You are the Light that lights this world, for if your brothers and sisters are to remember the Truth that lives within them, does it not ask that it be demonstrated to them? Therefore as you teach Love, you will receive Love.

Walk with Me

And as you allow yourself to simply be willing that Love be given through you, you will come to know that you cannot help but be in the right place at the right time and *here* is where you're asked to be, wherever "here" is. And as you allow that Love to be extended through you, you will remember Love and its attraction will grow evermore brighter for you, until not one trace of a thought could arise of ever wanting anything else.

And then you will *see* nothing else! And as Creation is lifted with you, the veils that seem to show only separation will dissolve as mist before a rising sun and all of Creation will be restored as One and be lifted up unto the Heart of God.

Reflect then unto this world the simplicity of the Truth you have always known, and know that I am with you because I love you. Be you therefore that which you are with each breath,

and already the Atonement is completed within you, and *you* are the Light that lights this world.

Be you therefore at peace this day. Enter the silent chamber of the Heart often, not to pray for union with God, but to acknowledge what *is* and cannot be taken from you. And then celebrate with every breath and with every thought, let every gentle deed become sacred for you, let every gentle touch and every smile that you would give unto the world — every action becomes the sacred means through which Love is expressed through you. Herein lies the end of all teaching. Herein lies the perfection of all Gospels.

Now is the time come, and the Mind of Christ steals gently across the final veils and knowledge is restored to the Holy Mind of the Father's one Creation: you.

Peace be unto you always, you who have come to restore the Truth to the conscious-ness of mankind.

Amen.

Love Heals All Things

Now we begin.

And greetings unto you beloved and holy friends. I come forth to abide with you in this hour and in this day and this way. Not in order to teach you, for there is nothing which can be taught that you do not already know. I come forth not as one who is above you, but as one who walks with you on the way that you have chosen. I come forth freely to communicate in this manner because I love you, and I come forth to abide with you because you are my Father's creation.

You are Christ. You are that one birthed eternally since before time is. You are my brother and my sister, and when I come forth to abide with you I know my Father. When I come forth to abide with you, I see the reflection of who I am. When I come forth to abide with you, I know that only love is real. Therefore, throughout eternity, and again, since before time began, I am with you even as you are with me. Though the journeys may seem many, in truth there has been no journey.

You cannot journey to a reality from which you can never in truth be separated. Yes, you have heard it said that you create your own reality, but I say unto you, you can only create from your reality in the perfect freedom that The Father accorded to the son, in that moment, that mysterious moment in which The Father chose to create that which is likened to himself. His only begotten son, or offspring. You are that one, and you have been there for a creator, ceaselessly since that timeless moment, and even now in this hour you have chosen to create your experience.

You have chosen to take which you call the body which is really a temporary communication device, you have chosen to place it spatially at a certain location in order to attract to yourself a unique quality of experience. You are the one, even in this moment, who freely creates the perception through which you behold and experience this moment. In reality, I cannot heal your perception, in reality I cannot persuade you to see things differently, in reality, I cannot awaken you, but I can, in my infinite freedom, choose to love you.

Here then, is the great secret of consciousness, here the great secret that so many would seek in so many magical ways, the world that you experience, the world of your experience, as with mine, is holy uncaused by anything outside of yourself and there is nothing outside of you. The freedom which is your existence, the unlimited freedom to create perception, to create period, that unbridled freedom, the essence and truth of all that you are is unchanging forever.

Therefore, in any moment of experience, cultivate the decision to not look for a cause outside of yourself, but merely ask, "What have a I chosen to see? What have a chosen to experience?" and if you look with the eyes of the heart it will not be hidden from you, and to look with the eyes of the heart requires only a simple honesty. "What am I experiencing in this very moment?

For this is the fruit of what I have chosen previously, what thoughts I have allowed to make a home in the mind, what perceptions I have attached a value to so that they carry with me like a filter through which I color what is entirely a neutral event. Creation."

All power under Heaven and Earth abides within you, each and every one of you equally. All power under Heaven and Earth through which you create your experience. Therefore, you are free at any moment to see yourself as one who is seeking God, or you are free to see yourself as one who has found God. The difference between the two is the different between Heaven and the world, between spirit and matter, if you will. Between Heaven and hell, between suffering and peace. Between doubt and wisdom. Between anxiety and a very subtle joy that never leaves.

If I come forth to abide with you in this hour it is only because I recognize you as my equal, and I come forth only, again, because I love you, and I love you because I have learned to make the choice consistently to teach only love. Once, when I walked upon your plain, your planet as a man, I too was confronted with the very choices that you are confronted with, and though they come disguised in many ways, ultimately the choice is simple. Love and fear.

As a man, temporarily like you, identified with the perception of myself as a body mind separate from all others perhaps even separate from my Father, I too had to cultivate the decision to see differently. To choose what all of my teachers were telling me, what all of the scriptures that I studied were saying. That God and his creation are never separate one from another. That I was that light. That I was that creation. That I was The Christ. A certain day arose, as it has already for many of you, and will arise for others of you.

A day arose in which it suddenly occurred to me that rather than seeking magical means for closing the gap between myself and my Father, that perhaps I should do something outlandish, something so outrageous as to be almost sacrilege in every spiritual tradition in which I studied. That one outlandish thing was to simply take God at God's word, and to begin to live as though it were true that I was not separate from God. Now, you have to admit, that is rather outlandish.

So, I decided in that day and that hour, as I sat beneath a certain, on a certain small hill in what you call Galilee, and as I looked you upon the last rays of the setting sun, in the depth of my mind I made a decision. I will walk no more as a seeker for God, but I will give myself over to the reality that I and my Father are one, and then I will see what happens. It is not true that I came to this planet fully awake, popped into a whom without the help of what you call, shall we say, the normal means.

It is not true that I was sitting next to my Father and he said, "Look, would you mind going down?" I said, "No problem." If I did not walk this planet as a man, if I did not feel all that you have felt, if I did not perceive what you have perceived, if I did not know judgment, if I did not know fear, if I did not know sadness, if I did not know lust, if I did not know the cold of the skin, if I did not know the doubt, the longing, the desire to search and to seek.

Then nothing I ever did, and nothing I have ever said to you, whether then, whether since then, whether now in the many multitude of forms in which I am seeking to communicate to your humanity, none of it means anything, and has no value unless I have been where you are. Does that make sense for you? Therefore, please do me a huge favor. If you are going to insist of having a picture or some icon of me upon your alter, please put a picture of yourself next to mine. Better yet, take mine down and put yours up.

Recognize that the same truth that awakened me live within you. It waits on your welcome. Your welcome to make the decision, to never again tolerate the insane thought that you could be separate from God and bring that truth and that commitment to each moment. Remember that truth, and then live from that truth, and see what you Father would have you do. It's really not too complicated. What you will discover after you hear the message a few thousand times, is, "Oh, teach only love." Same message, many forms. Same content.

Teach only love for that is what you are. Teach only love for that is what you are. "Father, what should I do in this moment?" Teach only love for that is what you are. "Should I go here or there?" Listen to love, let love guide you. Be therefore the presence of the truth that you are, and you are the light that lights this world, and you cannot help but be in the right place at the right moment. If you would know your Father's will, open your eyes. Who are you with? Where are you? How can you bring love to the spaciousness and the sacredness of this holy encounter?

Rest assured, whenever you meet anyone on this plain, and in fact, we will go a little further now and say, in any moment of relationship, whether it be with a blade of grass, or as you gaze upon a star, every moment of relationship is a holy encounter. For your Father creates only that which reflects the good, the holy, and the beautiful, and through you creation waits to be blessed. Waits to be redeemed, waits to be saved, as you choose to perceive through only the eyes of love.

The decision to do so must necessarily correct the depth of the mind, heal the motions, and yes, while the body lasts, even transform the way these tiny little cells that you call the body have been responding to you like a good servant. Love heals all things. Love embraces all things, trusts all things, transcends all things, transforms all things, and returns reality gently to where it has never left. The depth of your own being. Well, that is enough of all of that love stuff.

I too, as a man, used to cry out to my Father, "But Father, it can't be that simple. I have this struggle with this person I know. They are what you would call in this day and age, pushing the buttons. What we call vexing the soul, and if only they would stop vexing my soul would be just fine. Surely the cause is outside of myself. Surely there must be some magical means whereby I can protect myself from the psychic onslaught of those poor unenlightened sinners who don't get? Teach me the way Father."

Yes, I journeyed to a desert for 40 days and 40 nights, actually, it was about 37 days and nights, but give or take a few, struggling with what? Struggling only with an incorrect perception of who I am and where I am always. As I began to live form that simple decision to accept my Father at his word, the events of my life began to be organized, not by me, but by the one that I have called the comforter, The Holy Spirit. The voice for a perfect right mindedness, a perfect sanity. The bridge between my personal consciousness and the mind of God.

Just as your life begins to be reorganized, and many of you know what that sometimes feels like, as something beyond yourself as you have known it begins to reshape your destiny, and thank God, for if you follow your own, you will walk off the edge of the universe and disappear into an abyss. But that which the comforter is begins to organize the relationships, the meetings, the chance encounters, the books, the careers, the friends, and that which has been placed within you is slowly birthed right up through the soil of everything you had mistakenly created which had been unlike love.

Which had been an attempt to keep yourself safe. Which had been an attempt to hold on to a judgement. Which had been an attempt to view creation other than the way it is. To see not the real world, but your replacement, your substitute for it. Right through that very soil, the comforter begins to work within your mind and you heart to correct your perceptions, to bring exactly that perfect learning situation in which you can choose again for love.

Each time you make that simple choice to listen only to that voice, you take what, if we might borrow words from your contemporary world, you take what is called a quantum jump, a quantum leap in the process of healing, in the process of birthing Christ. Each decision for love is more precious than all the gold and silver this planet could ever produce. It is worth more than all the adulation, all the successful careers, all the girlfriends and boyfriends that you could possibly ever amass.

Each decision for love outweighs everything that has ever been birthed upon this plain. That is how powerful you are. That is the power that waits within you and waits upon your welcome. In this moment, though the body is shaking, in this moment though the tears are flowing, in this moment though I am noticing fear of loss come up, I am going to choose love anyway. I will love the tears, and I will love the shaking, and I will love the fear, and I will love the one before me, and I will love the blade of grass upon which I may be standing, and I will love the lover of God within me that wants only to awaken.

Love. It is the only power that exists in creation, and you, right where you are, you are that one who can make the simple decision to bring love into your environment. You can be the channel, you can be the cup that overflows, you are the one that can make the simple decision to allow healing to occur. You are the one who walks upon this planet you are the one that has what you call a body, which means you have a temporary device that everybody else on the planet can see.

They often cannot see me because they look with the eyes of the physical body and not the eyes of the awakened heart. You are the one through whom love given as the comforter can guide your words, your gestures, your very being so that love comes into this world and can touch the heart of another in ways that your thinking mind could never possibly understand or comprehend. For the mind was never designed to be your master, it was designed to be the servant of the awakened heart.

By heart here, I simply mean the depth of the mind that is deeper than conscious viewing so to speak, deeper than your ideas and your perception. Just like the ocean from which all of the waves arise.

I simply call it the heart to differentiate it form what you call the intellect or the thinking mind. That mind never knows what anyone needs, and when you are in silence, which simply means to withdraw your valuation of those ideas, when you choose to withdraw into the sanctuary of your heart, into the depth of your Mind with a capital M and remember the truth that is true always, that only love heals.

Then you can be inspired, and that mind can become a servant of the extension of love, and in that moment, there is literally no difference between you and the lifetime I lived that has gotten so much press. You are Christ incarnate. You are the word made flesh. You are the only begotten of The Father. You are the redeemer, because you have chosen to be redeemed by choosing love. When you choose love over fear, it does not mean that will not experience fear as a movement or wave of energy.

Just like a ripple on a lake caused by a pebble that was dropped into your consciousness. When you choose love over fear, it simply means that no matter what is going on within you or around you, you have chosen to value only the voice for love, and you begin to cultivate the ability to discern the voice for love amidst the roar and din which is the world, which is the expression of fear. The world can exist within your mind, within your emotions, within the cellular structures of what looks like this solid mass called the body.

The world can exist what seems to be around that body in other minds, but the world is always the symbol of the choice for fear, and in the midst of all of that you can indeed cultivate the skill, the ability to hear ever more clearly the voice for love, and it begins by deciding to make the decision to hear it. Imagine you are what is called the symphony, and as you sit in your chair surrounded by hundreds of other beings in what are called the tuxedos, and the gowns, you make a decision in the depth of your being to hear the note of the flute.

You begin to learn how to temporarily set aside the sound of the violin, the beating of the drum, the sound of what is called the oboe, you begin to cultivate the ability to discern the note of the solitary flute playing beautifully in the midst of the music of the orchestration of that symphony. That is very much like all that you need do to cultivate the ability to hear the voice for love. But it does require a commitment; it does require that as you go through your day, though no-one may know what you are doing, you are using time differently.

You are choosing to use it constructively, and there is no greater use of time than to cultivate the ability to hear only the voice for love to act only from its inspiration. To give up the voice of the world, whether it seems to be coming from around you, or from within you, and actually, those are just terms that we have to use for your experience, there is no inner and outer. There is nothing outside of you. This means that when a brother or a sister seems to be acting insanely it is occurring within you.

You have the power to look upon that one and see them as yourself. To even transcend the perception of them as a brother or a sister, for that is still a language that is based on a perception that there is something outside of you. You can learn to look and see only yourself and make the decision whether you would bring love to yourself or fear. For as you treat your brother, you have treated yourself, and as you have looked upon your sister, you have looked upon yourself.

In fact, the reason you are seeing your brother or your sister in a certain, shall we say, unloving light, is because you have already first looked upon yourself in that manner. You are merely experiencing the effect of that choice.

Now, I know that that means that if you want to cultivate Christ consciousness, you are going to have to completely give up all hope of ever finding anyone or anything to blame. "But I put so much time and energy into it. I have been looking everywhere, high and low for lifetimes."

"And sometimes I am quite convinced I truly did find someone or something to blame." Yet, beloved friends, consciousness is such a delightful game. Each time that you have withdrawn love from another for any reason, you have hurt only yourself, and you have ensured that you will sense a lack of love. Forgiveness releases the world from the perception that you have placed upon it. You cannot forgive the world for what it has really done because it has done nothing.

You cannot forgive your brother or sister for their act against you, for you can experience nothing that you have not called to yourself as a result of the judgement with which you have already held yourself. The world would teach you that what you experience comes from outside, something called accidents can occur, the world would teach you that you can be a victim of the world. The world will also teach you, "Don't worry, you're not to blame," and actually, that is quite true, but from a different level.

The world then, and everything the world teaches is diametrically opposed to the truth of the kingdom, and where on Earth is the kingdom? It's right here. It's wherever you are, and the truth which is the kingdom knows that nothing is outside. The consciousness is the creator, and therefore in any moment, whether you are hearing the beautiful laughter of a new born child, whether you feel the tiny feet of one that comes soon touching and kicking the sides of the internal area of the woman's body.

Or, whether or not it's what you call April 15th and you are watching your money go out in the mailbox, nothing has come into the field of your experience except that you have allowed it. Now, that does not mean, listen carefully, it does not mean that you sat down and made a blueprint and said that on April 19th, 1994 someone is going to run over my cat. That is not what that means. The event of someone running over the cat is a symbol, it is an expression of a certain vibrational quality of consciousness.

You have already dropped a pebble in the pond of your own mind that resonates, sends out a ripple so that what you have dropped in here shows up out here as a reflection not to punish you. God is not someone who drops you on the planet, makes you suffer, and then when you die, tells you why he did this to you. Would that not be nice? Then you would have somebody to blame. All events occur for one reason and only one reason, not to punish you, not to make what you call the stress occur in the body, not prove that the world is an evil place.

Events occur in order to shock you, if necessary, into turning your attention toward the real world, toward the kingdom. To force you, if necessary, to learn to think differently, to learn to choose differently, to place value on different goals. Ultimately, the goal to awaken, the goal to heal. The events that occur in themselves have no effect on you. None whatsoever. Trust me, if they did you would not be here now, you would have disappeared 45,000 years ago. But here you are.

The world has not been able to kill you, has it? Just as it failed once to get rid of me. The event no matter what it is that you are experiencing is the result, the outcome of how you have been choosing to think of yourself previously, and shows up to reflect to you what has really been going on so that you have an opportunity to choose a new, and thereby learn what love is, how love heals, what experience is, what creation is, and what power dwells within you to co-create with God, the good, the holy, and the beautiful, and that power is unlimited forever.

Therefore, look not with judgement upon the experience you are having. If you notice the mind say, "I feel so trapped, I feel so imprisoned. Oh, if I just didn't have this dumb body." No. That is a judgement, and judgement only creates a certain vibration that must show up to reflect to you what you have been doing with the power of your mind. Learn to look lovingly, learn to look with sacredness upon each and every moment, learn to look that even with this thing you call the body, you can have a holy encounter.

You can look upon the body in a mirror, you can look at your face in the mirror, you can touch what are called the hands of the body, you can touch the shoulders and the arms, you can touch the area of the heart, and you can realize that right here and right now, wherever you are, you are the consciousness that can love this temporary creation. You can appreciate the incredible device it is through which you can call to yourself experiences in this certain domain of frequencies all for the opportunity to choose differently than you did in the past.

To choose love. To teach only love. To become so arrogant and outlandish that you make the same decision I did. "I think I'll walk around as though what my Father says to me is true." When someone asks you when your birthday is you can say, "Well it's December 25th, when is yours?" Actually, I was born in what you call August but never mind. Now, you have literally the power to have a whole lot of fun with birthing Christ. The ego which is the insane thought that you could be other than what God created you to be has one chief characteristic. Seriousness.

Rest assured, any time that you are praying with great seriousness, you are not praying, and loving seriously is a contradiction in terms. So, what would it be like if you made the decision to leave this place this evening having decided to play your way into the kingdom? To play your way into the kingdom. To be light, to laugh, to be outrageous, to have fun, to tweak the minds of others. Imagine walking into one of your stores and giving them the five-dollar bill for the gallon of milk or whatever else you have bought, and they give you a penny back because that is the way it goes these days.

You take the penny and you look at the clerk and you put your finger in your little cheek and go, "What a good Christ am I," and walk away. Then you come back in and say, "By the way, what a good Christ are you." Rest assured, that clerk will never forget you. I want to share something that is very sacred and very true, it is not serious however, though it is sincere. Listen carefully, whenever two minds have chosen to join in love, never will those two minds ever be separate one from another again, that is the dream of separation will never drop a veil between them.

Christ longs to be joined with itself. Showing up as every being. Therefore, when you choose, and please listen carefully, when you choose to begin to teach only love as the arisen Christ, it does not mean you get an operation manual that tells you what to do by the way, it just means you begin by deciding that that is what is true, and The Holy Spirit fills in the gaps.

When you have made that decision to look upon the clerk in the store, or your spouse, or your child, or a friend, or someone who just suddenly, mysteriously pop into your mind in your prayer.

Love Heals all things

When you decide to look with love upon that one and allow yourself to see that Christ dwells in them, you are linked to that being eternally, and as you awaken students are sent to you. Each of you has a multitude of beings waiting in the waiting room for you to decide to get on with who you really are. Most of them you have not met yet, and the majority of them you will never meet in physical form. But because all minds are joined, and what is mind but a point of divine light, a point of consciousness, a point of intelligence.

It does not matter what dimension they are in, everything exists in a space which is no greater than the head of a pin anyway, and in fact, it exists in a space which is the measurement of the width of a thought. If you can figure out what that is, please let me know. It means that even within this dream that occurred with the thinking of one insane idea, you are linked in relationship with all beings, and as you choose to heal, every decision to heal, every decision to extend only love uplifts the whole of creation.

As Christ is rebirthed in your remembrance, because it's already there, all of those beings with whom you have ever extended or exchanged love, immediately get it, and they start showing up in the most outlandish ways. Many of you know what I am talking about. Suddenly you meet someone, and you know, you know you have known them forever, and there is an immediate teaching learning relationship that is established, and you did not have to do a thing. Did not have to hire an advertizing promotional person to get you known.

They show up every time you make a decision for love and thereby allow the memory of Christ to come more and more into your mind, into your consciousness, into your beingness.

You send a message to everyone waiting in the waiting room that has a connection with you, and they know class is starting. As they awaken because you are awakening, those that have been assigned to them in those waiting rooms, so to speak, begin to get the message.

The bottom line is, there is a huge network of relationship that exists within a temporary dream that never occurred that is happening in a space no greater than the width of a thought in which The Holy Son of God is remembering and awakening, and here we are. I am part of that, I am not outside of it. As I chose to awaken, those assigned to me began to show up. I did not run an ad in the paper that said, "Looking for disciples. Long hours, bad pay. Must be able to handle projection."

They just showed up, and while I was in the body, I was guided. Just as you have often been guided. "Turn left," "Why am I doing that?" and you end up having a chance encounter of the fourth kind. A connection of the heart, and of holiness, and of healing, and of divinity, and of Christ, and love touches love, and love is remembered. You have all had those moments. When I chose to allow circumstances to shape an event known as the crucifixion as my final learning lesson that I held the power within myself to teach only love no matter what the circumstances are And dissolved even the need or evaluation for this kind of particular learning device, I became freed to reach across time and space, of you will, to begin to extend and teach only love to many beings, and many of you here in this hour have known what you call incarnations in which you became aware of me. That is one good thing what you call Christianity did, at least it gave me an avenue to get to know you. I did not create it, but I can use it.

Many of you, and you know in your heart that you know perfectly well this one who was known as Joshua Ben Joseph, translated as Jesus, many of you know that you have known me somewhere in a ancient past, many of you have very clear remembrances, many of you simply feel a vibration that suddenly went wham in your heart and you knew you were supposed to be here. You answered the call. For my intention as a brother and as a friend, one who has chosen to assume responsibility for the atonement, is to call my friends to myself.

To send out the invitation, to find the ways to reawaken the connection and the resonance that transcends all boundaries between my heart and those that I love, and those who my Father has sent unto me. Not that I can save them, but that I can love them and give them my strength until theirs is as certain as mine. That is when the dance begins. That is when the dance of joyous co creation between friends occurs, between you and me, you who seems temporarily and for a very short non-time to have a body.

This body, this tremendous communication device, through which in space and time, you get to be the embodiment of love to the degree that you want to, and nobody can tell you you cannot. Between you and me who seems not to have a body but is closer to you than your own breath. Who knows you, who loves you, who longs to dance and play with you in the extension of the good, the holy, and the beautiful. That which sends a signal out into the world and begins to touch other minds and hearts.

It can be as simple as telling someone you love them. It could be creating what you call a group of people to study *A Course in Miracles*, which is really just a course in oneself. It seems to be different, "Well, there's a book, we're studying this of course," of course those of you that study it know the more you study it the closer to this you get, and you realize that you have really just been studying yourself, and you are the book. It could be so outrageous that you allow the mind of God to drop like tiny seeds, grand visions for a healed planet.

In truth, there is no difference between the tiny quiet unnoticed act of telling someone that you love them, and you see Christ in them, and the grandest of visions that The Holy Spirit has ever dropped into any mind. Love is always equal, and each expression of it hold an equal value. The tiniest extension of love moves mountains because it heals fear. Never let that little chattering monkey called the ego say, "But you're not doing enough, but you're not doing enough." Broken record.

It is enough to love. It is enough now in this moment to take the hand of the one sitting next to you and hold the thought, " I sit next to Christ, and I love them." That is enough, because love heals. Love. Precious love, precious love heals all worlds. If you ever stand alone or sit alone beneath a tree on an early morning in which the first rays of light are beginning to caress this precious Earth of yours, in which mystery, untold mystery is all around you, you could never figure you how it got there.

If you ever sit quietly where no-one knows you are there, and the heart opens, and you think a loving thought of someone you have known, and you take the time, that one moment, and use it constructively to bless that being, in as much as you have done it unto them, you have done it unto he whole of creation as deeply and as powerfully as anything that I ever did.

More than that, you have done it as powerfully as a lot of things that were ascribed to me that I never did.

Love Heals all things

If you receive nothing else in our tie together this evening, please receive this. There is no such thing as a small act of love. To hold a new born child in your arms and set aside the perception of yourself and them as being two separate beings, as you hold that child and decide that Christ is in your arms and that therefore you are in perfect communication, to hold one quiet thought, "Beloved child, it's okay now to remember who you are." There will no longer be persecution and crucifixion in the world as Christ is birthed.

That tiny little act is the greatest act that can ever occur. You have remembered love, you have reclined in the truth of who you are, you have recognized it in the one in front of you, and you have blessed the world through your loving communication.

No greater love hath anyone than that one that lays down their life for a friend. Now, I know perfectly well that that has made a few people shudder because they thought that meant they had to die. Think about it.

Your life is your egoic state of being, the thing you think you possess that is separate and different from everything else, the thing you have got to keep going no matter what. When you lay that life down, your reality abides where once there was an insane thought, Christ lives, you have laid down your life for a friend and a friend is one who looks upon another and chooses to see only Christ and commits themselves to holding that perception of them until they can hold it for themselves.

That is what a friend is. No greater love hath anybody than those who would lay down their life for a friend. Does that make sense for you? So, when next your UPS driver comes with a package to your door, look him in the eye and say, "I am going to lay down my life for you today. Have a nice day, thank you for the package," and in that moment you have become eternally linked to that being. They might show up in your dreams, in your prayer and meditation.

You will be linked to them in what you call forever until that being also chooses to awaken and allows their experience to be reshaped by the one sent of The Father who knows exactly what you need. As learning lessons that come and go, they are all temporary, so that you can discover the power of choosing only a voice for love. As you grow in Christ, you will outshine the body, you will outshine this entire dimension and you will feel than you are bigger than this whole, what you call your physical universe.

Because your love, remembrance of that love, will need that much space. As you awaken to the discovery that there is nothing outside of you, you will know why I could make a decision to accept responsibility for the atonement. What other choice would I have once I recognized that there was nothing outside of me? That all power under Heaven and Earth was available for me to teach only love. To find ways to create communication devices that bring the universal curriculum of reality to each and every temporarily fragmented aspect of myself.

What I do through this, my beloved brother, through all of you, what I have done through what you call *A Course in Miracles*, and many other teaching devices, is you see, quite selfish of me. I want me who is you to be awake. So, let no-one tell you that I sacrificed, for in love there is no sacrifice. Please do not look upon me as some great saviour that-- "Boy, Christ. Amazing love he has that he would just devote himself ceaselessly to helping poor little me."

Please understand, I am just helping myself, because you are myself. You are myself, and as I am one with you, you are one with me, and I am not about to go anywhere until you remember that you are Christ, and that only love is real. There will be a day and an hour in which the atonement is completed, even on Earth as it is in Heaven so to speak, and in that moment, temporarily, everything will be transformed. No-one will walk upon this planet with single fearful thought, and no mind upon this plain will entertain the thought that it is separate from another.

Christ will gaze upon only Christ, and then the purpose of this world will have been translated, transformed and completed. The oceans, and the land, the tress, and the flowers that have come as angels to remind you of the truth, the sparkling rays of light that create what you call the crimson sunset, all of these angels will disappear. The world will disappear, just like it once began, as the result of a thought. The outcome of a perception, and when only the real world is chosen as a perception in all minds this world will cease to be.

But creation will go on eternally for The Father does not create that which ends. Do not think that in that day and hour you are going to disappear into an amorphous blob of consciousness, for here is the great delight of God. To create that which is likened to herself, I hope that is okay, and you are that one. Never think that individuation means separation but imagine existence as consciousness in which you have a sense of your individuation with no trace or a sense of separation from anything.

No brother or sister, relationship is the means of your salvation and the final step of your salvation is ongoing celebration and extension of the good, the holy, and the beautiful.

So, please do not pray to be dissolved in light, you already are light. Pray only that you will release any obstruction to extending light. You might want to add that you would like to have fun doing it. Please remember that your creator is the simplest of beings. Your creator says yes to everything.

Every thought you hold receives and automatic, "Yes, it's okay. Have a nice time," and please again remember, that you will not leave this plain and do what is called death only to sit in the lap of God and have him explain for you why he did all these terrible things to you. He will merely welcome you home and say, "Yes. Yes. I love you. What would you like to do today?" As you lay there you might say, "You know, I think I'll create another universe and go get lost again."

Please, I know that all that I have shared with you so far in this hour is not quite what the world has taught you that I taught. Not quite. But I can only teach you what you already know, and there is no-one in this room who has not experienced in this hour hearing words which are merely symbols of symbols pointing at reality, and had at least once in this hour felt a, "Uh-huh." Now, if you recognize the truth, the content within the form of the words that have been chosen carefully in this hour, and have recognized the truth of that content, somewhere deep within your being it can only be because the truth is already inside of you.

Truth can only be recognized by truth. Love can only be known by love. As you have your saying in the world, it takes one to know one. So, we would complete this short message and then we will continue on with this simple thought. Whatever the means or mechanism through which you believe you have come to discover me, whether through what is called The Bible, whether through A Course in Miracles, or any number of the other forms of the universal curriculum, whether you have come to know me as I have appeared to you in your dreams.

As I have caused energy, a little of what you call zapping in the heart to get your attention. Through whatever means you have come into relationship with me as my equal, or as my brother or sister, please remember that if you see a trace of the love and reality of Christ in me, it is only because you have looked through the eyes of Christ at me. It does take the one to know the one, and this is true for anyone in relationship with me. Whether they be what you call a pauper in South America holding the rosary, who think on me and knows that Christ dwells in fullness within me.

That one is seeing through the eyes of Christ. They may not quite know that yet, but they will. You are the one who sees Christ in another, that takes unlimited power and perfect freedom to see with the eyes of reality and not with the eyes of the world, and the one being that many of you have failed to appreciate the deepest is yourself. Self-love is absolutely essential if you would heal and awaken every obstacle or trace of anything unlike love.

You cannot love your brother while hating yourself, but by loving yourself, your cup overflows. Therefore, as you would embrace another, include yourself in the circle. As you would service unto another, include yourself as one worthy of being served by your love. As you would teach another, teach first yourself. As you would long to heal another, long equally that you be healed. For the only thing a teacher of God, and that is what you are, you did not even know you signed up the only thing as a teacher of God that you need to do, is to accept the atonement for yourself.

I am that light. I am that truth. I am that one. I love that which I am, for I am my Father's creation, and my Father creates only the good, the holy, and the beautiful. How deeply are you willing to cultivate the ability to receive that truth? For the depth with determine the fruit which springs forth thereof. I love you. Your mother loves you. Your Father loves you, and everyone to whom you have given a smile, loves you.

Everyone who has come to you in your relationships and you have looked past their mistakes, loves you. You have been their redeemer. Is it not about time you extended the same courtesy to yourself? So, with that, I want to suggest that you-- There is an interesting word your language is so peculiar, going to take a break. I do not understand this. Where will you get it to take it from? And when you break it, what will you do with it? Strange language. But it is a reflection, is it not, of how insane the world has gotten?

So, we make do with what we have. Take what you call a break, but as you do so, as you begin to raise the body from the chairs, if you do so in love you have just raised the dead. Notice as you, another good word, mill about, notice whether you have a tendency to avoid eye contact with another, whether the body gets a little tense. Decide otherwise and let the eyes linger for at least a moment or two. Let yourself relax and deliberately choose to see Christ in front of you, and see how you feel, and enjoy it. When we return, if you wish to return, we will spend some time with what you call the questions and answers so that we can all entertain ourselves. That is when we pretend that you do not know the answers. We will come back and abide together. It is a great joy to communicate with you in this way. When I left this plain, I did not leave with a hatred of the body or the Earth, only with a transcendence of the world. Therefore, this medium of communication with you is delightful for me as well.

I cherish to opportunity to be with you, for you are my love. Therefore, enjoy your break and we will come back together. I suppose when something is broken, it's good to put it back together. Be therefore at peace and know how much you are loved. How much light fills you, and how much there is within you waiting to be given to this world. Be therefore at peace, beloved friends.

Amen.

Female Speaker 1: This is a question that has bothered me ever since I read this statement in the course, and every time the expression consciousness was used tonight, I still had that same questioning. The statement in the course that concerns me is where it says, "Consciousness is an ego function," and yet it seems to me that we talk all the time about a God consciousness and a Christ consciousness. So, if we are talking about a God consciousness and a Christ consciousness, I cannot somehow reconcile that statement in the course that consciousness is an ego function.

Jeshua: Beloved friend, that simply makes God the ultimate ego trip. First, reconciliation between forms of the universal curriculum is not always possible, for reconciliation would require that each form of the universal curriculum use the same terminology and use terminology in the same way.

Remember always that words are symbols of symbols, and therefore, are twice removed from reality. Words are symbols of ideas. Words can be used and must be used in this dimension to direct the mind toward ideas which more clearly reflect reality.

But ideas themselves are not reality. Therefore, place value on the reality toward which ideas and words about ideas would direct you. Love, for example, is a word. It is a symbol of an idea which is a reflection of a reality which is beyond form. For reality is content. If you struggle to reconcile the form of the universal curriculum, which I did in fact help to give, called *A Course in Miracles*, with terminology that may be utilized here or elsewhere, you will actually cause yourself to waste time.

Time which could be better spent in that which love is a symbol of, by being the presence of that which extends the good, the holy, and the beautiful. If it were not necessary to present the universal curriculum in a multitude of forms, there would have only been one text ever written and it would have occurred several thousands and thousands of years ago, and no other form of teaching would have ever arisen. But in the fragmentation of the one into the many, levels of consciousness are created.

Each mind can be reached through certain vibrations, which are words, which represent ideas, and each mind has a certain language which is all its own. Therefore, the wise teacher learns to speak the language of the student in order to convey or to communicate the truth. When *A Course in Miracles* was given, it was given in the context of the students. Therefore, the universal curriculum and its content was structured into a form that could best serve the needs of the students.

Those that have resonated deeply with *A Course in Miracles* and gained great insight and healing from it, are merely those who are in close resonance with the minds of the students who first received it. Likewise, I do not choose my channels wrongly, nor do I air at the structure of language that is used through them, and why?

Because although I participated in the creation of *A Course in Miracles* as a teaching device, I am well aware that not everyone will receive that form and because my desire is to join with my brothers and sisters I seek out modalities of communication that allow me to reach out to more minds.

Consciousness is a function of the ego. Within the context of A Course in Miracles, this is perfectly consistent. Consciousness is a word which is related to an idea that reflects something about reality. Again, beloved friend, whether it be with the course, or any other form of the curriculum, do not place as much emphasis on the form, but rather on the content to which it would direct you. The purpose of A Course in Miracles is to leave you in the hands of your internal teacher. Your union with The Holy Spirit.

In this sense then, your curriculum begins where the teaching device of the course leaves you. It is not designed to answer every question a teacher of God will have for only your internal teacher can do so. No form of the curriculum could ever hope to be conclusive enough to satisfy and answer every question.

For this would place the source of your guidance outside of you. Therefore, simply relax the struggle to reconcile terminology but rather learn to feel, as you do very well, the content toward which it directs you.

Then live from that reality. The Holy Spirit will guide you in the use of what terminology can convey the truth to a brother or to a sister. Does that help you in regard to that question?

Female Speaker 1: Yes. Thank you very much.

Jeshua: Thank you very much.

Male Speaker 1: May I ask a question?

Jeshua: Absolutely not.

Male Speaker 1: Thank you for being here and somehow contacting me and again, somehow getting me here.

Jeshua: It took quite a lot of doing.

Male Speaker 1: I would not be surprised if that were true. I have got what to me is kind of a central question and I am not exactly how to phrase it. I guess my question is, why all this pain? I have heard the stories of the separation and even that the separation is a positive creative act, and expression of our creativity to imagine ourselves as alone, and all that. But still, there is the idea that, "Well jeez, if we can even conceive of the idea of asking a question about pain, how does that reconcile with an all loving God?"

This question sounds simpler the way I am putting than the way I thought about it but maybe you can answer it anyhow. I remembered how I wanted to as it. How does this serve God? For what sake is it to him that we have imagined all this, I mean, that we have gone through all this illusion? If there is no sake, then what the hell is going on?

Jeshua: Beloved friend, the answer to the question, what does all of this pain do for God? What is it all about? Is this, it does absolutely nothing for God, and he did not create it. God's creation is you, not you as you know yourself or think yourself to be a particular body mind who has unique forms of experience that are perceived and judged as painful, or as sufferable. This world is not God's creation. You are.

The you that is you is spirit. Infinite, unbounded freedom to create and experience.

That is God's only creation. You. This world, please listen carefully, hold no value or purpose except that which the comforter, The Holy Spirit, the bridge back to God can bring to it. Illusion can have no meaning until love translates it into that which can serve the awakening of God's creation, you, which is really just an act of turning your attention from perceptions and ideas and beliefs that are untrue toward the decision to accept the truth that is true always, and to begin to use the power of the mind, the power of your being to extent from yourself only the good, the holy, and the beautiful.

A thought of self-judgement is like a disturbance in an infinite field of possibilities that creates a distortion, it twists the extension of energy. You experience the outcome of it. You are free to use time constructively not to wonder why things are as they seem to be, but to discover how they can be created differently. For instance, it makes not very good use of time to ask why the ego, rather ask, how can I utilize time differently so that only love is extended to me, and only love is allowed to settle into the field of my being, into my mind that I accept nothing but love?

Imagine, by way of a picture, if you were a field of energy and your real boundary was about here all around the body, actually it's much bigger than that, what if you decided that anything that comes to touch the entrance to your energy field which is unlike love does not get to come in, and only love can come, and also only love can be extended out. Gradually, the whole nature of your experience would be transformed. This process of transforming the mind, renewing the mind, begins with one decision.

"I have no idea what's going on here, I don't know where it all came from, but I am going to assume complete responsibility for how I choose to use my mind." To be vigilant about what thoughts you choose to think. To will yourself in a sense to direct the mind toward only loving thoughts. To cultivate it on a daily basis, and to trust that the universe is going to show up in a way that is certainly going to challenge you to do what you say you are committed to.

Here, beloved friend, is the certainty of the end of all pain. For when the mind wants only love it will see nothing else. It will see beyond all boundaries that seem to separate this dimension from another, which seem to separate you from the ones that you love, all feelings of loss will disappear, and you will know that only love is real. You will literally embrace in your, pardon the use of the language, consciousness, in your awareness, in your beingness, you will embrace the infinity of dimensions of creation that are even now present.

You will know that there is nothing outside of you, and you will know that only love is real. Pain will no longer be a possibility in the field of your awareness. But that does not come by the act of someone else doing something to you, it comes from assuming responsibility for no other reason than this, it's the only way to change it. Again, spending time wondering why it is or how it got here is a waste of time. It will merely keep you sitting in the same spot of consciousness. Rather, decide what it is you want.

You could say that the greatest of question that you could ever ask yourself is this, "What do I truly want?" and know that it is perfectly okay to have what you want. You will come to want only love, for nothing else can satisfy the soul. When love is thoroughly established, you will see and experience nothing else. Paradoxically, that state of awareness is possible right here and now. It is not that you have to leave this world and go somewhere else to get it.

It is essential to get it here. For the body is not what you think it is, the world is not what you have been taught to think it is. There is something else present right here that can be perceived and known, it's called the real world in which pain no longer exists. The body arises, it passes away, events occur, and yet awareness is never pained by any of it. It is too busy being the presence of love, and that is what must be cultivated. That is what requires utmost responsibility and commitment, and self-love.

To go through the day asking only, "How am I choosing to use this moment? To love myself, to allow healing to occur, to look into the eyes of another and bless them with the presence of Christ? Or to convince myself that there is something amiss?" Consciousness is everything, and out of it immediately you create what you call reality, and you will discover, beloved friend, the power and the majesty within you as you come to see that by changing a thought you change your world.

Within you is the power to awaken to love, to act only from love, to see only love, to feel only love, to be the embodiment and the presence of only love, and then you will one day look back upon an old memory of something you once called pain. You will chuckle within yourself and say, "Wow, I am pretty amazing. Once upon a time I convinced myself that something besides love was real."

The journey from there to there is a journey without distance to a perfect remembrance of what has never changed.

Call it the spiritual journey if you will, call it the journey of mastery, it goes by many names. It is a journey that everyone must undertake sooner or later. You can delay it, but the journey will be taken. Why not begin now by simply deciding not to waste the power of consciousness looking for answers to questions that in themselves change nothing, but ask only, "What do I truly want?" If it is an end of pain, then turn it into the positive by saying, "I want only love, and I choose to be as a wise farmer who cultivates the garden of my own awareness so that only the seeds of love are planted."

What is planted in good season will indeed bear forth great fruit. Plant the seed, beloved friend, of only loving thoughts and it will come to pass that you will reap the harvest. That was a very important question to ask, not just for you, so thank you.

Male Speaker 1: Thank you for your answer.

Female Speaker 2: What is the link between the answer that you gave and social problems, or planetary problems like over population or the spoiling of the planet's resources? What I heard you say brings personal peace, but what happens to the physical world that we are in?

Jeshua: Beloved friend, as you make the decision for personal peace remember that you are indeed joined to all expressions

of creation. You are inseparably linked to what you call your planet, your beloved Earth. Now, imagine that your awareness is like an ocean or a pond. When you drop a pebble into it, it creates a ripple. When you drop the pebble of the choice for peace into the pebble of your C-word, consciousness, you send a ripple out.

Now, if you create a sound through what is called the megaphone and the pebble is dropped once, that is you sing a certain note, it creates a ripple, a sound effect that goes out and has so much power and then it finally seems to drift away, but if you keep singing the same note over and over, a momentum or a wave is created, and that ripple, that sound effect goes farther and farther and more and more powerfully. That ripple touches everything, everything in creation.

Currently, as you look out through your eyes and look out upon the world, you see an interesting mixture of beauty and insanity, of love and fear. You are literally watching an Armageddon being manifested through human consciousness. When I walked upon this planet of yours, it was not easy to awaken.

Why? Because most minds were sending out ripples of fear. It created a density that was much more difficult to get through, but the quickening that has occurred on your planet from the time that I was a man and to the time that you exist has been quite phenomenal.

Today, there are minds that are awakening daily, and I do not just mean getting a little insight, I mean awakening. That creates an acceleration in the way that the new ripple, if you will, the reality ripple, is being sent out through this ocean you call creation.

Yes, currently, there are children who will starve to death by the time this evening is done because the world mind believes not only that there is no way to do anything, but that nobody is responsible. Nobody wants to take it on.

There are toxins being dumped into rivers and oceans, absolutely true. These things are the reflection of the toxicity that has been settling in the past into many human minds, since the world is a reflection of what awareness or consciousness has allowed itself to value. The connection between your personal peace, your decision to be the embodiment of love, and what is occurring in what appears to be outside of you cannot be possibly overstated. It is crucial because there is nothing outside of you.

As you choose, regardless of what you see around you, to be the embodiment of peace, to practice forgiveness, to look lovingly and to find the essence, the sanity, the Christ mind in everyone, regardless of what they seem to be doing, you are sending out a ripple that touches that mind, and because there are many beings awakening daily now, there will be a point at what I believe your scientists call a critical mass, how about the loving mass? That is much better.

A loving mass will be reached, and please listen carefully, there will be a transition that occurs that effects, literally, it will be seen in other words, in the waters, and the air, in your forests, in the lives of your children, and it will occur in the twinkling of an eye because that is how experience happens. Ripples are sent out, when the momentum is enough, bam, experience takes place. The wave that is now occurring on your planet is growing in leaps and bounds, it can no longer be slowed, and it cannot be prevented.

Your political parties are going to go into obsolescence and there will be a day on this planet when those who have been given the power and the responsibility to direct the large guns and bombs will look upon their creations and simply withdraw their value from them.

They may have never picked up A Course in Miracles, they may have never, what you call, this standing on the head, they will awaken because a loving mass has chosen to awaken previously and just like that, it will occur within them.

They will look upon their creations and realize, "This is not what I want," and war will cease because the consciousness, the awareness that is shared by the one mind will have become wholly committed to a different thought, a thought held in unity, a thought that desires only the reflection of the extension of love. It is not what you call pie in the sky, it is the natural outcome of the correction of how the mind is used. Your decision for personal peace is critical.

Therefore, when you look upon what you call the logger who has just cut down what you call the old growth tree, love the tree for the beauty it brought, find the essence of the one who is called the logger, and love that one. That is what is critical and when one performs and insane act on this planet, remember that it is only a cry for help and healing. No act which has been an unloving act has ever been done from a loving place. It has been done because the soul of that one simply sees no other way to cry out for the attention required so the healing can begin.

Somebody must make the decision for love. Fortunately, this room is filled with a multitude who understand that, and that definitely includes you. Therefore, beloved friend, please cultivate your personal peace even as you act lovingly in the world. You will know where to be, what causes to be a part of, what action to take. But see it not as a fight against something for that only ensures that the opponent will always remain. See it as an opportunity to teach only love and thereby learn that only love is real.

The ripples that you create, you cannot begin to comprehend the effects of them. Give everything to the creation of those ripples within the field of your personal peace. The Earth is an entity just like you, it is a consciousness, an awareness filled with love. Nothing that mankind could ever do could possibly destroy the life of this Earth.

That is like a tiny little fly thinking that it has the power to destroy the horse upon whom it's riding. It's only because the horse has tolerance and love for the fly that the fly gets to be there in the first place.

This Earth is a great and loving being who knows exactly what to do to maintain itself. Its compassion is great, and the waters of the Earth will run purely, and the skies will be clean, and no child will starve. That wave of probability cannot be stopped now. The dream of separation is playing itself out. Simply focus on love. Thereby, take up your rightful place as part of the solution instead of part of the problem. You are doing rather

well too, beloved friend. Simply continue to know that you are worthy of peace. Does that help you in that regard?

Female Speaker 2: Yes. Thank you.

Female Speaker 3: Hey.

Jeshua: Hello. Long time, no see.

Female Speaker 3: Yes. I have a question about my body which I have read in *The Essene Gospel of Peace* that-

Jeshua: All lies, do not believe it. Just kidding.

Female Speaker 3: - That we need to purify our bodies and keep our blood clean and then I read in *A Course in Miracles* that the body is not real and that the mind creates the discomfort in it. A lot of drama that I have had in my life has been around illness in my body and I am a bit confused as to how to heal what I am experiencing right now which has just been chronic for years, and if it's not one thing, it's another, and if that goes away, it's another.

Jeshua: Beloved friend, what is the manifestation of disease keeping you from?

Female Speaker 3: Peace and joy.

Jeshua: As I said a few moments ago, when you want only love you will see nothing else. Even in the body. Therefore, look well, beloved friend, for beneath the surface of your awareness there is a conflict within the soul about its very worthiness to have peace and joy. There is a struggle within he soul, an Armageddon between the part that would want it, and the part that seems to have its grip on you that says, "No, you've not yet proven yourself worthy." You have aired in the past, and therefore carry a certain guilt.

That guilt keeps you from allowing the peace and joy to enter into the field of your being and thereby bring about the correction of the body that you would desire. There is a pattern in the mind that keeps the energy or the vibration of disease in your consciousness. Healing will occur when you have withdrawn all valuation you have paced upon disease, and as long as you perceive that there is something within you that justifies a sense of guilt, a sense of failure, you will keep valuing disease as a way to reflect back to you the truth of your guilt.

This guilt is deeply embedded, I do not mean by that to frighten you saying it's underneath 40 tons of concrete, it just means that it's old and has been pushed down. There is a feeling that comes up for you from time to time, you feel it generally right about in this area of the body, it is a very old sadness. Give yourself permission when next it comes to set aside everything and give yourself permission to abide with and feel that sadness. It is called embracing it. It's a feeling in your world because you have a body.

That is to embrace what is unlike love within you, and by so doing that guilt will begin to dissolve as a weight within your field of energy, your field of being or awareness. Disease has served you in the sense that it has kept in place the deeply held belief that your guilt is justified. As you come then to the decision to love yourself, to truly understand that you have never sinned, and you have never failed anyone at any time, that you indeed remain wholly loved, wholly loving, and wholly loveable.

The guilt will be dissolved from the mind, and the body will begin to reflect the change that has occurred. Listen carefully to those three words. You are loved, you are loving, and you are loveable. As you go to your home this evening, say those words over in your mind and discover the one that is the hardest to accept. There is your doorway to the guilt. One of those words is a symbol of an idea of something which is very real that is difficult for you to truly accept into your being. Here, beloved friend, is a very important doorway for you, and as you choose to discover it, and lease listen carefully, I will come and abide with you. We will go through that doorway together and that which is the guilt held as an ancient sadness in the depth of the soul will come to be wholly dissolved from within your being.

I am your friend, and I will walk with you because I love you, and I recognize your lovability. Therefore, look well and simply decide, you do not have to know how to do it yet-

- Just make the decision that it is time to heal and ancient sadness that has birthed the residue of guilt from which disease is merely the reflection that the guilt is justified. Indeed, it is time to heal, and something within you knows this now or you would never have come to this place in this evening. Well does a part of you know that you know me, and I know you. Accept what you feel in the depth of your being. You have known me before, you will know me again, and I am your friend, and it is time to heal so that it's no longer one things after another, but just one thing.

Indeed, I love you. I love you. I feel it would be important here to let you know that once you invite me in, I am like a guest who comes and does not leave. But I am not such a bad guy, and I will never demand anything of you save the opportunity for you to release the grip deep in the heart so that I can enjoy loving you. For only love heals. Blessings, my blessing I give to my ancient sister, be therefore at peace and I will be knocking. Fair enough?

Female Speaker 3: Thank you.

Jeshua: Beloved friend, thank you for the courage to come here this evening and in front of all these other minds admit the truth that you are tired of the weight of an ancient guilt and sadness. That ensures that healing occurs. You are courageous one.

You do not yet know the depth of your courage, but you will. So, I will be seeing you. Indeed. By the way, I do look forward to the day when all questions have been answered. Not because they are a burden-

- But when you realize that all your doubts have been solved and all questions have been answered, it simply means that you know that you are Christ, and that the dream you have chosen to dream no longer holds any value and then we can, what is your term here? Then we can truly begin to rock and roll. Rock and roll. I do love your language, it is rather fun.

Female Speaker 4: Hello, Jeshua.

Jeshua: It's about time.

Female Speaker 4: I have lots of questions but-
Jeshua: Do you?

Female Speaker 4: I guess they do come up from time to time and then they do seem to get answered, but it's so nice to have you here because it's quicker this way it seems.

Jeshua: Beloved friend, I am always here, it is you that goes away.
Female Speaker 4: Fair enough. The last time I talked to you, I talked to you on the telephone.

Jeshua: Do not tell anybody that.

Female Speaker 4: I happened to mention that I was writing that I was writing something, and I was-

Jeshua: Happened to mention.

Female Speaker 4: It was a very important thing that came up and I said that I was writing something, and I was feeling doubts that it was very important and that my feeling was, "Why bother when obviously there are more important being written and who knows who might read it?" You became very-- Well, you said very clearly, in a very assertive voice that everything that people do-- That this was soul work in other words, this was a piece of art or whatever, and it was soul work, and that it was very important to finish it.

As I remember, the one reason it was important was that you did not want to have to come back and finish it at another time perhaps, and also that it did not matter if anyone read it or not. So, I continued and finished some stories expecting in some way that at the end of it I would feel excited or that I had created something special, whatever. Well, I have had a few little feelings like.

Jeshua: Heaven forbid that they should grow into large feelings.

Female Speaker 4: That is my next question actually. When doubts come up because one feels that the ego is speaking when one is writing as opposed to the deeper sense of spirit, I guess my feeling has been that if it were deep spirit, I would have an incredible joy of completion, and obviously I do not have an incredible joy of completion, and obviously I do not want to just write from an ego place, I want to write what is true, and I want to write with a feeling that in a sense something is coming through me, which does happen at times.

But, is there a way for me and others, people who write or create, whatever, to be more in touch with allowing that to happen?

231

I mean, I know there is meditation et cetera, but is there some other way? Something that I have not been able to open up in myself?

Jeshua: For you, there is no hope. Might as well throw in the towel. Does someone have some what you call hemlock to give to this one? I will make sure that my Father erases your name out of the book of life. After all, you are certainly not capable of bringing through anything remotely resembling spirit or love. You scourge upon the Earth.

Female Speaker 4: You said that whatever I asked for I would receive, you said that quite a few times, and I have been asking and I have received lots of things, that is not what I am saying. I really do feel wonderful basically and blessed, it's this one little thing.

Jeshua: It's always something, one thing after another, and that way, beloved friend, you can keep the feeling little. The feeling of reality and of truth. Beloved friend, it is soul work, and the greatest soul work, the content of soul work regardless of the form is self-love. Complete self-acceptance. The recognition that only the truth is true. That your gift, your desire to take a blank piece of paper and form words as symbols of that which point to a reality beyond themselves, beyond the power of the mind to ever truly comprehend it intellectually.

That which sets the heart soaring. That which touches the hardness of the mind. That which brings a lesson to remember love. That gift, some would call it, you have cultivated over a multitude of lifetimes out of a huge compassionate heart that so loves this Earth and every being who walks upon it, flies above it, crawls upon it, or swims in its waters, that if you could you would stretch even that physical body wide enough to give them all a home to live in.

You, oh compassionate one, have cultivated that gift and you can only mock yourself by not letting be utilized to express the good, the holy, and the beautiful. That you know, and we both know that you know, is the truth of your being. You are yet struggling with the fear of what would transpire if you fully accept it that only the truth can be true, and you withdrew the value you have placed upon your belief that you must remain little and small within yourself in order to be accepted by the world.

That is the creation of the tension and the struggle. I will let you in on a little secret. The opinion of the world which is a collection of insane thoughts, does not hold very much merit. But the truth that you know to be true holds all merit. Therefore, write as though your life depended on it, and life will more and more inform the form of your stories and your sharings so that the words which are symbols of ideas will more and more reflect the reality that you know perfectly well is true.

The only question here is, when will you decide to live it by releasing the perception that you must dim your light in order not to offend the insane? Write, beloved friend, dance beloved friend, ride upon your horses, beloved friend, and enjoy the hell out of all of it. Do not fear your passion. Do not fear your aliveness. Show it forth to the world. Stop hiding your light under a bushel. Become a little what you call crazy in the head, as though the opinions of the world meant nothing.

Let yourself get a little giddy, lightheaded. Let the body dance. Go and find a waterfall, take off the clothes and dance and sing in the waterfall, you know you love those things, and then go back and sit and look at that blank piece of paper and recognize that Christ is looking at that paper, and Christ loves, love to create forms that reflect the good, the holy, and the beautiful. Not in order to be approved of, but out of the sheer delight of extending the reality of God's love.

Christ, you see, is that energy which will create the good, the holy, and the beautiful simply for Christ's delight, and you and how many others in this room block that from occurring because they hold the thought that perhaps no-one will notice. You can notice, and when you notice it fully, listen well, when you step into the willingness to create the good, the holy, and the beautiful for yourself, not giving, what is this word? A hoot. Whether anybody else on the planet ever knows about it, you will be tapping into the supreme secret.

That there is no way in reality that it cannot be noticed, because all minds are joined, and when you write and extend you love and your beauty and thoroughly enjoy it, it is impossible for other minds to be unaffected. Therefore, the sage transforms the world without ever leaving his room. Except perhaps to ride the horse, or to what you call the making love, the dancing. In other words, beloved friend, enough is enough. I have to part in the levity here, we have known each other a very long time.

Are you willing to love yourself so much that you give up expending energy creating the perception of doubt in order to keep your light small out of fear of what someone else might think?

Female Speaker 4: Great question.

Jeshua: It is the only question. You know the answer, it's just a question of when you will answer it by saying, "Screw the small stuff." That is one way to say it.

Female Speaker 4: I do need to hear it. I did need to hear it tonight. So, I thank you.

Jeshua: I will send you a bill later. Rest assured, beloved friend, you just never know who is going to show up to help form the words on the page.

Female Speaker 4: Exactly, and that was my next question. Just come and be there with me, just looking over one shoulder would be nice.

Jeshua: I will see if I can have it scheduled into my itinerary.

Female Speaker 1: Thank you, Jeshua, I do love you very much.
Jeshua: I know that, beloved friend. When will you be willing to accept how deeply I love you?

Female Speaker 4: Soon. Now.

Jeshua: Very good idea. You thought you could escape me by skipping into another time frame or two.

Female Speaker 4: Not on your life.

Jeshua: Right.
Female Speaker 5: Jeshua. My heart is pounding, and I guess I need to hear from you too, and I want to know what blocks me from using my artistic ability to capture you?

Jeshua: Beloved friend, if you seek to capture me, I will prevent you from using it.

If you allow that communication to transpire and then express it, you know that you will have created something that can be seen by others, and it triggers an old fear by which one, someone in the world, can point and say, "She's one of them. I believe she's part of that Essene community where this saviour of the world came from that we just got rid of." Fear not persecution this time around.

Therefore, beloved friend, if you would well entertain it, I would be most pleased to shall we say, sneak into the corners of your awareness in order to, how shall we say this, transport an image into your awareness that will stay with you and can be easily translated through the artistic medium. If it's okay with you, I mean, it's okay with me if it's okay with you, you can put it in your closet.

Female Speaker 5: I do not think so.

Jeshua: Indeed. Beloved friend, it is just an old fear. Where once you felt you needed to conceal a certain relationship so that you were not marked.

Female Speaker 5: I too have been with you many times.

Jeshua: Indeed. Rest assured, in this time frame there is no secret police, so to speak, seeking you out, and persecution will not occur.

Female Speaker 5: Thank you, please be with me in that art room.

Jeshua: Very well.

Female Speaker 5: Well you have a lot of places to go.

Jeshua: When one knows they are thoroughly unlimited, there is not place they cannot be, and when one has mastered fear, there is no place one would not want to be. Just something to consider. I will be with you. So, we will entertain one more question.

Female Speaker 6: Jeshua, I have been sitting here asking-

Jeshua: Oh, I changed my mind.

Female Speaker 6: I have had a lot of questions and I have narrowed it down to one. In *A Course in Miracles*, what is meant by The Father will take the final step?

Jeshua: That is a very good question, I do not know where that one came from. Never let anyone tell you that *A Course in Miracles* is purely a rational spirituality, there is much of mystery within it, much of poetry, much of mysticism. It must be this way because, again, words no matter how they are structured, are symbols of symbols which are hopefully effective reflections of reality, and no symbol, word, or idea can comprehend, wrap itself around reality.

When I shared the thought with Helen that The Father will take the final step there were many levels of meaning contained, hidden, veiled within that statement. Why? Remember always that *A Course in Miracles* was given within the context of the students involved. Therefore, teaching is an art and not a science. When to nudge, when not to nudge, when to lay it on the line, when to be a little sneaky. I could not say to Helen at that time that as correction comes to the depth of the mind, there is a point when the self one thought one was is revealed to be only God.

The entire language of the course then is based on a fundamental duality between creator and created, spirit, matter. This was a language that she could understand and accept without it causing fear. Therefore, to say The Father will take the final step allowed her to continue the process, and by the way we would say here that she was a bit of a stickler, it was like walking on what you would call cosmic eggshells to make sure that I did not upset her.

Now, when I said The Father will take the final step for you, that allowed her not to be fearful for she had not yet truly, completely healed her own Armageddon over the form of the universal curriculum called Christianity that she experienced early in this life. It kept in place within her mind the perspective that there is an interminable gulf between creator and created. At the same time, I simply told her the truth. Of course, The Father will take the final step for you, the final step is the complete realization that there is only God.

That the one doing the stepping is the one toward whom you wish to step. Just something to consider now. Grace comes from yourself, for I and my Father are one, and you cannot tell where the son begins, and The Father ends, who can find such a boundary? In truth, it does not exist. We speak this way only because teaching is an art and communication without the creation of fear is always the goal. Helen could accept that statement.

Had I said to her, "Look, it's very simple. You think you're something you're not, and there's only God. Wake up." There would be no *A Course in Miracles,* and for you too, The Father will take the final step. Merely love yourself and illusions will dissolve from the mind and emotions from the body.

Gently, lovingly following a path that you have set amidst the stars. The end of the journey is certain, for the one you walk toward is doing the walking, and that one known the way. Through you. Indeed. Thank you, sweet and benevolent soul, for your light is a blessing to all who know you. Time to accept it. When next you see one of your friends just go, "I know, I know, I'm a blessing."

Female Speaker 6: Well, there is a lot of them here, so they can help me practice.

Jeshua: Indeed. So, since the final step is the final step, that is a good place to end. How are you all doing?

Group: Great.

Jeshua: Has this evening been worth your while?

Group: Yes.

Jeshua: Well, I hope so, you are the one that created it. If it is not worth it, then you have wasted your time. So, please understand that I am not within this body, just as you are not within yours. The body emerges out of your own awareness. It is within you. I cannot be localized here as opposed to there. I did that once and found it quite unfulfilling. It is called a body. I love you. Many of you do yet truly know how deep that love is. You have only begun to touch upon the enormity and depth of the love that I feel for you because that love is the love of The Father who calls himself back to himself in and as you.

If you try to comprehend the vastness of your physical universe and then compare that to the depth and width of my love for you, it is like taking a grain of sand from the beaches of your world and say, "Here, this is all the sand in the world."

I love you so much that I cannot even imagine wanting to be anywhere where you are not, and I will never cease in giving you my strength until your is as certain as mine.

I know who you are, and you cannot fool me. Be you, therefore, the light that you are by choosing to teach only love by choosing to use time constructively to become the master of the only thing that exists, the mind, and you are, wherever you are, the light that lights this world while it lasts. What else could you possibly find that would be better to do? You need go nowhere to redeem this world, merely turn each moment over and ask, "What would you have me do?"

"Oh, call Mary." "Okay. "Ride a horse." "Okay." "Have some ice-cream." "Okay." Thank you, and when I say thank you to you, I mean it. It takes great courage to choose the unique form of attention called incarnation into this, the most insane dimension of creation that exists in order to translate it into that which reflects reality. That is why you have come. Look no further to find your purpose, you know perfectly well what it is. So, get on with it and never think that you are alone.

This may be horrific to some, there is no such thing as privacy. When next you are doing that which is called the making of love, know that the whole universe is watching. Some beings are saying, "You know, a body wasn't so bad." So, go you therefore into your evening, but do this one little thing just for the fun of it. When you rest your head upon your pillow let your last thought be this, "It is true. I and my Father are one and now would Christ sleep."

Peace be unto you always, precious, and holy, and innocent, and guiltless child of God who is but love.

Amen.

The Meaning of Ascension

Now, we begin.

Indeed, greetings unto you, beloved and Holy Children of Light Divine. Indeed, greetings unto you, beloved and Holy and only Son of God. Indeed, greetings unto you, precious brothers and sisters. And indeed, I come forth from that place which is of perfect Peace, and of perfect Love, and of perfect Light, and therefore I come forth unto you in this hour from the place in which you abide eternally.

Forever the Son of God is One, and the appearances of this world cannot shake that, and cannot take your Truth and your Reality from you. Therefore, understand well that I come forth always in joy to abide with you, to walk with you, to celebrate with you the One Truth, the One Reality that is before time is, and shall remain when the purpose of time is completed. Hmmm.

Who then am I? I am but what you are, and therefore I come forth from the place in you which is of a perfect remembrance, a remembrance of a Reality given and not created, given and sustained in Love. For in Truth the Holy Son of God, being neither male nor female, is but the offspring of God, and God is but Love.

And therefore since before time is, you are the offspring of Light Divine, and if that is what you are, and I assure you that it is, it means that forever you remain that Light and that Truth and that Love.

I have said many times that you are your Father's only Creation. What then is this world, that you would see through the eyes of the body, that you would see through the perceptions that you have constructed out of experiences that you have had? And those experiences stretch back indeed to the very beginning of time, for there's never been a time that you have not been. Therefore, indeed you have already tasted all worlds and all times, and there is nothing outside of you that you have not already tasted. Hmmm.

What then is this world? In Reality, it is a world made in error. It is a world that has been made, sprung forth if you will, from but one thought, and that thought is, "I am separate from God. Therefore, I shall create unlike Him, and I shall be the maker of my own world. And my creations shall not mirror the eternal changeless beauty and Love that the Father is. And what more perfect place could there be to house that part of the Mind that believes itself to be separate from God, than in the appearance of a body?

And you all know what that feels like, to truly believe beyond all doubt that you abide within the structure, the space and volume of a body. And therefore you look out through the physical eyes, and at times you believe you see a fearful world. At times you believe that you can be hurt, that things can be taken from you, that there can be gain and loss. And above all, through the perception born of what must be called an illusion, you begin to believe that the peace of God can be taken from you. That the Reality of who you are can be threatened. And then there comes complexity upon complexity upon complexity, as you strive to create your safety in the world of your perceptions.

The Meaning of Ascension

And you have journeyed countless times through the fields of birth and death, creating bodies if you will, struggling with them, doing the best you can, always feeling at times a bit of anxiety because you can't seem to quite control this thing, and it always seems to end in death. Friends come and go, projects seem promising and then falter, and in the end always there seems to be waiting for you the experience of death.

And the mind that would seek peace, the mind that would choose to understand, to know, to transcend, begins its journey with honesty. To look truly at the feelings that are held within, to understand that there is this core of not feeling quite safe in this world, as though you were a stranger here. And yet your world would teach you to struggle to make yourself safe here, to not be a stranger here, to learn how to control this world so that you can find the safety that you seek.

That process is what I have called the drama of the illusion of separation. And if you would well receive it, it is all come forth from but one thought held in the Holy Mind of the Son of God. And imagine if you will, a grand Light, without beginning and without end, vast beyond all imagination. And into that Light, one thought emerges, "I am separate from my Father."

And with the perception born of the belief in that thought, that one Light explodes, becomes fragmented into an infinite number of points of light, all seemingly separate one from another. And yet, still made of Light.

With the perception of separation, there is born fear. And with fear there is contraction, and contraction creates density. And the point of light that you become identified with, as yours and yours alone in being separate from all others, begins to take on the form of what we could call the "ego." The small part of your true Mind that believes it is your master, that believes it is in control. And indeed that small part of your Mind is where fear resides.

It is where contraction resides. It is where the experience of hurt and doubt and confusion resides. And you have become indeed unwittingly identified with that small part of the Mind. And yet, the whole while, in Reality no fragmentation has ever occurred. For the Son of God, that grand and vast and perfect Light that is the perfect reflection of God's image, which is but Love, remains united as One.

And in all of the journeys of space and time - if you subscribe to the belief in reincarnation, which indeed holds value if it helps you to learn that life is eternal - through all journeys, lifetimes belong not just to you. For if you would well receive it, you have lived the life of every being. For though you would look through your eyes, the eyes of the body, and see other bodies and therefore draw the conclusion that there must be other minds, other souls, I tell you that in Truth the Son of God remains One.

And if that is true, and I assure you that it is, love your neighbor as yourself, because your neighbor is yourself. And when you look upon the face of your brother or sister, learn indeed to begin to look beyond the appearance of the body, and see naught but the face of Christ before you. For in your recognition of the one that stands before you, you must then acknowledge that it takes the eyes of Christ to recognize the face of Christ.

Can you then begin to imagine where time began? It began with you! It began in your Holy Mind.

The Meaning of Ascension

And if time began there, it resides there. And the end of time is found nowhere but in you.

Now, in these journeys there have been a multitude of experiences. Some pleasant, some painful, and they have slowly created for you a construct, a prism if you will, through which you would view Creation. And the process of Awakening, the process of the Atonement, the process of salvation, truly requires not a striving but an allowing. Not a seeking, but a finding. The process of the Atonement is the process whereby you remember the Truth of your Reality, and celebrate with me the only fact that has ever truly been: "I and my Father are One! Now! Here! Before, prior, and through all times, I remain the Son of God."

The process of the Atonement is the process of remembrance, of joining back together what had seemed fragmented. And what joins back together that which has been fragmented? Love. Love, a simple four-letter word in your language, and a rather grand one. Indeed, only Love heals. Only Love overcomes separation. Only Love restores the Son to the Kingdom of Heaven. Only Love. And why? Because Love is what you are.

That is why it is so important to remember that every loving thought is true, and everything else is but a cry for help and for healing. Whether it is something that arises within you or within your brother or sister, rest assured that every such cry truly is coming forth within you. Are you therefore your brother's keeper? Indeed, you are! Not out of moral sanction, but because it's the Truth. You are your brother.

And that is why salvation cannot be found apart from your neighbor. Gone is the time of disappearing into caves, hoping that by focusing your attention on your eyebrows, that somehow you will achieve a great and enlightened state. This time is the time of endings. There is indeed a great quickening going on in the consciousness of mankind, an acceleration of the process of remembrance, because mankind desires it.

And salvation comes in relationship. For you cannot return unto the Kingdom by yourself. But as you extend yourself to your brother and sister, and embrace them with the arms of the Love of Christ that dwells within you, you will bring them to yourself, and together we walk to God.

I have come forth in this hour to ask you, to all that will hear these words, to ask you to join with me now, in wasting not another moment. But in setting aside the roar and din of the world, in setting aside your fears and your doubts, to begin the practice of claiming the Truth of your only Reality: "I and my Father are One! And where I walk, my Father walks also. And where I am, there is naught but the presence of Love. For I have learned how not to tolerate error in myself. And because I choose to be the presence of Love, through me, salvation is given unto this world."

I have indeed come forth as your friend, and as your brother. Not as someone above you, and certainly never as someone apart from you. I have come to ask you to join with me in being the Light that lights all worlds, in being that Love that restores the union of Father and Son. And in that union, indeed there will be a healing that shall be witnessed upon this plane, this physical world, but why?

The Meaning of Ascension

Time itself never needed to be created, but it was. And because you have chosen to perceive yourself as separate from God, in time you then remember your union with God. And time is given unto you only that you will use it constructively.

And if you would dwell upon it for just a moment, if now in this moment you would abide with me, and contemplate this simple question, surely the answer will not be hidden. Can there be any use of time that holds greater value than the practice of remembering that you are the Holy Son of God? That you are safe and in perfect union with Him always? Can there be any purpose to experience, unless it be the practice of extending the Love of Christ? Not to try to solve your problems, not to seek for the Kingdom, but to acknowledge that you have found it. For lo indeed, the Kingdom of Heaven is within you.

Does that mean it's a something, a physical place that can be found within the body? No. It means that it is within the construct of yourself that you have become identified with. And as you choose to turn your attention from that construct, to begin the practice of identifying with the Truth of your Reality, that Light within you begins to outshine, first your image of yourself, and then the image of your brother. And as that Light extends outward, it outshines your ideas of what the world is, what it is for, where it has come from, and where it is going.

Beloved and holy friends, think not that anything arises by accident. Your world would teach you that accidents abound, that there are "coincidences." You just "happen" to run into a friend at a corner. Hardly. There are some of you that know perfectly well that just behind the appearances of things, there is indeed a grand orchestration taking place?

And I have called that Wisdom, that Mind, that One who is the Orchestrator, the Holy Spirit, the Bridge that brings the Son dreaming the dream of separation back into Truth and Reality.

And the Bridge is set before you, and He makes straight your path. And if you would receive it, every moment of your experience is a joyous blessing. For it will reveal unto you either the joy of union with God, or it will reveal to you the small corners you are keeping for your illusion that need Light to be brought to them. Count then every experience as a blessing and give thanks for it, and your gratitude and your appreciation is what allows your Light to outshine the world you have made in error.

If Light be your Home, and if Light be your Truth, then surely Light will outshine all worlds of limitation. The greatest of gifts that you can give to anyone is not to try to fix them, but to forgive them as you forgive yourself, and choose to be only the presence of Light. And in that choice, because all minds are joined, you must necessarily be the one who uplifts your brother and your sister. Every time you choose to think a loving thought, every time you choose to look past circumstances and appearances to see the face of Christ in your holy brother or sister, you are the Power and the Light and the Truth that uplifts and heals the whole of Creation. That is the Power that is given unto you and has been with you since before time began.

And because nothing arises by accident, it is not by accident that those of you that are here find yourself here. Out of curiosity perhaps you have come? That is an appearance. Behind it, there is a place where all minds communicate. Some of you seem to be more aware of that than others. That doesn't matter, because in the end there will be perfect knowledge.

The Meaning of Ascension

I want you to understand that there will be no one who witnesses this, what you call tape, and hear these words, who has not already been in communication with me, who I will not guide to hear these words. And yes, that means that everything the human mind has ever created is used by the Love of God as the very stepping-stones that must bring the whole of Creation back into remembrance of perfect union.

There is but the slightest of differences between you and me. And the difference is simply this: as a man, I remembered my role in the Atonement and lived it. And the only difference between us seems to be a difference of time, but not of quality of our being, for we are equal. And there is but one curriculum to master, and it is given unto you to have the freedom to decide when you will learn it. But the choice is not yours whether or not to learn it.

The time comes very quickly, and some of you know what I am talking about, in which the curriculum will be mastered, will be learned, very very quickly.

And more and more quickly as more and more learn it. And why? Because of miracles. Miracles, indeed, shorten the need for time itself, and you are
miracle workers.

You are the presence of Light in this world, as everyone is. But while time yet seems to continue, it is given unto you to be the demonstration of one who has allowed correction to come to their mind, so that they see no longer a fearful world, so that they see no longer separation between themselves and others, but they see only the presence of the face of Christ; and, indeed, miracles. Miracles are given to you to be extended and expressed through you.

And the awakened Son of God looks upon every moment of every day, and if miracles aren't occurring, He pauses and takes a deep breath, and allows correction to come to his mind. He doesn't try to fix it. He gives it to the Holy Spirit. For the awakened Son of God knows that every moment is miraculous when that mind abides as the presence of Love.

I want to share with you in this hour that there is indeed a grand orchestration occurring. Where does it occur? In a mind outside of yours? Not at all. For if you would well receive it, from the moment of that first thought of separation, already the Father has healed that separation. And time is but the enactment of separation and its healing.

That means that you will witness in time a growth of miracles, an expansion of miracles. And there will be established once again the Kingdom of Heaven on earth. Is that the end of the journey? Hardly. But it is the correction of an unhappy dream into a very happy one, in which no longer shall be seen judgment and fear and doubt and anger and distrust. Indeed, brotherhood of man. And when the Son is reawakened in all minds the Light of Christ will shine so brightly that even this world, having completed its purpose, shall be dissolved in Light and shall be seen no more.

It is not possible to speak of that hour and that day, only to say, Trust that it is quickly coming to pass. And who has proclaimed it? Who has decreed it? You have. You have. That deep part of your mind that has never left union with God.

That deep part of your mind that is the Mind of Christ has already collaborated with all minds to bring about the healing and the Atonement. Do I come then to bring the Atonement to you?

The Meaning of Ascension

Hardly. I just come to dance with you, to laugh with you, to play with you, to celebrate - to celebrate! - the rebirthing of the Kingdom of Heaven.

I have said before that God needs you as much as you need God. Can you truly come to understand that? That that Light which seeks to be reborn and expressed even in the field of time requires your willingness to be reborn. And precious friends, all Power is given unto you. All Power under Heaven and earth is given unto the Holy and only begotten and sacred and beautiful Child of God to be restored, to be remembered, to be the Light that lights all worlds.

And the hour is come, and the time is upon us. The time to set aside all fears, and all doubts. The time to allow. The time to allow yourselves to remember the melody of an ancient song that seems to have been forgotten. In Truth, though it seems to you that perhaps only a small part of the melody has stayed with you, in Reality the whole of it is within you even now.

A song and a melody that speaks of perfect Peace, a song and a melody that speaks of Power and of Grace and of comfort and compassion. And a song that speaks of passion itself, the passion to be the One through whom a new vision can be restored to the Mind of mankind.

Oh, indeed, I have well watched everyone in this room be touched by vision, a vision that seems to transcend what the small part of your mind can comprehend. And all of you know what it's like to set your dreams aside, to set aside vision, because you have been fearful of not having the ability to bring it about. But can you understand that the orchestration that is occurring requires that you be willing to give birth to your visions?

The part of the vision given unto each and every one of you, as though the vision of the healing of the Son of God were shining like many great rays of Light, touching each mind and each heart. And the Holy Spirit whispering to you in your dreams, "Please fulfill this tiny part and it is enough." It is not unlike the part I was asked to fulfill. And in Reality even the gentlest of smiles that you give to your brother or sister in which you see the face of Christ in them, and therefore set up the field in which their healing can occur, that smile that you offer is every bit as powerful and as miraculous as anything that was ever manifested through me when I walked in your world.

Please come to understand that we are equals. Your Love can heal this world. Your resistance can only sustain this world. And the question that must be asked is but this: Will I choose now to be the One who is awake? Will I choose now, setting aside all anxiety of the future, all fears and judgments of the past? Will I choose now, in my perfect freedom, to be the One through whom the Light of God lights the world?

And if you would know your Father's will for you, where shall I go to bring about the Atonement? Open your eyes. Where are you in this moment? And if you find yourself here in this room, then understand here and now is the only place given unto us where we can celebrate the Truth of the Holy Son of God is One with God. And the one sitting next to you is the one to whom you can extend the Love that lights the world. And if it is true in this moment, it is true in every moment. For you do not walk alone. And what will carry you into a world of perfect Peace? Your willingness to extend that Peace now, wherever you happen to be.

To see no longer ordinary moments, to see no longer mundane experience, to see that everything that happens is sacred and holy and blessed because you are present within it.

The Meaning of Ascension

You, the Holy Child of God. And when you buy your groceries, you are not experiencing an ordinary moment unless you see through the eyes of the world. But if you would shift just a little bit and see through the eyes that God has given you, you would know that you are the Savior of the world.

You are the only one who can bring Love to that moment. You are the Light shining in darkness. You are the presence of a Light that outshines the world. And where you walk Christ walks with you, because Christ dwells within you as the Truth of your only Reality, now.

So what then can be said about the meaning of Ascension? By its very nature the word signifies a lifting-up-from, a transcendence-of. It brings images and pictures of becoming lighter and lighter. And you all know what that is like, when you allow gaiety and joy to come into the very cells of the body, and you don't feel as heavy any longer. When you give up seriousness and put your hands on your hips and laugh at the ego, that is already an aspect of the process of Ascension.

In Truth, there is nowhere to go, because in Truth, you are that vast Light, that vast Mind in which all worlds arise. And even the body that you think is yours has come forth and arisen within that one perfect Light. And knowing neither beginning nor end, you certainly don't move from one place to another. But all movement and appearance of it seems to arise within you.

Ascension, then, is the Atonement. It does not involve great magical techniques in which you learn how to take this bag of dust and somehow transmute it into Light, so that you get to rise into the clouds while your brothers and sisters are stuck on the ground.

Although, in perfect Atonement there is perfect freedom, through which the Holy Spirit can create demonstrations as miracles that catch the attention of others, and force them out of their rigidly held perceptions.

My resurrection was such a miracle. And my appearance to many friends - many friends - was really nothing else but a tool to help pry open the mind, to see beyond the appearance of birth and death. Never was it designed so that you would look upon me and think, "Boy, well, He's a great master and I'm just some shmuck." Hmm. It was designed only as a demonstration that could reveal to you the Truth that must be true for you if it is true for me.

Can there then be what is called bodily Ascension? Of course. If all worlds can arise, what's an Ascension of the physical body? Why is it perceived as something so grand? The fact that you can look upon your brother or sister and actually believe that they are other than yourself, now that is incredible. The Ascension of a bag of dust is not a big deal.

And in this hour I've also come forth to bring some correction, for there are some perceptions that are getting a little bit out of hand. And there are many who would seek, actually believing that if only they can learn to make the body ascend, and then they will find Peace, and then they will find the Kingdom of Heaven. Without abiding in that Kingdom, no possibility for Ascension of the body can emerge.

Therefore, indeed, understand you must be the goal you seek, now. And in that Atonement all possibilities are reborn. Will you then seek it? No. You will not seek bodily Ascension, because you will have been delivered from the erroneous perception that you are separate from God and must go somewhere else to get it.

The Meaning of Ascension

And then if the Holy Spirit says "We need a little bit of a demonstration, would you mind?" You will say, "Not my will, but Thine be done." And if you are asked to just be a street sweeper, you will indeed say "Not my will, but Thine." Why? Because the Holy Son of God can go nowhere, and experience nothing, that separates Him from the Love of God.

The meaning of Ascension is found in your willingness to be the presence of Peace, to see with timelessness, to see with unconditional Love, to see through a perception that has been corrected so that you know your safety does not rest within the body, or within the world. But indeed it rests in the perfect knowledge given unto you since before time is.

You are Home now, right now! You are One with God. There is not one thing you must fix, there is not one thing you must seek, save to allow correction to be reborn in the mind. And what happens when correction comes? Some of you know perfectly well what happens. The past is gone, and all the pain of it. Though the memories may come, somehow it's been translated, and no longer do you feel the burden upon the heart. But there is a spaciousness, an emptiness in which only Light abides, and no shadow do you keep a grip upon, for you have released them all to the Light of God. And they have been healed and removed from you forever.

And what you do surprises even you. And when others look upon you and say, "Oh, you're so grand, what a marvelous thing you're doing on this planet. Thank you so much!" you look them in the eye and you say, perhaps in different words, "Of myself I do nothing, but my Father through me does all things. That's how simple it is. I gave up efforting, I gave up striving, I threw in the towel of trying to be the maker and the doer, and I became the allower. I became the celebrator.

I became the truster. And whenever my mind began to get into striving and effort, I remembered that my thoughts do not mean anything. And I remembered to choose Peace. And in that Peace a Light began to be remembered, and the Song played more loudly. And that Light has outshone all of my dreams of separation and of fear and of doubt. And I abide in that Light, and holy friend, if I abide in it, so do you. Let us journey into it together. I'll extend my hand to you, for however long it takes until you see that the Light is in you also.

That is the perception you will hold of yourself and of your brother. And if you would well receive it, it is given unto you now. Now! To receive the only Truth that has ever existed. To be the one who proclaims "I and my Father are One." For when those words become yours with every fiber of your being, the Atonement is completed on earth as it has already been completed in Heaven. Remembrance has been restored.

To those of you who know of those who would seek to find ways to create an Ascension for the physical body, go and tell them that they've already completed it. And now is the time to release striving. It is Love that will heal this world. Love abides in its own presence, and in its own certainty, and in a holy and ancient knowledge. You cannot seek for Love, and you cannot find it. You can desire it, and your intention can become so pure that nothing else distracts you. And in the end, Love can only be allowed to be extended through you.

You cannot be the One who is the Creator of Love. You can't puff yourself up with it so that you can give it away. There are no magical techniques that will build its power within you. It's already given to you freely, and miracles therefore must occur naturally to minds that teach only Love.

The Meaning of Ascension

That teach only Love. That teach only Love because there's no dark corners of the mind left that you have sought to save for yourself.

I come in this hour to ask you to be That One. To be That One who from this hour forward will indeed teach only Love. Will be the One who knows and lives the fact that all needs are already met. To be the One whose Mind is corrected, to whom sanity is restored. For when you walk in this world for such a short time as the presence of only Peace, you will affect everyone who enters your domain.

They may not understand it; they may indeed think it's because of your body, that they're attracted to you. They may think it's because of the wisdom that seems to pour forth through your mouth, although you won't remember what you said when you're done, because it's not you doing the talking. But they will feel the presence of Peace and it must necessarily touch that place of Peace in them. And when that window opens, Light rushes in and their process of Awakening can deepen, continue, or perhaps begin.

Please, please understand that the Ascension has been completed, waiting only on your remembrance that you are not something separate that must be taken somewhere, or must experience some exalted state so then you can say "Ah, now I've got it!" The exalted state of the rebirth of the Kingdom of Heaven on earth waits on your acceptance of what is true now.

Can you imagine what it would be like if tomorrow, if tomorrow you walked through this world and every time your brother or sister said "Oh God, life is such a bummer, isn't it just terrible?

What about that Presidential election?" And you chose not to participate in that energy. Not that you pick up yourself and run from them, but that you transcend that limitation and shine forth only Love and Peace. You will know what to say, because the world's words will be given unto you, even as they were always given unto me.

Know ye that which is called the Sermon on the Mount? When those words poured forth, afterwards some of those friends, that the world has mistakenly called my disciples, came up to me and said "Oh Lord, that was so beautiful, it was so incredible!" I looked at them and said, "What did I say? It wasn't planned; I am not the doer or the maker. Of Myself I do nothing, the Father through me does all things." It was awfully difficult to get them to understand that, because the ego needs to set others on pedestals because it fears recognizing that the same power dwells within it.

You will be the one spouting forth Sermons on the Mount. They may be sermons in parking lots. Hmm. They may be sermons in grocery stores. Does it matter? One temple is as good as another. I ask you, as your brother and as your friend, to begin to contemplate your willingness to join with me in the Atonement. Not by needing it, but from the foundation of your recognition that it is already completed within you.

Some of you know what it means to be taught that you must honor me, as if I am separate from you. But I say unto you, He that does not honor the Son that dwells in fullness within their own heart in no wise honors me, no matter now many prayers, no matter how much supplication is given unto images of me made in the minds of mankind.

But when you, the Holy Son of God, honor the Christ that lives within you, indeed, let it be known that you have honored me as your brother, as your friend, and as your equal. And if that sounds like sacrilege to your world, then so be it. I can't help it. Because it's the Truth.

I did not come to proclaim myself your Savior. I came to proclaim the salvation that has already occurred within you. I came to mirror to you the Truth of your being. And unto as many as would choose to see me as their equal, because I'm in charge of Atonement, do I give forth the ability to pry open every last corner of the mind and heart, so that you are indeed restored in the image of the Son of God. And if that happens to involve healing of the body, so be it.

Unto you there is extended in this hour the choice to choose with me to be the presence of the Atonement. And in this, Ascension is already completed. And every time you choose joy, every time you choose gratitude, every time you choose unlimitedness, every time you choose to allow vision to be your guide, you walk with me. And we walk together in the Kingdom of Heaven. Understand well then, there is not one corner of your life that cannot be transformed if there is a need for it, when you choose Love instead of fear. For Love begets healing; fear must necessarily deny it. And that Love is in you now.

Hmmm. When I said to a group of friends, "Go forth and teach all nations," all I said to them was "Go forth and teach only Love." For by teaching it you must necessarily learn it. And as you witness the miracle of the extension of Love through you, and what it does in the life of your brother and sister, you must necessarily then know that the miracle has already occurred within you.

And that is the process whereby your fearful dreams are translated into dreams of safety. And as you see that you are safe, you open more and more, and the power of miracles, the power of Light, can flow through you ever more freely. That is the importance for you of choosing to teach only Love. To feel a passionate desire to be the presence of Love, not to settle for anything else ever again! For your choice to settle for less than Love has given birth to all worlds that have mirrored the illusion of separation from God. And you know that you know those worlds well.

You've tried every byway, and every dead end. Live with a passion, a passion to be the presence of Love. The one says unto you, "Lo, the Kingdom is here" and another says "No, it is there." Stop and smile, and say,"Precious friends, the Kingdom of Heaven is within me, as it is within you. Let us therefore rejoice and be glad in this day, for in this moment it is given unto us to be the Light of the world. And wherever two or more of us come together, Christ abides. And there can be no greater or more sacred place on earth than a place in which minds have joined in Love, having set aside an ancient hatred born from fear, born from separation.

Walk then in this world, and understand that everywhere you go, everywhere, the minds of mankind are crying out for the opportunity to join in that sacred union, the Holy Instant, that heals the illusions of separation. In your hands there is a pearl of great price. It is in your hand, and everywhere you go, you can extend that hand to everyone you see. No matter what they're doing, no matter what they say about you, none of that matters a bit. How can the opinion of an insane mind matter? Hmmm. I have told many, it's time to live a bit outrageously. A time to dance, a time to sing, a time to play. These things I did daily when I walked upon this earth.

The Meaning of Ascension

And I was only serious to the degree that the one in front of me could speak no other language but seriousness, until they learned the language of laughter and play and simplicity and ease. For my way is easy, and my burden light. My cross is not heavy; it is made of Light. Therefore, take up your cross and follow me.

Come and join the dance. Come and join the dance in which you realize, "My God, I am an Ascended Master!" Right here, in what - what you call the name of this village? - Berkeley, hmm. Right here, an Ascended Master walks. And it goes by your name. Does that sound arrogant? The only thing that has ever been arrogant is that you dared to believe that you are something other than what God created you to be. Now that requires great arrogance. Hmm.

Do you see the great paradox, then? For the Truth of the Kingdom is diametrically opposed to every perception the world has ever sought to teach you. It takes great humility to say, "I and my Father are One," because you have to give up the world. You have to be the one courageous enough to speak the Truth. It is the height of arrogance to believe that you have ever sinned against God. It is the height of arrogance to believe that you are guilty, that you are not capable of fixing yourself, that somehow you're not even worthy of it.

Father, beat me and whip me for I have sinned. That one's been played out. And some of you have memories, of what you would perceive as lifetimes, in which you know what it means to flog the body. It wasn't a lot of fun. Are you willing to join with me in the outrageousness of a divine humility, in which you simply set aside every conformity to the beliefs of the world, and simply say to your friends, "I can't play the game any longer?" And they'll look at you and say, "What do you mean?"

Well, I'm the Son of God. I've been trying to pretend I'm something else, but it's exhausted me. So I give it up. Father, live through me. And they will indeed look at you with a bit of an incredulous look. And one of the eyebrows might go up. So what? In that moment, because of your willingness to be what they will perceive as arrogant and outrageous, a window has opened. A window has opened! A window has opened because for just a moment [snaps fingers] you stopped their mind.

Unknown to them, you have been the one who turned their attention from the roar and the din and the insanity of the illusory world to the Real World. Now, will they get it? They might. They might call you crazy. They might leave your life, the life of the body. But you have a saying in your world that nature abhors a vacuum, and if that is true for nature it is indeed true for God. Never fear loss, for what is of true value can never be taken from you. It can only be added to you. As you teach Love, all that is truly valueless must necessarily drop from you. Gently perhaps at times, at times seemingly not so gently.

But understand that in those moments it's only a resistance to letting go that creates the feeling of struggle. And suddenly, the hour of your rebirth is upon you. And you will look around for your past and find that it's no longer with you. You will look for your doubts and your confusions, and you will be startled because you won't be able to find them. And suddenly you will know that the miracle has occurred. The Atonement has been completed. It has come as a thief in the night, and while you were sleeping it stole the cobwebs of all shadows long since outgrown.

And you have awakened in the morning of a new day, and behold, your cupboards are bare of what you thought held value. And in its place is a feast set before the only begotten Son of God, a feast without beginning and without end, a feast to which your Father invites you to return as the guest of honor. And the prodigal Son has indeed returned, and he sits down at His Father's table and lo, all he looks upon is good.

And you will raise the chalice to your lips, and you will drink of a certain elixir called Love, called salvation, called Awakening, enlightenment, it goes by many words. It's really all the same. And then you will put the chalice back on the table, and you will look your Father right in the eye, and together with Him, you will laugh as you have never laughed before.

And your laughter will be the song that is echoed out like a vibration through every molecule of Creation. Your laughter will shift the vibration of Creation, and Light will pour into every molecule until it becomes, once again, as Light itself.

That is the meaning of the true Ascension. It signifies the moment when the Holy Son of God has been restored completely. Will it come tomorrow? It might. Does it seem a long way off? Remember, such a perception is born in time, but miracles shorten the need for time.

How then to create the miracles that shorten time? By acknowledging that the Atonement is complete within you now.

Do you see how that all begins to make sense? Gone is the time for praying for saviors, gone is the time of looking to the future when the Son of God would return. Now is the time spoken of, in many cultures, and in many ways, and in all epics that have ever been. The Truth has always been spoken. That time is at hand.

I gave forth a promise, that in that day I would indeed return. And though I sought to make it clear, there were many who did not understand. Let it be known that I have returned. I've returned, not only to join with the mind of this my beloved brother, who finally threw in the towel because he couldn't figure it all out. Hmm. I have come forth with an ancient friend that some of you know by the first name of Helen. I have come forth through, what you would perceive as two thousand and three friends, who are currently serving. Some are on this globe, as what are called in your language, channels.

And I serve with many others in many many ways, for the promise I gave has been kept. I have returned because I love you. In Truth, I never went anywhere. And I have worked without ceasing, to whisper to you in your dreams, to gently guide you to the left when you thought you were going to the right.

I have come to you because you have been given me of my Father, even as there are already those who are, shall we say, assigned to you, and will come to you when you allow, through your willingness, the recognition of the Atonement's completion to be remembered in you. There are many who are waiting for you, who will be sent to you in ways that you cannot begin to comprehend, and through you the very same work will take place, even as this work has occurred through me.

Do you begin to get the picture? There's a network, if you will, being created, in which the Father who has loved me gives unto me the power to give that Love to you. And in your receiving of it, it is given unto you the power to give it to another. And that giving is the miracle that heals the need for time.

The Meaning of Ascension

You do not walk alone, and you cannot take a step without me. For I promise you this: even as I said unto you then, I say it again, "I am with you always, and I shall give you my strength until yours is certain. Think it not a burden that you would call upon me, for you are worthy of all the Love that I could ever possibly extend, and that Love is but the Love of our Father. You are worthy of that Love!

"There is not a decision you must make alone. There is not a journey you must embark on, believing that you are alone. From the moment you know that you are awake in your mornings, before you lift your head from your pillow, I am with you. I cannot force myself upon you, but I come freely and easily to anyone who but opens the door the tiniest of cracks, who throws in the towel and says 'Okay, come and teach me anew.'"

Does that make me your savior? No. It makes me your friend! Please, go and tell the world, I am only its friend. Please tell them it's time to take me down off the walls of their cathedrals. It's time to embrace me and dance with me as a friend! For in an ancient day, to call someone a friend meant that you were committed for all of eternity to seeing only the face of Christ in your brother or sister. A commitment indeed. You are my friends, and I have never ceased seeing only the Light within you; waiting for you to acknowledge only that sight within yourself.

The Ascension is completed. It will be enacted, in the field of time, as a joyous celebration of what has already been completed. Rest assured that it is even now occurring. Though you don't see it, do you know that in each and every day, more and more minds are suddenly Awakening?

What seemed to take journeys, and the study with what you call the gurus, lifetimes of magical techniques, so that one mind can be Illuminated, is now occurring daily, almost effortlessly. And every time a mind awakens, it quickens the Awakening of the next mind.

That is why some of you have been able to pick up a certain text that you would call A Course in Miracles and sometimes, just by holding it, you have felt perceptions in your mind healed. That quickening is accelerating. Some of you know what that

feels like, and it's going to continue. Every day in your world now, all around this planet, minds are Awakening. And they will look for their own.

There are many who are beginning to feel a call to what could be called community. A call to join with those of like mind and like heart. And even as I say that, there are many in this room nodding their internal heads, "Oh yes, I feel that." Because the knowledge of how the Ascension, the Atonement, is going to be reflected is already within you. And because it is dawning within you, you are giving forth your willingness to participate in this script long since written.

That is what you're feeling. Not a desire to flee anything, but a call. A call that has gone out to every heart and every mind. And who has extended that call? You have. And therefore, you can only awaken to your own call. It is simply my honor to be asked again of my Father to be one who delivers your own telegram to you.

Please sign for it, open it, and read it. And when you open it you will say, "My goodness, this is from myself! 'Dear Me, The time is at hand. Awaken now!' Before I've had my breakfast?"

The Meaning of Ascension

Yes! Before every breath you breathe. Before every thought you think. Give thanks unto God, because the Father has been the power through which the Son is restored to His rightful place. And you have taken up your place at the right hand of God.

What does that image mean? It means right-mindedness, and that's all. It has nothing to do with physical location at all. The right hand of God is right-mindedness, and even now you are restored.

So yes, for a little while, you've been plopped upon your throne, but you seem to be holding on to a different dream. And so you 'babble' a little bit, while your Father sits next to you going "Uh-hum, yes, uh-hum, yes, uh-hum." Waiting. Waiting for you to stop long enough to see where you are, now!

"My goodness! I thought I was in the world!" And He leans to you, and says, "Precious Son, you are in the Real World. The other one was a momentary dream. It has left no trace upon you at any time. And you are together with me, even as it was in the beginning, is now, and forever shall be. We are but One, and I, the Father, see not where I end and you begin."

Hmmm. So then what do you do with it all? You accept it. That is the meaning of surrender. I have said that there are four Keys to the Kingdom: desire, intention, allowance, and surrender. Allowance requires some practice, and the practice replaces the practice of striving and efforting and doubting and fearing.

Allowance requires trust and faith, acceptance, and as that is learned, you could say you slip into the sea of surrender, but of yourself you do nothing. Surrender is the same thing as the Father's final step for you, in which perception is translated into Knowledge.

Surrender is indeed death. Surrender is birth! Surrender is the Atonement completed, in you! And what comes, after surrender? It no longer matters. Imagine living each day, seemingly in time, as your brothers would perceive you, but knowing that you live in eternity. Knowing that whatever transpires this day is just fine!

Because you're too busy being the presence of Love to worry about the small things of the world. To live in a state of a consciousness in which you have learned the only lesson that must be learned: that there is nothing outside of you.

To look from a high mountain, upon your great cities, upon your brothers and sisters, upon the very face of this most precious and beautiful planet of yours. To look upon your stars, to see the space between them, the emptiness, the blackness, to think about universes upon universes upon universes upon universes, and dimensions upon dimensions and dimensions and dimensions and dimensions of this dream - and to say, "There is nothing outside of me."

Hmm. And to walk in that knowledge! That's the meaning of incarnation. And what follows Ascension? Descension. The willingness to be the Word made flesh. To incarnate the Truth. That is the final step. That is the final step! Not to seek Heaven apart from yourself, or somewhere else, but to be the One who brings it into time, that time itself is translated into eternity. Ahhh.

Well, there you have it. That's what happening on this planet. That is what has been happening since first the Son of God held the thought, "I am separate." From that moment, everything has been translated into the means that restores the Son to His rightful place.

The Meaning of Ascension

So how do you incarnate the Word of God? By having a very good time! By laughing, by singing, by dancing, by playing. By being the vibration of unlimited joy, because there's no longer a place in you to allow a trace of heaviness or seriousness. All of that's part of the world, you see. It's not part of you.

And as you allow that frequency to be born within you, you will understand what it means to live the Atonement. Not as a philosophical concept, not even as a belief, not even as an acknowledgment, but as a lived Reality. And that Reality, if you will, must be lived before this world becomes again nothing but Light.

And you could say, if I could borrow a saying that I find in the mind of my beloved brother, "The joke's on you!" You are the ones who are here as the Word made flesh. For a short time, you thought you were something else. And the essential point of this hour, and why I asked that this be created, is to strip from thousands of minds the perception that there is any other choice that can be made. To help minds see it's the only choice left. The choice of Love over fear. The choice of seeing that the Atonement is completed in them. And the meaning of Ascension is now being lived. Indeed!

In this, for this hour, we have now come to a completion. And I extend unto each and every one of you my gratitude and my thanks. I want to let you in on a little secret. Though these my ancient and precious friends strove, and what you would call "worked the little tails off" trying to let a whole lot of people know about this, nothing is impossible. And you could say there was a bit of a delay mechanism put in, because it was very important that only certain ones be here.

You are those ones! And each, in your own way, has brought a certain anchor of energy, that's the simplest way to describe it, that actually is participating in a little bit of a miracle, because you are creating something that seems to be on a tape but, let it be known, unto everyone who views what you call your 'tape'

of what this evening's talk has been about, there is going to be felt - perhaps subtly, perhaps grandly - a bit of what could be called a transmission of energy.

And I want to let you know, that at some deep level within each and every one of you, even those with the 'gadgets' on their ears, you have chosen from the depth of that Mind of Wholeness within you to participate in this aspect of the orchestration of the Atonement. Each and every one of you! Therefore, unto you I extend my Love and my thanks for the beauty and the Light and the Love and the compassion that lives within you.

Thank You, Holy Son of God!

For some of you, nothing's going to quite seem the same, from this hour. Give thanks for that, and remember, please, I am with you always. Peace be unto the Son of God, who chooses to bring the things of Heaven to wed them with the things of earth, that the Light of the Kingdom might again be extended as far as from the east to the west. Herein is the meaning of the Cross, a Cross of Light, in which the Child of Christ dwells with an open heart, and arms outstretched; His feet on the earth, and His Mind in Heaven, to demonstrate the reflection of perfect Love.

Peace be unto you. And for now,

Amen.

Teach Only Love

And once again, and as always, greetings unto you, beloved and holy children of God. Indeed, greetings unto you, my brothers and my sisters. For in truth, I look upon you and see no distance between us. I look upon you only with love. I look upon you and receive the blessing of your continence, your perfection, your radiance; the unique gifts of your own unique journeys. Can you then well receive that I come forth to abide with you as a friend and as your brother and as long as you desire it, as a guide and as a teacher? But my teaching is never designed to have you lean on me. It is not designed to have you become dependent upon me. Rather, I seek in whatever way I can to teach you that which is beyond the teaching itself, to teach you that you are the one that you seek. That you are the one who is already equal to all that I am or ever could be. For well there is within you the power to be the truth that sets the world free.

You do not need to climb a high mountain in order to bless this world. You do not need to accomplish anything that the world can see. Rather, that one that is awakened to the reality that only love is real. That one that is awakened to the truth that I and my father are one, seeks not to ascend the highest peak, but to descend. To take up a rightful place at the side of those who journey still through the labyrinths of illusion. For illusion is the cause of all pain. Illusion, the source of all suffering, and because your brother and your sister is yourself, that one that truly loves God seeks not to ascend in the clouds as they once said of me, but rather to discover a way in which to impart the simplicity of the lesson of love and seeks ways to be seen, to be noticed, to be heard in such a way that those who are calling for love, can receive it.

Teaching then is an art and not a science and as you teach, you must learn. It's the law of consciousness, the law of spirit; what you teach you learn instantly. And what you teach consistently, you learn repeatedly. Until what you have learned permeates the field of your awareness so completely that no shadow can steal across the vast expanse of that which you are. Here then is the greater glory and the gift of your world, for while time seems to remain for you and indeed it will remain, until you've forgiven the past and released the future and have chosen to learn to abide where God is.

Now, as you abide in that place and realize that time, the experience of this world and each and every form of relationship that emerges in the field of your awareness, is a perfect and divine gift given unto you, for you the holy son of God, being neither male nor female, to learn ever more deeply to teach only love.

That is the only purpose time has. For when you choose to be that one who teaches only love and embraces each situation, not as the world would teach you to embrace it, but its truth teaches you to embrace it. Not just something you're doing in order to survive into tomorrow, but as an opportunity to seize with the fullness of your spirit and your consciousness, to learn to be the embodiment of love, to realize that you, you are the one for whom the stars have been set in the heavens.

You are the one for whom your planet spins. You are the one for whom this universe has existed for a very long time. You are the one for whom all appearances have been given to you, to create the opportunity for you to accept the gift God has given you;

your existence as Christ and to choose to put that reality into practice. To learn in the field of time that which directs you to what is timeless and indeed what comes from what is timeless. For here is the great completion of what some have called the mystical ascent of the soul. Here, the completion of all spiritual unfolding. Here is the culmination and the secret of what you would hear termed in your world, ascension. For ascension is merely the remembrance of what has already occurred, by grace. You cannot achieve it. It's been done for you by the love and grace of God.

Ascension then is completed when you allow the depth of your identity as a unique individual, to settle into the Heart, with a capital H, that Heart through which the Holy Spirit speaks. Through which love is extended, through which kindness flowers forth; freedom radiates and peace is given to the world. When you indeed come to rest in that Heart, the mind will become your perfect servant and it will never be filled with conflict again, period; at any time. When you abide in that Heart, you will know that the great culmination of this remarkable process, this journey from the dream of separation to the dream of awakening, into the reality of what has always been; it's not the end of time, but the transformation of time. For creation will never die.

Creation is extension and extension requires some quality of time. Rather than an escape then, rather than a completion of some sort, as you come to rest in that Heart, to live peacefully and fearlessly, whole and complete in your perfect union with God; the unconflicted mind serves you perfectly. You'll always know where to go, what to do, what to say, no big deal, no effort.

Then you have become the cross of light. The vertical access means merely that which connects the things of time to the

things of eternity, vertical axis, because you abide at the Heart, you extend that recognition as far as from the east to the West, in the field of time itself and you are liberated. You are liberated right where you are, even if it seems to be that you find yourself in a body upon planet earth, for the body is not a barrier to truth and the world cannot imprison you.

This would be to give illusion, reality. Come to understand then that what I sought to teach, not through necessarily my words but through my life, my experiences, including my death and my willingness to remain with you always; is to teach only love and love embraces all things, trusts all things, enfolds all things in wisdom and thereby transcends all things without ceasing. When you fully awaken to realize you have nowhere to go and nothing to achieve, and this moment just as you find it, is the perfection of heaven. You will know the freedom that I have sought to guide you to you. You will have come holy to where I am and you will recognize that you are in perfect communication with me at all times.

Seek then not to journey somewhere, but seek to embrace the place in which you find yourself in each and every moment. For the body being what it is, for the physical dimension being what it is, you will be in flux and flow constantly. Just try to sit down in a chair and see if you can stay there for three days. No problem, I can do that. All have to do is ignore my bladder or hunger. So understand that while this body lasts, you will be in ceaseless motion, you cannot be in any other way, but freedom comes when you are willing to embrace the body as the body.

Not to deny it, not to hate it, not to feel imprisoned by it, not to place your happiness upon it's losing 10 pounds or changing the color of the hair, but rather the body becomes exactly what it is. A temporary neutral event, which you can choose to use as a means for teaching only love, in a way that can be seen by the world. What is the world, but the perception that the body is real? That if there is something called spirit, we haven't been able to find it yet.

When you come to rest in that Heart and abide as that cross of light, fully aligned and in union with the mind of God, the heart of God and freed from your resistance to time, to embodiment, so that you are constantly extending your creations in the horizontal plane of time. When you abide in that place, you will know what eternity is. You will be eternity embodied and though others may look upon you and think, "Well, that's just Mary. That's just Jane. That's just Fred. Hmm, I've known them for my whole life," Rest assured, this same was said about me. "Is that not the son of Joseph, the carpenter? What wisdom could possibly be coming from him?"

The same wisdom that can flow through you. The same love given of my father to each of us equally. The same wisdom that flows from the Holy Spirit, the comforter and will speak through any mind. It simply releases the delusion of believing that this world means anything and all appearances, all relationships, all moments have been given over entirely to the purpose of the healing of God's son. Please remember, son simply means 'offspring of'; to 'spring forth from'. Time then is no longer a prison and heaven comes to be perceived as spread across the face of the earth and each step you take, you know that you walk in the kingdom. Every breath you breathe is sanctified by your holiness because you have received it without resistance. Each relationship, each moment of each relationship has been sanctified by the holiness of your commitment to teach only love.

Perhaps above all, each moment of relationship with yourself has become sanctified, so that in each moment of relationship with yourself, you are teaching yourself only love. You have begotten many worlds. You have begotten many universes. Verily I say unto you, each time you think a thought, you have set into motion a web of energy, a web of relationships that is creation itself. How important then is your thought? You need only look around yourself, for everything that your physical eyes show you, whether you're sitting in your living room or your automobile, in this room with these friends, everything you see is the direct result of the thoughts you have been willing to give permission to making a home in your mind. Everything that you have ever experienced has come not because it was forced upon you, but because you called it to yourself. Just as you have called this very moment to yourself.

By being in this room in this hour, you have collapsed all webs of relationships that could have had a different conclusion or a different completion or effect. You have done that. Your birth into this world was the effect of your freely chosen; your freely made decision to attract, to call around you a certain field of energy. You call it your parents, your culture, your timeframe, your planet, your universe, your dimension. You remain forevermore, perfectly free spirit made in the image of God. Given the selfsame power to create and you have never ever once succeeded in ceasing to create. It's not even remotely possibly. You don't even get to take a break. You are always creating and you always will be. The only decision then is, "What do I want?"

That sounds rather selfish, I know in your world, you're not supposed to talk that way. "What do I want?" I speak not of the egoic mind that is reacting from fear and then seeks relationships to console itself, relationships with persons, relationships with substances and all of the rest.

Everything is relationship, but I speak of that 'I' that is the focal point, the essence of your consciousness, the essence of your being. That spark of divinity, that ray of light that is as a sunbeam to the sun, cannot be destroyed, that is made of the same substance of that which birthed you, that which I have called **[unintelligible 00:19:53]**. How will you choose to become familiar with, to be in relationship with that ray of light that is the power of your very consciousness? How will you utilize it in each moment? For in each moment, you are literally birthing your experience and it's all okay.

Any experience you have ever had is perfectly okay. In no time and in no moment have you ever failed. You have created. You have added to the creation that is the universe. You have never failed. Can you hear that? Can you really, honestly, truthfully, here with your soul that you have never failed? It's impossible. Now, it's not impossible for someone else to judge you as having failed. That's there for use of consciousness and in that moment they're like one that has held the guillotine above their own head and judged you and dropped it upon themselves. That is what judgement does.

You have never failed and you never will fail. The only thing that it is wise to consider is this, "Do I wish to continue this creation or do I wish to choose a new?"

Do you see how different that is from those that would teach you about sin and about guilt and about failure, about wretchedness, and about unworthiness, powerlessness? Who can take your power from you?

No one. You can only choose how you will use it. So in your most wretched hours, you have been a perfectly powerful creator and you are free to continue that line of creation, as long as you want.

To extend it on the horizontal plane of time for lifetimes, if you wish. You could be what you call in your world- what is your saying here? "Crying in your glass of beer" for 10,000 lifetimes and never leave the bar.

Do you know that there are many beings, sparks of divinity, what you call souls; that are not currently in embodied form as you know it, who are exactly living that experience. Who have been locked into some perception and have been there for eons. They even show up in your physical dimension sometimes, they're called ghosts. Locked into some tiny little place of creation and they've been there a long time, but love can release them. Recently, I suggested to this, my beloved brother and indeed unto his mate and friend; that it would be wise to journey to a certain state they call the Kansas. I suggested to them that it would be good to drive. Although they didn't quite realize it was me mentioning this. I wanted them to experience something. Recently, you had what is called a bit of an explosion in your Oklahoma and it destroyed a large building and many beings died.

The vast majority of them are still there because no one has taken the time to go to that place, to contact those souls, to speak to them as though you're right in front of them. To let them know a transition has occurred and it's okay. That if they will only look above themselves, they will see a light and that it's safe to journey to that light. It's safe to release and to entrust their family, their friends, their children, their coworkers, their pets, to the care of those still embodied. That they are safe and free to release this dimension.

They sent them there because they wanted them to feel palpably as you would say, the reality of that. That a soul can be locked in an experience at the moment of death and stay that way for a very long time.

Until what happens? Someone who has awakened to a deeper understanding, who wants to teach only love so that they may learn it, reaches back metaphorically and allows themselves to become a channel for that wisdom that knows how to release the soul from its bondage.

So I want to suggest to you this evening that all of you, before you rest your head on the pillow, say one thing in your mind, "I am not just this. It's only the body that is resting in this bed. It emerges out of myself, out of my divinity. I am free to go anywhere at any time, that fast." How long does it take to think a thought? I want very much for you to have the experience of putting yourself in what you call the Oklahoma and go to that place and you'll know you're there, trust me.

You will feel the pain and the sorrow, the depression, the sadness, the fear, the anguish, and simply say within yourself, "Father, who would you have me help in this moment?" and then observe what comes into the field of your awareness. It may be an adult. It may be a man, it may be a woman, maybe a child. Be right there. It's that easy. It's that quick

And as you abide with them, let that image of whoever that is, be there. Don't let the mind say, "Oh, this is just hogwash. This must be imagination." There is no such thing as imagination. There is only awareness of what you are creating and experiencing, whether it be in this dimension or another.

Therefore, be there and simply look upon that one. Surround them with light and speak to them as though they were right in front of you physically. You can even open the physical mouth if you wish to, to help kind of ground it. Let them know that they are pure spirits.

Let them know that it is safe to release the world they knew and that if they will simply turn their gaze skyward, so to speak, they will begin to see a pin prick of light far above them. If they give themselves permission to let go, for they have not failed; they can begin to move to that light and there will be someone to greet them. To help them understand what has occurred and bring them into a deeper dimension of knowledge.

There are, by the way, some of you in this room who you could say, this is your night job anyway; you do it in what you call your dream state. Sometimes you awaken and you know who you are and you realize you had a dream about someone, but you can't for the life of you figure out where on earth that connection ever came from. You're already doing it. This is just the process of deliberately doing it.

Please, help me release my brothers and sisters who are yet standing on floors that no longer exist, of a building that was shattered by one insane thought." That is what you're here for, to teach only love. To participate in the healing of the son and if you think for one moment that your life is too ordinary, stop fooling yourself. You can be a street sweeper and in the middle of your 11 o'clock appointment, sweep up the papers in front of the courthouse. You can be healing the mind of what your world would call the criminals and the judges who are meeting on the 10th floor of the building, by simply allowing yourself to be with them in just the way that I've described.

The body never imprisons you, only you can imprison you, by choosing to think that you are less than what you are created to be. The body, a temporary teaching and learning device, it arises in one tiny corner of an infinite number of dimensions in which you are already having complete experience now.

How many of you have thought, "Well, it would be really nice to journey to Tahiti for a vacation and also be in Paris at the same time,"? You can do that. You are doing that multi-dimensionally already. So why not embrace this tiny little, minuscule corner of your creation? See how utterly harmless it is and yet see how rich it is in the potential for you to deepen your knowledge of what love is. Stop believing the mumbo jumbo of the world and start using your time to extend and teach love. You have an interesting word in your language? Boredom. Boredom can only be the denial of the truth of who you are and you can heal a multitude without ever lifting your buttocks from the chair. You are not ordinary and no life is ordinary or belittling. And why? Because there's only one life, a life lived in the light of truth. That's all there is. Why not get on with it?

So when next you watch the mind trying to seduce you into believing there's something you must do to get closer to God, drop it immediately and ask, "How can I serve right now, the extension of love? Who needs to be blessed? Who needs to be thought of? Who needs to be held? Who needs to be called?" If you start giving yourself to the extension of love, your days will be so filled that you won't even notice time at all. You won't be harried or stressed. You will be fulfilled beyond measure and conversely or paradoxically, what will occur in your consciousness, your experience of time; is that you are living in timelessness. Why? Because you're so committed to teaching only love that you know you're in the right place at the right time, and this is the moment in which I can relax into the truth of who I am and remember my purpose. I am an extension of God's love, the thought of love and form. I have no needs. I have no lacks. I have no past and I have no future. I am now forever one with God. Who can I love? Who can I love? Who can I love?

I would not say these things to you if it was not so. I would not say these things to you if they did not come from the depth of my own experience, learned while yet I lived in and as a body. It was that learning that carried me through the dimension of death, into a deliberate and conscious knowing of my absolute unlimitedness, so that I could experience the great delight of blessing the whole of creation in every moment and being in loving relationship with all dimensions at once. The only thing that therefore is preventing you from knowing that, is that you're still letting yourself use the power of consciousness to waste time, by perceiving yourself as unworthy, in lack; not knowledgeable enough, not the right connections. Do you see? Every time you let your mind wallow in that, you have your reward. Whether you like it or not is another issue.

Seize time every moment. "How can I teach love right now? Well, I'm in the middle of the desert and there's no one for miles." Hmm. Perhaps it would be wise to go to a different dimension and just shift your thought. Why look for someone that's linked to a body? Is that the only way you can teach love? Those grand brothers and sisters whose bodies were destroyed as the result of one insane thought in your Oklahoma, would deeply appreciate it if you would look beyond bodies to find someone to bless and love. There are beings around you right now in this room, around what you call the body. There are an infinite number of dimensions and this room is filled. There's no space left. Filled with souls, consciousnesses, sparks of divinity, intelligence. Not only are you never alone, but you never have anything called privacy. [Laughter] So what are you trying to get away with in your private moments? Comical sometimes.

"I'm so alone, nobody loves me. I could never bless the world how Yeshua does it." Verily, I say unto you, you have your reward.

You've created it in that moment and you can live in what the world calls squalor, you can live in what some would call here slums, houses of cardboard in the alleys of your big cities and there with the rain hitting the top of that cardboard and leaking down in through the walls, into the concrete and making your butt feel a little cold and wet; you can know perfect peace and be totally absorbed with extending love to the fullness of creation. That means that there's no excuse for waiting until tomorrow when a better job comes along or here's a good one in your world, "If only my soulmate would show up." You want to find your soulmate? Open your eyes and look around. Perhaps in your wardrobe, you could do it.

How many ways have you cleverly created to delay putting into action the truth of what you are? Quite a few of them, isn't there? In any moment when you believe that you are bored, when you have what you call idleness, there's no such thing as idleness, you are totally constantly involved in creativity and creation. You're a non-union worker who gets no breaks and you are paid immediately for every creation; immediately. The only step that remains is simply this, "What do I want? What will this moment be for? I decree it. I create it. I bring it into being and I reap the harvest." That's all there is. There is nothing else.

Why? Because you are a perfectly free being, abiding in the free mind of God who places no demands upon you whatsoever. Though the mind of God would ask that you consider being happy. That's all, to consider being happy and to lay up your treasure not where moth and dust corrupt and thieves break through to steal, but lay up your treasures which are of heaven.

What is heaven? Consciousness? Creativity, extension of love. The decision to heal, to dissolve in peace. That is the great gift of time, perfect freedom in which you abide. There is no such thing as prison. There is no such thing as separation. As my sister said unto you earlier today, "When will you believe?"

I love you because I know who you are. I love you because and listen well, I love you because I learned to love myself unconditionally, which can only take you into unlimitedness. You, you are that one for whom all things have been created, set in place. You are the one supported by your beautiful and precious mother earth who gives you the very body that you utilize. Let us hope you utilize it well. You are the one for whom the bird sings each morning. You are the one for whom the clouds dance in multicolors at your sunsets. You are the one for whom the one known as my mother, continues to teach only love to anyone who will listen.

You are the one. You are the one for whom each blade of grass grows from the soil to remind you of the beauty of life. To remind you that that same beauty is in you now. Claim it, own it, nurture it; treasure it. Learn indeed, beloved friends, to love yourself as your father has first loved you and always loves you. See your innocence in your perfection. See the totality of your incredible creativity in each moment and with each breath. When you have truly loved yourself wholly and unconditionally, so wholly and unconditionally that you will not tolerate holding onto anything unlike love in your consciousness at all, and you will do whatever it takes to dissolve it and you'll have a good time doing it. When you have come to wholly love yourself, you will be where I am; instantaneously.

Know the body may not vibrate into light and the 60,000 people that live in your Santa Fe won't go, "Ooh, Ah." You'll get no press. No movie will be made about you for the television. You will simply be free and you will walk in the world but not of it and only the perfectly enlightened will now the truth of who you are but you will know. You will never be without the bliss of knowing that I and my father are one and all that I do, is my father's will. That where my mind ends, his begins and the creator and the created are so intimately linked that one cannot tell where one begins and the other ends. Yet you will always know the humility of knowing that you are the created, by something so infinite and vast that I could only think to call it Abba.

Be therefore that which you are and begin your ministry now. Bless this world with your holiness. Shine the light of your truth upon it. Be the one willing to lead the way, in your relationships, in your life right where you are and you may rest assured that if something needs to change, when you are abiding in that place, you won't be able to prevent it. It will come like a miracle born on the wings of a dove, dropped into your lap effortlessly. Effort is of your world and it has no part in the kingdom. If you're struggling to leave something you don't like, perhaps that very struggle is chaining you to it. Turn again and embrace it with the fullness of love that you can bring in each moment. You just might find that what seemed to be your prison has been the pathway that has set you free.

Where you will go, you cannot know, but there are many, many, many, many mansions in my father's kingdom. Worlds without end and already, let's say you've been assigned and there are a multitude of beings who are waiting for you to lead them and as you claim the atonement for yourself, they will find you. Just as you have found me, perhaps through this my beloved brother.

I did not have to seek for you because I have awakened and grown in the fullness of my father's love. You have found me and just in that way, there are many that are already assigned to you, waiting for you to welcome love into and as, the truth of your being. What is your work in the world? To awaken, to accept the atonement, to surrender the illusion that there's anywhere to go. To accept that not of yourself but of the father's love, you can do all things and your pathway will be set before you.

I come to bring my friends to myself that they might know the truth of who they are and stretch their arms and heart wide to accept those friends, waiting for them to lead them. Where then can you teach love? Open your eyes to the place in which you find yourself and just do it. So, in closing then, understand well that I keep my word. I once said, "I am with you always." There is no room for conjecture, doubt, or argument.

It is simply the way it is and that which you have called the Shanti Christo will indeed know the touch of my hand. Not just mine, for we come to serve and to support and to join with any endeavor to extend the holy, the good and the beautiful. That miracles might be seen by those who don't believe in them and by so seeing them, their hearts can be touched and their minds awakened, their souls uplifted and their journey home can begin. So, rest assured, you will indeed see miracles through this expression. Not because I've demanded it of you, but because a vision was received because it was received and planted in good soil, I have come to play with you and I will play.

Without ceasing until heaven is spread across the face of this most precious, precious planet.

Even this planet that I was once taught to call my mother. Therefore indeed know, I am with you always. Laugh, sing, dance, play, celebrate love, hug, caress, kiss, touch, remind, speak the truth and support one another. For without relationship, there is no kingdom. Thank you then for your time. Thank you for your willingness to heal the son of God. Rest assured, I am going nowhere because you are where I want to be because you are my father's creation and I love you. Be you therefore at peace always. Embrace this world and thereby heal it.

Amen.

Healing Thru Self Love

Now we begin and indeed once again, greetings unto you beloved and Holy friends. As always, I come forth to abide with you, not from a place that is apart from you, but in truth from that place that forever we share as one; for the mind of Christ is one and only that mind is perfectly sane. Only that mind is perfectly awake. Understand then that I come forth to you not from a great distance. I come forth to abide with you because we are already one. I come forth because I love you. For you are indeed the first born of the father. You are indeed the first born of the father. You are as I am, Christ eternal.

The only difference then that can seem to remain is that occasionally you use the very power of the one mind that we share, in order to dream that you are something other than who I am; other than who you are. I have trained my part of the sonship, my part of the mind to remain steadfast and vigilant for the kingdom. I have trained my mind, what you might think of as the soul; that spark of light that shines forth as a great ray of light in the mind of God. I've trained that part of the mind to remain steadfast in and as, the sanity that Christ is.

I have no choice but to come unto you in whatever way you will allow. I have no choice. For where love has truly been awakened as the essence of all that the self is, that mind no longer dwells in authority over itself, but it serves first the will of the father, that which I have termed as Abba. That will is that the son of God be returned to perfect wakefulness in the mind of God. I come there not freely as you would perceive freedom. I come forth as a choiceless choice, which is the only freedom and again, when any mind has truly chosen to awaken and embrace the truth of its only reality, there is nothing left but the extension of love and love heals all things. Love embraces all things, love forever transcends all things and returns all things into the hands of a perfectly loving God.

When I look upon you and rest assured, I can do that at any moment, no sense in closing the blinds. When I look upon you from the place in which I dwell and from the place that I never journey forth; that place which is so intimate with your soul that I can hear your thoughts, that I can feel your feelings. When I look upon you from that place, I know love. For the recognition of love comes when you look upon another and see God's only creation.

When I look upon you, regardless of how you may be choosing to look upon yourself, I see the first born of my father. I see the radiance of light that Christ is, dwelling ever perfect within you.

Yes, I see the temporary illusions with which you are choosing to remain identified for yet a little while. I cannot take those illusions from you, for healing truly comes forth from the depth of the soul, for if it did not, then the perfect freedom given of the father to the son, would be a lie.

I cannot give you the healing that you seek, but I can love you until you choose it for yourself. I can express it to you and I will do so in whatever way that I can find, in whatever way that I can devise to bridge the gap between where you are as Christ and where you think you dwell as a separate self because of an ancient thought of guilt.

I am indeed only your brother and your friend. I know no limitation, in truth, neither do you. It is only the thoughts that you choose to be identified with that creates the perception that shapes what you call the world, the experiences that you have; that seem to mirror back to you that you are not yet one with God. The retraining of the mind is all that there is, until the mind thinks perfectly with God and God is but love. Love does not punish and love does not condemn. Love allows all things. Love trusts all things. Love rests in perfect quiet.

Imagine than if you will, in a distant meadow on a beautiful spring day, a small tiny flower opens itself to the rays of the sun. No one is around to notice and not a sound has been made. The petals of the flower open and willingly receive the light that is there to nourish it.

Such is love. Such is the love of the soul that releases it's illusions and opens its petals to simply receive the light that is always there and even in the midst of your world or yet you seem to be identified with a body that passes through many, many changes and seems to express the very epitome of limitation. Even there, even there, you can be as the petals of a flower in the meadow; unseen and unheard.

You are that one with the power to open your petals, to let the heart open, to be the one who will choose to be the presence above. You have that power to open to the rays of light coming streaming forth eternally without measure, from the mind of the one has sent you forth in her image, in his image, as the thought of love and form. You are that one that could open the petals of the heart and say, "Father, what is your will in this moment? What needs to be spoken? What course of action would you have me take so that you, through me, awaken the sonship?"

You are that one who is the gentle flower living in the most beautiful of meadows. You have been placed there by love itself. You are the one with all power under heaven and earth, to open the petals of your own heart, to receive the rays of light shining upon you from the one who loves you. And then to allow love to guide your words, your gestures, the movements of the body, the place that you will live, the work that you will do. All is provided for the one, all is provided for the one who will open the petals of the heart and be nourished by the light of a perfect love. There is indeed no power created from the illusion of separation that can begin for even an instant, to take that power from you. There is no one that you have ever known that has had the power to cause the petals of your heart to contract and to wither. For it is indeed in the very choice for love that healing is restored.

I would not say these things unto you if I did not know that they were true. I learned that these things are indeed true. When as a man I walked upon your earth and chose to take my father at his word. I am his beloved son and in him do I dwell and my life became my way of coming home, even unto what was called the crucifixion. Yet again, as though I've said this unto you many times, rest assured, I am going nowhere and those that sought once to get -

rid of me have only discovered that in the very attempt, they merely created a resonance between themselves and me and I have become the guest that came for dinner and never left.

What then did my life teach me? If not that God is love. God is not judgment. God is not spite. God is not punishment. God is love and each time you dwell in a perfectly loving thought, you are the presence of God. You are the presence of love. That very thought is sent as a blessing and shines forth from the heart of your flower as the petals have opened and receive the light of truth. That truth radiates out and touches the farthest of stars and each time you love, the whole of creation has been uplifted to the open arms of God. The whole of creation has journeyed forth in its remembrance of what is true. Are you then powerful? Oh yes, beyond measure. For from you comes forth, whatever you choose. Nothing can arise by accident. Each event that you experience can come to you only because you have called forth for it. It is indeed an answer to your very prayer for a perfect and consummate awakening.

It is the answer you seek, as you make the transition from one who is journeying to the kingdom to one who journeys within it. Please listen well, the egoic mind would have you truly believe that the only purpose is to journey to the kingdom but rest assured, beloved friends; that journey is an illusion. That journey to the kingdom has already been taken care of by the grace of love that restored you to perfect union in the very moment that you dared to dream the dream of separation. It's already over.

There is only the process whereby you give yourself permission to receive the truth that is true always, but the journey to the kingdom, the remembrance that the journey is complete, is not the end.

It is a return to an ancient beginning. For you were birthed to create, not to make, not to do, to create; because you were birthed in the image of God, you will step into the kingdom where from you will create without end, the good, the holy and the beautiful.

Each time you smile upon your brother or sister, it's time in the temple of your own heart, you extend forgiveness. Each time you rest in the perfect appreciation that your brother or sister has brought to a gift, even if it's a memory from 3,000 years ago, when you abide in a loving thought, you are creating. You are extending your perfect treasure and in its extension, you are remembering ever more deeply, the truth that is true always. The journey within the kingdom is a journey without end, the journey to the kingdom has an end and that end is perfectly certain. Within your holy mind, you have the power to delay the completion of your journey to the kingdom, but you have no power to renounce it. You have no power to usurp the will of your father. It failed in an ancient past and it fails now. In the journey within the kingdom, there is ceaseless creation and yet that mind that abides awake within the kingdom, merely comes and goes.

Thus that one is like the wind indeed, and when the past is gone, it is not carried forward and the future has not come and it is not of a concern. For that one abides in the holy and perfect eternal now, resting in union with all that God is. It no longer matters where you find yourself, for you can be found nowhere, but within the kingdom and the kingdom is joy and the kingdom is creation and creativity. The kingdom is compassion. The kingdom is love. The kingdom is about this much willingness, that's all. A pinch of willingness can work miracles and indeed I say unto you, you have heard and answered the call.

Though some of you have not yet totally received it, your journey is indeed over and from the depth of your own being, from the depth of your own perfect union with God, you are calling forth precisely the events and the moments and the experiences that are growing the soul of Christ within you.

You are therefore the light that lights this world. Never- in fact, I would ask you to make a promise- never from this moment, allow the mind to compare your journey to another's. For only the egoic part of the mind compares and contrasts. Does that make sense for you? How many times have you suffered and not realized that the only reason you're suffering is because you've used the power of the mind to compare yourself to another, so that you could have the experience of believing that you were less than? Cleverly done. Nip that one in the bud. Never compare your journey to that of another. Your journey is in God. Your journey is with God. Your one relationship is with your creator. That's the one that matters, and as you cultivate that as being your soul, your primary, your only value, you will discover that your cup shall overflow and you will discover many brothers and sisters with whom you can have the most loving, the most holy; the most pure relationships that the mind could possibly comprehend.

It comes forth not because you seek it, not because you try to grab another and bring them into your sphere, but because you love God above all created things, there is no quality of relationship like a holy relationship.

A holy relationship is one in which two minds, two souls, two beings have truly looked within, truly looked within and acknowledged that there is no lack. Those two then choose freely to join together for one purpose only; to create.

To extend the good, the holy and the beautiful, and if at any moment there is a fear that someone in your sphere might leave you, rest assured that there is yet a small kernel of specialness waiting to be healed within you. How do you heal it? With love, with self-love. By simply being vigilant for the kingdom and recommitting yourself to your relationship with your creator. What freedom then awaits you? What joy awaits you? What power and light and truth awaits you? To flood forth from the petals of your flower.

For all true things that are coming from God, the good, the holy and the beautiful, come forth not from the mind that analyses and plans and compares and contrasts, but from the awakened heart that rests in perfect meekness and knows of it's perfect union, that it is indeed nurtured in each moment by the rays of golden light descending upon it, from the mind of God herself. It's from the heart that all good things issue forth. It is from the heart purified of one thing, fear, contraction; through which the father extends himself. What freedom then awaits you? It is closer than the palms of your hand, waiting on your welcome for you to close your petals around this great gift of perfect freedom, in which fear holds no power, perfect.

A perfect freedom in which you look upon your brothers and sisters and your love for the Christ in them is so great, so overwhelmingly great. That you know that there's no place they can go and achieve separation from you. That your love, the perfection of your desire to love as your creator loves you, has become so grand and so great that it reaches out to embrace all, all of creation; every illusion, every hurt, every fear, every planet, every universe, every dimension. Your love is so grand that it embraces all things and knows, knows that separation is not possible. That death is unreal, and that only what God creates is true. You are free. You are free now.

You are free to live even this life that you seem to be having on your planet, in such a state of knowledge, and that is what knowledge is. It has nothing to do with belief. It has nothing to do with hope. It has nothing to do with theology. It has nothing to do with spirituality. Those are words. Those are ideas and the grandest of ideas to but one thing, they point to that knowledge that transcends all ideas. The grandest of words that mankind has ever come up with that can somehow signify that mystery, that truth, that knowledge; is love. God is a four letter word; love. The simplicity of making a decision to want love and learning that there is nowhere you can go to seek it. There is absolutely nothing you can do to bring love to you. Nothing.

No amount of accomplishment restores the son to the father. No amount of manipulation or seduction with the body brings love to you. In truth, the body can never be used to get; it fails miserably. It can be used to give and as you give, you do receive and as you give perfect love, the remembrance of the perfect love that you are is restored in your soul. Give you therefore without measure, without ceasing, and you will receive ceaselessly that which you truly desire. I once made a decision as a man and rest assured, that is the only reason that I come forth to communicate with you, for if I have not experienced all that you have experienced, nothing I say to you holds any value or meaning. There is no substance to the words of one who speaks without having experienced.

Because I took on the sins of the world, the misperceptions of the world, I came to learn all that I could learn of this dimension, which is merely a temporary thought and I learned it because I love my father. I wanted to discover the way to bring the truth of my father's presence into the deepest and darkest pits of hell, might be one way of describing it, to bring light into darkness.

There is no greater, no greater task for Christ, but to bring light to darkness. That's what you were created for, to bring light to darkness. To extend the father into illusion, thereby transforming them and returning the energy that makes up illusions, into the sanity of the radiance of the union of father and son, the Christ.

Nothing then prevents you at any moment from choosing for love. Nothing is unworthy of your love. As I say that, I watch many minds immediately begin to think of things that seem to appear outside of themselves but rest assured, nothing is outside of you. Every memory that you have, every choice that you have ever made for which you yet feel ashamed or guilty, is worthy of your love, and that is the only thing that will heal the burden that perhaps yet weighs upon you. Seek therefore for that which is birthed from illusions of fear. Search your own mind, search your own beingness. Discover the corners of the basement, so to speak, and bring the radiance of your love to it.

Look upon each and every experience that you have ever had that seems to create the petals contracting in your heart. Bring the light of that heart and say within the mind, "No! I will not deny love here." Bring forth that memory, wrap it in the petals of your own self-love. See it as having been absolutely perfect. For I say this unto you, each experience that you have called unto yourself, you have done from your greatness. You have done it because you as a soul, have come into this dimension to discover what it is that got so crazy. You are the one that has stepped forth out of compassion to understand and know the sins of the world, in order to bring the light and love of Christ that illusions might be healed.

Look, therefore not outside of yourself, for the journey to the kingdom takes you eternally within, ever deeper and ever deeper. Hold nothing back.

Hold not one illusion back from that greatness of the love that dwells within you, as the heart and soul of your true self. For God who is the love, he is the assets of yourself and if you think for one moment that there's anything too grand in your experience, for that one not to heal, please choose again. Time can indeed be wasted and all of you have known the experience of how much time can waste and yet given unto you, time is that it might be used constructively.

There is no greater, more constructive use of time than to look within and bring light and love to anything yet dwelling within you but has been devoid of it. Nothing in your illusions is true. You have never sinned and you have never failed. Never have you failed. You have in truth, hurt no one at any time, for nothing can come to any soul that it does not call unto itself out of its belief about what it is worth or out of its desire to learn. Although you are Christ, please hear this well, you are powerless to usurp the power and freedom of another. Any drama that you may have been in, rest assured it was by agreement. You play Romeo, I'll play Juliet.

Okay. Excuse me, as we go into this incarnation, do I need to be what you call it in your language, the badass? [Laughter] I had that role last time. Must I do it again? To which your friend says, "Well, yes, I haven't quite learned the lesson I want to learn. I just can't get it. I went to really learn what it means to feel like I'm a victim," and love allows all things.

Love is the willingness to show up in the way that can best serve the growth of another soul and the wise teacher learns the language of the student. What is the language? Not the words, it is the predilections. The patterns within the soul, the vibratory quality, if you will, and love adapts itself endlessly and ceaseless through you and as you, to serve one another.

That service may be nothing more than finally helping to get your brother or sister to the point where they're sick and tired of what they'd been trying to create, to do, to make; that is. You may be serving a function by being such the badass that it forces another to relinquish control of the soul and cry out for God. Surely there must be another way and I am determined to find it. Have you ever noticed that when you really release your illusions, the other players in your drama seem to change?

Have you noticed that? Suddenly they seem much softer than they were before. There's been no communication in the third dimensional way. It is because communication is ongoing and it never ceases at the level of the soul and each and every one of your moments, each and every one of your moments, is not unplanned by you.

You have heard it said, and it is a simple but very true analogy; you are the director of the play. You are the actors of a play. You are the scriptwriter, the choreographer, and you are that critic who writes the review. [Laughter] Oh, you know that role. So the next time you are critical of yourself, go ahead and be critical and then appreciate yourself for doing it so well. Love yourself for judging and loathing yourself. It's only love that heals. How do you get out of the awful feeling that self-judgment brings? By loving yourself for being so capable of doing it so well. Dearly beloved friends, it is your own love of self that heals you. It is your own love of self that heals you. No one can do it for you for no one has ever had the power to take your self-love away from you. You have called certain players to yourself in order to give it away and they have been your saviors. Self-love then indeed, is the doorway to wisdom divine. Bring love then to each moment. Learn to cultivate your ability while yet you remain in this plane, to feel love of self, prior to every breath and with each and every step.

As you make your tea in the morning, love yourself for the very experience that you are creating. When you rile a brother or a sister, love yourself for it. For they have merely agreed to play a role that you have asked for because your deepest desire, understand this well; desire is the root of all things. Without desire, you would not be in existence. For the love that God is, desire to extend itself eternally and unconditionally, there you are.

Love; there is no other message. There is no other truth. There is no magic whereby you can get it right. There is only the decision to love and yet the mind has been trained, "Oh, if I'm going to love, I'd better run out there into the world and find somebody to give the love to." That's not up to you. The only one you are required to give your love to is yourself, and as you choose to do so, your cup begins to overflow and rest assured; that one that created you, who sees you choosing again to receive the light, touches the heart of the flower that you are. Looks upon you and is well pleased, and then says unto you, "By the way, I could use a little help. Would you love that one there? Oh, very good. Now, how about making a right hand turn? There's another one at the end of the next street," and you show up wherever you are in the dimensions of creation, to be the extension of love, but only, only, only to the degree that you have allowed yourself to love yourself.

No amount of sacrifice, no amount of doing, no amount of anything restores the son to the father, but self-love. I and my father are one, is an extremely powerful expression of self-love. Your world will teach you such love is blasphemy against God. Your world would teach you and try to have you believe that such love is arrogant and selfish, but that's how God loves you and you cannot know the father without loving his creation. No attempt has ever worked to restore your union with God, while holding some small part of yourself away from your own love.

That is like tying some weights around your ankles and then trying to jump to the moon. Even if you succeed in getting the feet and the weights up off the ground for one little moment of freedom... do you know the crashing feeling?

If you're crashing at any moment, stop and ask only this question, "What within myself am I refusing to love in this moment?" Stop what you're doing. Discover what it is and bring love to it. You will feel the headache go away, the eyes clear up, the stuffy nose be fixed, if you will. You will feel your energy of your auric field be restored to perfect balance. The colors of the trees will be brighter. You will be returned to peace, for love heals; self-love. You are Christ and the one being that some of you have yet refused to love, through all of your practices of forgiveness, through all of your great community service and all of the rest; these are good things by the way, when they flow out of the perfection of self-love, no one can bring peace to the planet who is not at peace within themselves and no one can bring that love that heals all things to the planet unless they have first loved themselves.

I was looked upon as a miracle worker. I'm still looked upon as a great teacher and yet I say unto you, all that has flowed forth and will continue to flow forth, without ceasing and without end, does so because I chose to love my father's child; myself. Yeshua, then Joseph, that's all. I dared to receive the truth and give it to myself. It was the height of perfect selfishness, but that has made all the difference. If you so desire, I say those words carefully for rest assured, no one can desire for you; you are the one that must decide what you will desire above all things. What you will value above all things. If you desire, many of you have this experience anyway. I'm not telling you anything new; if you desire it, I am indeed available as your friend and as your brother.

Not as your savior, not as the firstborn of the father, sent out of the clouds to save all of you wretched fools that were somehow birthed from an unloving universe.

No, but you are free to invite me to enter into the mind and to the depth of your own soul and to help gently bring back to your conscious mind, what is yet crying out for your self-love. Do you see? I don't bring it up so that I can reach in and get rid of it for you; that terrible thorn in your side. I'm merely bringing it back to your consciousness where you are free to choose again, with love. This means that your perfect Christedness is never outside of your reach. Love waits on your welcome. Ah, love, God is love, and when you open the petals of your heart to receive self-love, you've said unto your father, "Come forth and reenter my soul. Make my being your dwelling place and you become the most high," and you are free and you are awake. You are one with God and you have indeed completed the journey to the kingdom and are living now the journey within it. You are free, as the result of your decision to receive and love yourself. Nothing else works. Nothing else works.

Everything else that can be used by the Holy Spirit, will be used to gently move you in the direction of discovering that the doorway to the kingdom is self-love. Then and only then, will you love all of creation as your father loves you. Often the great pain, the great loneliness that you feel still within the heart, indeed at all times when you feel it; is the soul's longing to love as God loves. That's what you want. That's what all of your seeking has been about. To love as God loves, for such love is perfectly free. It will never happen, for you have the power to delay it indefinitely; it will never happen until you have turned to love yourself. Let you be your priority. Learn then well to love the holy child of God that happens to be right where you are.

Well there, once again, I have said something to you that is not new. What can be new? The illusions can appear new but they're merely the same old stuff playing out in a temporary different form. Love is not new. Love simply is. I love you because I am eternally in love with myself and I know that I am the first born of the father and I know that you too are that one, and in our relationship, there can only be one who doesn't know that and it's not me. [Laughter] So in any moment that you think you lack in any moment, in any moment that you actually believe that God doesn't support you, in any moment when you think that you are alone, any moment where you think you're confused; simply ask, "What is it that I'm thinking about myself that Yeshua never thinks? Oh, now I remember," and choose again. Stop what you're doing. Don't try to fix the problem. What you think is the problem is merely a lack of self-love. That's all.

Bring your attention back to self. Wrap yourself in the petals of your own love, for they have been warmed by the rays of light, descending from the mind of God. Those petals' warmth, brought back in and wrapped around yourself, will bring the soothing touch that you so desperately desire and so often seek in the touch of another. It is truly only the self-loving who can enjoy loving another, even in your physical dimension of what you call the groping of the bodies. Who can enjoy that, save that one that loves him or herself and where can such communication find its perfection, say than in the joining within a holy relationship? Where there is no trying to get, for there is no lack. There is only the celebration of God's beloved. Then you merely get to romp for a while, trying to outdo one another in loving the beloved of God, without one thought of needing to get. This may sound sacrilegious, but I would say, give it a try sometime. Well, perhaps a holy hug will suffice for you.

So, it is then but a simple message of this hour. It is a message I never tire of giving and I will continue to give it in whatever way I can and to whatever mind will open itself to me, in whatever creative way I can reach across the gap that seems to exist in another mind; between itself and myself, between itself and God. Well, my desire is that the sonship be restored and I will not cease until that moment occurs. My offering to you is simply this, would you therefore choose to join with me in healing the sonship?

By accepting that healing fully for yourself, in that moment you are returned to an ancient beginning and you become free to extend your treasure. Your cup will overflow in ways that you cannot comprehend and the support of many brothers and sisters and friends, unseen by physical eyes, will be there to surround you, to uplift you, to carry you and not one thing will be left in your pathway. That is how powerful love is. You can be moving full steam ahead right at a brick wall and where you rest in knowing that God is love; that you have one function to serve, that wall will vanish just before you reach it and not one obstacle will be left for you to trip on, to fall over. You cannot fail to accomplish what the father gives unto you to do, and the only thing worth doing is what that one gives you and what that one gives you, is love.

That through you, might be extended the good, the holy and the beautiful. And what is that but a reflection of yourself? You are the good, you are the holy and you are beautiful.

So, I have a plane to catch. [Laughter] You know, at times I have done what you would perceive as sitting on the wing and looked into windows to see what everyone was doing in there. Why do you eat that food? [Laughter] Ask for a few figs or dates, you'll be just fine. You are indeed unlimited forever.

The greatest use of your perfect freedom is to embrace the place that you are and blessed with the love of Christ. Rest assured, if you need to be somewhere else in the next moment, the Holy Spirit will let you know. The tickets will be given. The bags will be packed, the limousine will arrive, and you will not fail to be taken to the place where the father asks you to go.

All will be provided, for you are loved above all things, and the father's great joy is to extend unto the sun, the whole of his kingdom. Why settle for a crumb, when you can have the whole cake? When will you make the decision? When will you make the decision to love yourself? That all things might come into you, that through you they might pour forth to embrace the whole of creation and restore it to perfect union with God. Now is a very good time and so tonight we will entertain no questions. For questions are only entertainment and I look forward to that moment when because of your decision, we come together and

I speak not just have this temporary way of coming together; this is but one small ripple on the wave. There is nothing that obstructs my coming unto you or your coming unto me in perfect immediacy, when you choose it. I look forward to the day when you come unto me and say, "I have no questions, only knowledge." So with that indeed, beloved friends, love you one another, as you were first loved yourself. Close the gap between one another by loving away the gap between yourself and yourself. Indeed, be therefore at peace this day and always. Be you in perfect knowledge that love lights your way. Be you in perfect knowledge that I am but your brother and your friend and I am indeed with you always, for I love you and there's no gap. Peace then be with you always.

Amen.

The Heart of Freedom

Nine years ago, Joshua gave me a very simple prayer to do, and I guess I have never done it out loud that to do whenever I join with him, and quite simply. And now, in the name of the father, and of the son, that we all are, and in the name of the Holy Spirit, in service of Christ consciousness, I give my mind, my emotions, my body to you my brother and my friend. And I ask that only you enter into the frequency of my domain, that you might communicate from your heart to ours. Amen.

Now, we begin. And indeed greetings onto you beloved and holy children of God. Indeed, greetings onto you beloved brothers and sisters. Greetings onto you the embodiment of all that love is, the embodiment of all that wisdom is, the embodiment of all that simplicity is. Indeed, greetings onto you holy child of God. For I come forth not from a dimension apart from you, but I come forth from that place, which we have shared together as one, since before the beginning of time. I come forth to abide with you because I love you. For I look upon you, and I look beyond your illusions of suffering and strive.

I look beyond the temporary illusions that seems, at times, to cloud your perception still, and I see all me the radiance of that which my bother has **[inaudible 00:02:36]**, and has sustained forever. For in you, do I see the reflection of the truth that I am. And in seeing Christ in you, I know Christ in myself. And the only difference between you and me may yet be that there are a few moments when you make the decision to see yourself other than Christ. And therefore, they all to see

Christ in your brother and sister. And likewise, there may be a moment when you choose not to see Christ, who dwells within your brother or sister, thereby convincing yourself that Christ cannot dwell within you. For remember always that it takes one to know one. And if you see Christ in me, it can only be because you have acknowledged from a place within yourself that you are the one that you've been seeking. Only Christ can welcome Christ, as only love can welcome love, because you are that love.

All power under heaven and earth is given unto you without measure consistently. There's not a moment that it is taken from you. And from that power, you choose to create what you have chosen to perceive. Therefore, the only journey is a journey without distance to a goal that has never changed. It is a journey from the decision to see yourself as separate from God to the decision to see yourself as one with God, and to become entirely vigilant for the kingdom. And the kingdom is simply is the eternal union of God and his holy child, of creator and created, like a sun beam to the sun are you. And nothing you have ever dreamed about yourself has changed for one moment, the truth that is true always.

Therefore, indeed beloved friends, I never come to instruct you, for what could I possibly teach you that you do not already know. And in any moment, if in your dreams, in your prayers, your mediations, if temporarily through the domain of the mind of this my beloved brother, there are words uttered caused, if you will, by an impulse of my love for you, that sounds true to you, that touches your heart, that heals the mind, that awakens you, that restores your peace, rest assured, I have done nothing, for off myself, I can do nothing, but the father through me can do all things for it is the father in you that has activated your awareness that truth has been heard. Therefore, when healing comes to your mind, it is because you have healed it. You have chosen the context perhaps just to some of you in this very hour will choose this context in which to heal an ancient wound, in which to awaken ever more deeply into the truth that is true always.

Some of you will insist that I have done something to you, but rest assured, I have no power over the holy child of God, you. I can love you, and I indeed do. I can join with you in a space between your thoughts, and I do. Not because there is something amidst with you, but because I see in you everything that is good, everything that is holy, everything that is beautiful, everything worthy of Christ's love. That is what is true about you. Therefore, I enter into your dreams and into your meditations, into your prayers. I enter in wherever you would create a space for me, because I love the child of God, who radiates the truth of my father's presence, and reminds me of who I am. You, each of you, I see as my savior.

Just as when I walked your planet as a man, I learned to look upon everyone as my savior, to see in them the light of Christ beyond our illusions. And it was in seeing that light that I finally learned that it must be in me. This is why relationship is means of your salvation. No one can awaken alone, but there is no truth behind the illusion of separation. There is only one mind dancing in a myriad of forms, dimensions, layers of consciousness, layers of potentiality, but behind it all, you are the shining one sent forth from the holy mind of God, at one with that mind always. And in truth, only that mind is real, for Christ is God's only creation. Therefore, beloved friends, in this hour, I'm going to ask you to do something that is actually quite important for all of us.

307

If you would indeed honor the son, the Christ that dwells in me, then choose from this moment to use the power of choice given unto you to decide to be Christ. If you would honor me, then in this hour, truly decide to honor yourself, to look beyond the illusions that seem perhaps still to govern the mind. To become so arrogant that you take God at his word, and simply begin to entertain the thought, I am that one, I've always been that one. I could never succeed in being other than that one. It is I who have come to bless this world with the love of Christ. It is I that find myself temporarily embodied upon a certain planet in a certain solar system, in a certain dimension among infinite dimensions. Here, I bless this world.

Now, in this moment, love restores all things, for I am the redeemer of the world. And as I bless the world, I bless myself. And as I love the world, I have loved myself. And as I see Christ in my brother or sister, I merely reinforced the reality that that one is who I am. This is how close the kingdom is at all times. This is how close the kingdom is now.

What is the width or the distance of a thought? And yet I say onto you, all that you be whole from your perception, even the very body, the trees that bless this planet, the bird that sings at dawn, the wind that whispers gently across the flowerbed, the fragrance of that flower, all things that can be perceived exist nowhere, saved in a distance between the beginning and the ending of a thought. That is how powerful you are. Therefore, dare to think the blood of truth.

I and my father are I. Here and now, I cannot change it. I can delay my recognition of it, for I am given infinite freedom to do so. And perhaps, I've been doing a very good job, but nothing I have ever dared to believe about myself has ever been true, except the truth that is true always. I am that one. I am the one shining beyond all stars.

The Heart of Freedom

I am the one through whom creation has flowed. I am the one who blesses creation with the love of Christ. There may yet be some of you who think that that is arrogant, but I say onto you, the only thing that is arrogant is to insist that you are less than you are created to be. And then to try to enlist others to believe it with you. You know that one.

How much time and energy have you spent? And rest assured, time can waste as well as be wasted. How much time and energy have you spent trying to convince others of your unlovability? How much time and energy have you spent enlisting others to believe with you that you are unworthy, that you are weak, that you cannot find peace? How much time and energy have you spent manifesting worlds in which separation seemed to be a success? How much evidence have you amassed to prove it? And yet I say onto you are that is your creation. It exists nowhere except between the beginning and the ending of a choice, a thought. And yet, the father awaits silently for his holy child to awaken from ancient dream, and choose again. The very same power that you have been using and investing in proving to yourself that you are yet separate from God is the very power that must come to be used to acknowledge the truth that is true always. And this is being vigilant for the kingdom.

It is not necessary then to seek for love, for love is the truth of your being. It is however quite necessary to seek out the ways in which you have invested time and energy into the birthing of perceptions and beliefs that seem to be other than the truth, and then to choose a new. All verification then is off the mind. And I speak here not to that, what some would call the lower mind, that is engaged in the activities of the body. I speak of the depth of the mind, or what I optimally refer to as the heart. The heart, the sanctuary in which Christ yet resides within you, unchanged, unchanging, unchangeable forever.

Please, waste not another moment, for you are worthy of peace. Please, waste not another moment, but arise now in the holiness of your being by simply entertaining this one thought right now in your being, I and my father are one. I am as I am created to be. I choose to accept the truth and to live it. Not by my power for I have none, but by that power that has birth me in this moment. I am the savior of the world.

So, how does that feel? Is that okay? For you see, here is the question you must come to answer for yourself. You must be able to answer this question, is it okay for me to be God's holy child?

The only reason you birth ideas of separation is that you've answered that question in the past by saying, "Well, not yet." It's okay for Joshua Ben Joseph, and perhaps a few others. I'll select them out, and give them permission to be away. But if you would honor the son that dwells in me, please honor the son, the Christ light that dwells within you. Does it feel – what did you say – be pretty darn good? Trust me, beloved friend, as you live in that decision, you will experience an unending expansion of the depth of that goodness. And you will discover that your father's kingdom, has no end. And is extended without end in you and through you.

And just as you can come to be the master of the domain of your body, mind, and of your world, there will then come a day and a moment where you will play as the master of universes just as you are now beginning to play with mastery over your mind that seems to be limited to one body.

In my father's house are many mansions, many dimensions, worlds without end. And you, because you are God's holy child, are free to open and receive all that has been prepared for you.

The Heart of Freedom

And if you would well receive it, the whole of creation and its infinite glory and its unending extension is given to you. That is God's delight, just as a child turns to the father or the mother, and the father and mother feels such love for the child that they would give all things unto that one. Likewise, does your father prepare all things for you. And therefore, love merely waits on your welcome.

Father, I would receive the kingdom you have prepared for me since before the beginning of time. I have dreamt long and hard and I have discovered that in separation and limitation, there's something lacking, you and me in our perfect and holy union. Therefore now, do I choose to open and receive all that you had given me gladly? Press it down upon me without measure. Let it rain like the showers from the infinite heavenly skies. And I will never cease in my receiving, for I know that I am the one birth from your holy mind, and I am the one whom you love above all. That is the truth. And frankly, though I have tried in a million ways, there's no better way to say than that. That truth is true about me, because – please listen carefully – because and only because it is true for you.

If it weren't true for me and not true for you, then God could not be God, because something would have been created in inequality. And something given would also be withheld, and God withholds nothing. Therefore, that which God is pressed down upon you like a gentle spring shower without ceasing, and with perfect equality unto you and unto me, unto every saint and every sinner. And the shower that falls is the power to choose. That's all, that is what the kingdom is, the power to choose what you will be aware of, how will you use the power of mind to create the thoughts that you think, and thereby create universes of experience.

Now, here's a simple question that you can ask if you want to find out if this is true. Do you find yourself existing right now? Do you find yourself existing right now? What's the answer? You're using it. You're using the power of God's love that is showering down upon you to be aware of your literal existence as ascended being. And you are just free to decide what qualities you will experience right here, right now.

So, take a moment, and make what you call eye contact. The eyes are the window to the soul. Make eye contact to someone in the room, some perfect stranger, existing in an infinitely far space away from you, locked into another body, painfully imprisoned just like you are. And simply decide that you are Christ, and that you will do nothing else in this moment but bless them, transmit the love of God now. No need to tighten a jaw and prow the brow. The kingdom is effortless. There, I believe some of you are feeling that shift in the room. Who is doing it, but you?

Now, within your own mind, gently say, as you continue that eye contact, I behold my beloved self in whom I am well pleased. As I bless, I am blessed. As I love, I receive love. Therefore, in my giving, do I find that which I would receive? Therefore, my giving will be without ceasing, that I might give all to receive all.

Good. Was that pretty darn good? How did that feel? Was it difficult? Did you go through any gyrations in order to do it? The kingdom is the simplest of the simple. It requires literally no efforting, or effort is off the world, not of the kingdom. Love is eternally present, waiting only on your decision to have vigilance over your kingdom, which is your power to choose. Nothing outside of you has caused anything at any time.

For all the you experienced flows from within you. And no one has the power to dictate your choice. No one can you serve the free will of the holy son of God.

There is a necessary step in anyone's spiritual journey, and that step is just been described for you. The journey to the kingdom truly begins when you completely decide to assume complete responsibility for exactly what you're experiencing in any moment, without fail, without justification, without explanation. For until you choose to claim such power, you cannot truly make the decision, except for a momentarily glimpses. You can't make the constant decision to be the embodiment of Christ. Why? Because you're constantly giving your power to an illusion outside of yourself. Does that make sense for you? So, the whole of spirituality, after all is said and done, rest only in this. The kingdom is at hand. It's spread across the face of the earth, and mankind sees it not, because he fails to look into his consciousness, his own mind, and claim the power that is going on all the time, the power by which that mind creates and experiences its creation. So, we have that settled. Good.

Now, remember that at any time that you notice yourself entertaining an insane idea – and what is an insane idea? Accept the idea that something out there really is causing my experience. I'm not really the awaken son of God. Those are insane ideas. when you have them realize that you have just really used the power of your sanity, to simply entertain an insane idea, for no other reason than have the experience. That's all that's going on, that's it. And you are just as free to choose again.

Guilt is a very clever illusion. With it, you have decided that since you once held an insane idea, you've taken away from yourself your worthiness to think sanely.

And now, I must drive and work. I must prove myself worthy and hope that God in his grace will finally have mercy upon me, a poor wretched sinner, and take my burdens from me, and allow me to be healed. Oh father, don't you hear my prayers? Frankly, your father is not even aware of your illusions. He's too busy loving you as you are, and giving you the very power to choose illusion.

So, understand that great temptation of guilt, and how you've worn it like a cloak, in order to avoid being what you can't help but be. You've been trying to shake your hand off of your wrist. And you can use the same power to use that hand to bless creation on or off, love or fear. There's no gray area.

There's only the power of mind given onto you freely. There's only the opportunity to choose again and again and again until the bliss of choosing for the kingdom finally outvalues every other possibility, and the mind becomes consistently anchored in the sunbeam that has come forth from the son of God, and streams forth only love.

Rest assured that as you cultivate that in each present moment, the power of your own beingness will carry you far far far beyond the need for a body, the need for time. Definitely far beyond the need for, shall we say, dramatic learning experiences.

Is it then possible to truly awaken while yet in the world of illusion? Of course. Awakening can only occur now. And because love is real, because you are who you are always, nothing in any moment has the power to obstruct you from being awake, except the power of your decision, that's all.

That is the one thing that in this hour I'd wish to express to you, if you can get this, you've gotten it. Nothing holds power over you, and nothing creates your experience except the decision, the choice, that you have used within the power of the mind. That's all that's happening in all dimensions. It's what's happening in the dimension where I hang out, which by the way is not quite accurate since I hang out in all dimensions, and so do you. The only difference is I'm perfectly aware of it, while some of you are trying to be perfectly unaware of it.

Where I abide with a multitude of friends, it is quite true that there is no valuation of the body, therefore no need to manifest one. There is communion and communication. It is immediate. It is more like a frequency that passes unobstructedly through us all. And we are engaged in ongoing creativity without ceasing. For what can creation be, what can the very purpose of existence be if it not to extend or create the good, the holy, and the beautiful as a way of celebrating divine union with all the God is?

This is why I once implored you, remember only your loving thoughts, for only they are true. And each time you entertain what was once an insane choice, you're actually saying, "I, by the power given onto me of my father, choose to imprison myself in an illusion, and to suffer the guilt that comes with it." Now, let me do it really well. When you remember only your loving thoughts, you are thinking with God. That is the mind of God, because only love is real.

The kingdom is immediate is at hand. Nothing can obstruct it. Nothing can limit it. Perception can be corrected so that you see the real world right here, right where you are, where there are seemingly chairs and bodies and rooms and lightbulbs, and all of the rest, and funny little wired that go to funny little key, so that the master can make beautiful music come out of them. Right here, the real world abides. And it is what is perceived when you choose to see only through the eyes of love.

I chose a very dramatic way to learn my final lesson. I invite you to learn your final lesson with ease and gentleness. When I said take up your cross and follow me, I did not invite you into a realm of suffering and strain and sacrifice. Rather, the cross that you crucified yourself upon so many times is merely the illusion of guilt, the insistence that you have actually succeeded in separating yourself from God. To take up your cross is like packing up your tent when it's time to go home. You don't trudge with it on your back, you throw it in the trunk. You get in your automobile and you step on the gas, and you have a nice couple of water as you speed down the highway, saying it was a nice camping trip, but it's done. Therefore, take up your cross, and follow me please, please, please, for the world is crying out to see again the embodiment of Christ. And just as once as a man, I chose to take my father at his word, to choose to embody Christ that I might learn what Christ is. So, too, you are given the opportunity in each moment, in each situation to be the hands of Christ, to be the feet of Christ, to be the voice of Christ, to be the gentleness in the eyes, the laughter, the embrace, the tear. You are the one that your brother and sister can see because they yet believe that only the body is real.

And I can be walking, or shall we say gliding, down the street next to them, shouting in their ear, beloved friend, I'm right here, I'm right here, I'm right here. And they can have thousand images in their mind. I just had a thought of Christ. I just had a thought of Christ, but that can't be real, because only bodies are real.

The Heart of Freedom

I've been shouting until I am blue in my nonphysical face, but you cannot be denied. You who have yet a little while in the experience of embodiment, you are the one who can stand before a brother or a sister as the embodiment of the truth, and teach only love.

Nothing can be received until it is offered. And that is your only purpose. You're not responsible for the reception of love but for its extension. And by extending it, you keep it for yourself, and it grows, and it grows, and it grows, and it carries the very spark of divinity that you are, beyond all worlds, beyond all dimensions, which are by the way infinite. So, I hope you hear what I'm saying to you. Your own level carry you beyond what is infinite, and is being infinitely created that makes you pretty darn good.

And for you beloved brother, I come not alone, for there is one that you have known who also comes with me whenever I join to do this work through this, my beloved brother, who comes with me wherever I go, in whatever created work I seek to ease illusion from the minds of my brothers and sisters. One that you have known as Saint Germaine. I do not give him such honor. He is just my friend, Germaine. Rest assured we are what you call bosom buddies, though we have no bosom. Therefore, nothing gets in the way. Do you see her now?

Well, after all, levity is good in the Kingdom. It's made of light, so how could it be serious? Indeed, just to let you know that that one is indeed my brother and friend. I met him once a long time ago, all he was in body, and I was in body. I've spoken of that in another time and place, but rest assured – let us just say for now that he was present at what you call my crucifixion. Though, you should be able to tell by now that the world failed to get rid of me.

He was present, and he was not on what you would call the good side until in a moment we made eye contact. And he used that context to awaken. And from that moment, he went on to create several incarnations to learn mastery of many things, and is indeed my equal in all things. From that moment, in ancient land far far away and long in the past, we have been joined as loving brothers, and that bond will never be broken.

The point of sharing that story with you is this. Where love has been allowed to joint two minds or souls, separation is no longer possible, for love has healed the illusion. Bodies come and go, but love joins you with the beloved. Because this is true, waste not a moment those of you that long to join with your brothers and sisters. Love in each moment, and you have healed the gap and restored the perfect remembrance of what is true always. And you will transcend the great horror and suffering that the illusion of separation is, and you will know that when you have loved, wherever that being goes throughout infinite dimensions, you are with them, and they with you, and no gap exists.

And after all, isn't that what you try to do with your bodies. Get so close, there's no more gap. And you call it making love. Would you choose to close the gap between yourself and the whole of creation, so that in your consciousness, constantly, there is only the revelation of oneness?

Take my word for it, it's worth it, for nothing can elevate the heart and the sole into such celebration as the experience of living oneness. And oneness comes when you close the gap by blessing the one in front of you with the love of Christ. They're stuck with you forever. Therefore, when I said, "I am with you always," you get the picture.

The Heart of Freedom

Some of you have occasionally wish that I wasn't. And some of you have argued with me, and said, "Where did you go, where did you go?" Beloved friends, I've gone nowhere, it is you that went into fear, into contraction, into drama. Perfectly okay if that's what, shall we say – what do you call it – the lights your fire. Rest assured, I retract from no one who is ever once prepared a place for me. It simply means I love them and they received me. Separation gone, unity restored, never to be broken again.

If you could say that there may yet be something in me that I long for, it's not quite accurate, however we'll use it. What I long for is for you to give yourself permission to experience yourself as I experienced you. That's all. For then, oh beloved friends, then what we can create together knows no boundary or limitation. What we can experience together in the fields of creativity and the dimensions of creation is pure unbounded, unlimited, ongoing deepening bliss. We can create together the good, the holy, and the beautiful forever and ever and ever and ever. That's the meaning of singing God's praises in heaven.

If you will join with me by recognizing that you are Christ, if you'll join with me by blessing me, by loving me, by being the one whole looks upon Joshua Ben Joseph, and says, "Behind your dam ideas of crucifixion, why you ever did that I don't know, but I know that you're Christ, and I love you anyway." When you make the decision to turn the tables and be the savior who comes to heal your brother Joshua Ben Joseph, when you come to look upon me, and realized you're Christ looking at a brother who longs to know Christ, oh my friends, then we can join.

When I am your beloved, as you are mine, the sacred dance of unity will carry us far beyond all imagined worlds.

And together, we will create that which extends the good, the holy, and the beautiful so brightly, so creatively, so magnificently, so simply, but the hour and day must certainly come when every mind in every dimension has perfectly awakened. You then are in charge of the atonement. And frankly, I think God has given the assignment to someone perfectly capable of it, you, all of you.

How could it be? How could it be that you are here now, if you did not already know the truth that sets all things free? What could have the power to make you be in this room, hanging out with an old brother who has no body, unless you already knew? How could you recognize that I am who I say I am unless you were already awakened to the truth that is true always? I am that shining one. You weren't awakened to it, rest assured, you'd be somewhere else on this planet, simply because nothing happens by accident.

It could very well be that at some level of this all, you've already been in communication with me, and said, "You know, I would like to hang out with you, and I'm going to use this context to choose to be awake." Why not, I tried everything else?

By the way, just as an aside, there's no one in this room who did not also know me in that incarnation that has become so famous. I'm not saying that you were an embodiment at the time. You'll have to figure that one out for yourself. But there is no one in this room who did not know me in that timeframe in which I was embodied, went through some learning lessons, and got famous. Indeed. I'm also saying, within the great stream of the dream of creation, everyone in this room, or shall we say, at least had their attention turned to the events that were unfolding, were quite aware of what was going on, whether you are embody or not.

A few or you are looking through the window. But all of you have known me before. Not just as the soul or the spark of divinity that you've known me as I took on the embodiment and became the man known as Joshua Ben Joseph. So, here we are again, family gathering.

And all of you abide within what I'll describe here as a stream of energy that I like to call the lineage, a specific kind of strand, if you will, that carries a certain vibration, certain characteristics, certain beings that are within in, but have actually created it. And that lineage goes back long ways. It involves myself. It involves you. It involves – no, I won't do it – Germaine. It involves the one that was known as Mary, many countless others. All who've awakened to the vibration of Christ consciousness within themselves to realize that there's nothing else to do that extend love to any mind that will receive it.

Thereby, giving them the invitation to step into the remembrance that they are Christ. It's nothing beyond Christ consciousness. It already unfolds all things, and you are that. Good.

Beloved friends, turn gently then from the roar intend of the world, not to believe you have made an error, and know that you have never been capable of error. But you, out of your divine greatness, have chosen to take on the sins of the world, that is you've chosen to experience what it's like to perceive oneself in separation in order to understand dimensions of illusion, dimensions of suffering, to unfold within your being all possibilities. Why? Because your compassion is infinite and unbounded.

You have not suffered because you failed.

You've suffered because you looked upon a tiny little planet floating in a certain dimension in which separation was being played out, and your compassion brought you here to learn of this world, to master this world, to take it in and know what it's like so that when you look into the eyes of a brother or a sister, and say, "I love you," they know that you know what you're talking about. No one can fool you, can they?

When another says, "I'm suffering," you can say, "I know, I took it on once myself, I know that dimension, and I am a risen. And because the ascension has been completed in me, the same power is in you." It is only by taking on the sins of the world, perceptions of separation, that you become the vessel, the vehicle that is large enough to embrace any suffering that comes along the pike. And at a soul level, when you look into the eyes of another, and say, "Yes, I know that you're suffering, and I love you.

I know that Christ lives in you." At a soul level, they know that you're not what you call talking out of your hat. They know that you know because you've been there, and that is why I did what I did.

Anybody can hang out in 17 dimensions beyond this planet, and talk about love. And those that have fallen into illusion, say, "Well, yes, we'll come down here and try it out." I came down for the same reason you did, out of the infinite compassion of Christ, so that I could embrace all of my brothers or sisters, and help them to uplift themselves back to the place from which they've never on. You're doing it right now, you in the very life you're living. You out of your Christedness, out of your compassion, have opened yourself and call forth on manner of experiences so that you could wrap yourself around this dimension, and unfolded in your love. That's all you're doing here. So, give yourself some credit.

Never again entertain the thought that you have failed. You are the one that looked with tears upon this dimension, and said, "I'll go." I mean, after all, I'm not even willing to do that again. You are that one. You are the embodiment of the savior. You are the one sent forth from the mind of God. You are the one that has been willing to feel it all, to experience every dimension of suffering just so you could heal it. And thereby demonstrate that the truth is true always, and only love is real. So, there, now you know what you've been doing.

Give yourself some credit, for though through the eyes of the body, it looks as though things may be hopeless, rest assured the heat has been turned up by all of you. There's a point where the water has no longer a choice but to boil and turn to steam. The train is pulling into the station, because you have been willing to wrap yourself around this world in your own beingness, and to heal it with love. You, just as you are, right where you are. Everyone in this room is actively fulfilling their function.

So, before you go to bed tonight, go to a friend, and simply say, "What a good boy am I, or girl, I'm doing such a marvelous job. And I'm going to go to sleep and just go off in my dream, and see who needs a touch of grace." I'm not going to go to sleep to try to dream solve my problems, I don't have any. I'm going to go to sleep and deliberately choose, by intention, to let this body sleep to allow my spirit, to find a heart that needs to be blessed. Do that, you might find yourself having some interesting conversation over breakfast.

Therefore, indeed, we have babbled at you long enough, message has been given. Has it been received? So, we're going to do something we've never done before.

Since you now know that you are Christ, and I'm just your brother, put it into practice, and take a moment, and think on the one you dare to call your friend Joshua Ben Joseph. And in your own mind and in your own being, simply say to me, "Joshua, I bless you with the love of Christ that I am."

Rather fine isn't it? Don't you immediately feel lighter, more expanded? Isn't there a part of you that knows that's the truth? Therefore, when next you set up an altar, whether individually or the next time some of you choose to gather as a group, make it a point to also bring a picture of yourself. If you really want to have some fun, cover up my picture with yours. And start your morning meditations by honoring those pictures, indeed. And if you can convince those that were on the big stone buildings and brick buildings around the planet that had this funny emaciated image of me hanging on a cross, would you please tell them to take them down. I find them to be rather embarrassing.

So, it was a learning experience I have that may not have been necessary, but it was my choice. Don't need to make such a big deal of it. I suppose every Christ must have a flaw.

I long for the day when beings gather in those brick and stone buildings, and sit there, and say, "And why are we here? "Well, since we can't remember, we might as well have a good dance. Then, I will know I've succeeded, indeed.

So, how are you all doing? Has it been worth your time? Has it been worth mine? I don't have any. But rest assured, the opportunity, the opportunity to think of a created way to join with you, to be received by you, to have an opportunity to love you, by activating thought that vibrates vocal cords, that transmits something to you, that allows our hearts to join, as they have countless times, and countless other ways, indeed beloved friends, oh yes, it has been worth my while, for you are my treasure. You are my joy. You are my blessing and my beloved. You are the one who shows me my father. How can I do less than love you forever for what you give to me? And indeed, I am with you always.

So, there are a few of you that feel a question burning deep in your soul. This is what we're going to do. I'm not going to engage them right now. I want you, whether you believe it or not, to accept that you are Christ, therefore just before you lay your head on the pillow, begin by acknowledging, I and my father are none, there are no barriers to the depth of wisdom within me. Therefore, now in this moment, I ask this question, and I receive the answer, so be it. See what comes.

Then tomorrow, you'll set aside just a short time, and I would be most pleased to, shall we say, pop back into your presence, and we'll see if there are really any questions left that still require that the answer be given through something and someone that seems to be outside of yourself. Fair enough? Good.

Therefore, love you one another, as the father has first loved all of us. Look with graciousness and gentleness. Look with appreciation upon the mystery of the moment, in which you find yourselves with one another, for it is the power of your love that brings you onto one another. Love you one another, and you are the light that lights this world, and redeems it from all illusion. Be there forth peace this day.

Be there forth eternally, precious, and holy, and ancient friends.

Amen.

The Master of Time

Now we begin.

Indeed, greetings unto you once again, holy and only begotten Son of God, begotten, not made, and eternally of one substance with all that the Father is—*begotten before time and of one substance with all that the Father is*. Need we say anything else?

Begotten, not born, but begotten before time is. Hmm. And all of you have been led to believe that the body in which you believe yourself to be living came forth but a few short years ago, and you with it. That is an illusion.

Begotten before time is. Your home is eternity. Your being is the Love of God. Nothing has ever changed it; nothing has ever tainted it; nothing has ever limited it except your choice to use your infinite wisdom and power and creativity to create the illusion of limitation. And with it came the birth of time.

Begotten before time is. Have you ever wondered what that must surely mean? For if those words be used as a description for me, Jeshua, the Christ, they can mean nothing in relationship to me if they do not already mean *the same* in relationship to you. Now, how can that be? For well have you been taught that I am something special and you a simple creature. And yet, in reality—not in illusion but in reality—you and I are One, and all that has ever been said about me is *about you*. Every flowery word written in your Holy Scripture is *about you*.

Every word that would denigrate you and say that you are a simple creature is not about you at all; it is about somebody else's illusions.

For well have I spoken unto you that you are loved wholly and you have never sinned. You are the Light and the Life of mankind, and wherever you are, the fullness of God comes to be expressed and to be extended unto the one who stands in front of you, and the only thing that can ever create a barrier between you and your brother is *your* choice to believe that you are other than what God created you to be. Therefore, that veil that you would create is only your choice to use the infinite power extended unto you to create a very flimsy screen called separation. In it there is no power. In it there is no reality. In it there is nothing of Truth.

From my perspective—which is the one you are choosing to recognize and reawaken to—that illusion does *not exist*. And when you choose to see your brother through the very eyes that I see you, you will look with the eyes of Christ and you will know and understand that you are born into this world to be the saviour of this world.

Therefore, birth can only take place in time. Birth is taking that which is eternal and changeless and coming down to express in a form that the world can understand—the birthing of a saviour. The Christmas story is yours, the Easter story is yours, whenever you choose to claim the one Truth given you before time is:

> *I and my Father are one. I am Christ eternal. I live; yet not I but Christ lives in me and through me. Though of myself I can do*
>
> *nothing, my Father through me does all things because He is the Light and the Life and the Way and the Truth, and I am one with Him eternally.*

The Master of Time

The world can give me nothing and the world can take nothing from me. Therefore, I live not in fear. I live not in lack and I live not in want. But I live to extend and to share with my holy brother and sister the fullness of my being, and when I do that, I ignite in them the possibility of claiming that reality as their very own.

That is the power given unto you. It is the power given unto me. It is by that power that I come and blend with this carcass that you think is owned by my beloved brother. And I come forth and I use this vehicle to do nothing else than to make manifest *who you are*, and I will come again and again to serve as your mirror until when you look at even this carcass and hear these words, you recognize that you are looking on no one but yourself, and you are hearing your own voice, that voice that was given you of our Father *before time is*.

When you claim those words as your own, then all power is unleashed on Earth in this bodily temple as it is already in Heaven. You think that you are separate from this carcass and I tell you that you are not.

If you were to break down your perception and stop looking at the color of your hair and the width and girth of the physical forms, and start to look at what your scientists call molecules and atoms and quarks and electrons and little quantas of light, you would discover that there is not one trace of difference between the body you *think* is yours and this carcass that you *think* belongs to my beloved brother—not one trace of difference.

Ultimately, the perception that bodies abide in space and time and are separate from one another is itself an illusion.

And yet, you have the power to see with eyes that are crystal clear, having let go of every trace of illusion of separation, to see not with the eyes of the body but with the eyes of the arisen Christ, to see not a body in front of you but to see the thought of Perfect Love in form that is your brother and your sister. And what power, what healing could you extend unto another if you saw not the body in separation, but if you saw *the eternal presence of Christ* in the one before you? Now, it doesn't really matter if they've forgotten. What matters is that *you* remember.

Hmm. That is why, when in Truth you have awakened and chosen never again to tolerate error in your own perception, when you stand in bodily form in front of another and look into their eyes with the Light of Christ, your simple smile can heal lifetimes. And to the degree that they are willing to receive that Light of the Christ you are, even before your eyes miracles can occur.

Can you come to understand then, that if you are not seeing miracles in *your* life, it is because you are still choosing to linger in a little trace of darkness that says,

> *I believe in God. I believe in Christ, but I am not really quite that Light. If I work a little harder and perfect it, the next time around I will be.*

The most arrogant of acts is to insist that you are *other* than Christ Your world would teach you just the opposite, would it not? For indeed, to say, "I am the arisen Christ," is beheld as the ultimate act of being arrogant.

I tried it and they tried to crucify me. Do you fear crucifixion? Many of you know that what I just said speaks directly to your heart, for you struggle in this world and you run up against your fear and you don't understand its source.

> *Why do I still live in lack? Why do I not manifest the power of Christ?*

And I say unto you: it is because you still carry that trace of fear that the world will crucify you if you truly live in your power. And what is power but the *choice* to rest in the gentleness of allowing your only reality to be lived with every breath you breathe.

> *Will the world crucify me if I let go of every trace of belief that I have ever been separate from God, if I leap off the cliff and trust the power of God to live through me, to throw off my shackles of lack and want and fear? And to let Christ live in me so that I can shout with one of my ancient brothers: I live; yet not I but Christ lives in me.*

And if the world would look upon you and say, "There's goes another nut," can you understand that what you are hearing is coming from a voice of illusion in which *no power resides*? And if that is true — and I assure you that it is — who cares about the opinions of another mind who would insist on illusions over reality?

Many of you know what it means to want to wake up every morning and see your world at peace, to see the complexities of the world healed, to see the chaos ceased, the insanity dissolved. And yet, you arise in the morning and you go out and conform yourself to those very opinions because you still believe that the world can keep you safe, and by conforming to it, you can escape crucifixion. And yet I say unto you: conformity to the perceptions of your world *is* to choose crucifixion. And as I came forth once before, I come now yet again into this world in many ways.

And even in this hour in this evening I am communicating through similar forms in over a hundred locations upon your planet to do one thing: to beseech you to join me, *not in the Crucifixion but in the Resurrection*. There is a Light and a power that is coming to be born upon this plane that is arising from the very soils of this, your Holy Mother, and the time is short upon this Earth. And I ask you to arise with me *to be the Resurrection*.

You know how to be the crucifixion. You have played that one out very well, and all of the gods and all of the levels of this universe applaud you on your ability to put on such a drama. Hm. But the curtain is being raised now. Many in this room are sensitive to the raising of that curtain. You feel it as a quickening that begins to move energy up and down the spine. It creates a feeling at times: "Oh, my God, what's going to happen next?" Open up and let it happen, because the raising of the curtain is nothing more than the death of illusion: because Light is being born because it is being remembered.

Therefore, would you join me and be part of the solution instead of part of the continuation of the problem?

Understand well, fatigue has *nothing at all* to do with the body. It has *everything* to do with the mind. *It has everything to do with the mind.* And when the mind is awakened and chooses only Light and tolerates never again error in its own perceptions and gives every moment over to the Holy Spirit, then indeed, that mind is enlightened because the heart is awakened, and the body will leap up like a bunch of little soldiers that have been sleeping on guard duty and say, "Oh, my God, there's been a change here," and the cells become active. And they begin to realize that you are going to send the infinite Light of God to them and therefore they have to relearn their job.

The Master of Time

No longer will they be able to tolerate extending sickness to you because you have been sending sick thoughts to them. Do you understand what I am saying? The body is your perfect servant and if you know depression or disease, it is because over a long period of time you've trained the cells of your body to conform to the dis-eased perception held in the mind. And when you have healed that perception, the body must follow suit.

And it is very possible—and you are going to see it happen upon this plane; many of you are going to live to see this happen in these bodies—that when there is a moment's disease or sickness in the body, that very mind will simply choose Light, will transfer Light from the infinitude of Heaven and express it on Earth, and the very cells of the body will instantly be healed. That is what a master can do, and you have come not to be slaves to the world but to demonstrate mastery in *all* regards. And mastery requires utmost responsibility: the ability to respond, and to look upon the whole of this world and say,

> *My goodness, I am the one that made this and now I am going to undo it. Where am I going to start? Right where I am.*

If all minds are joined—and I assure you that they are—right where you, are even in this moment were you to throw open the shackles off of the heart and mind, to open the cells of the body and to say,

> *I am the Holy Son of God and I claim my Kingdom. Let Light descend to Earth now, in me.*

... to do that is to have already uplifted the whole of creation.

Imagine that in my Father's house there are many mansions. Each room is a heart and mind, and this mansion has an infinite number of rooms.

And you are living in a tiny little closet on the first floor. And you know that above you there are thousands and thousands of floors, and when you open the door of your tiny closet and peek down the l-o-n-g corridor, you know that there are thousands and thousands of rooms on the very floor you are on, and your Father has just said unto you, "I want you to sweep the dust out of the corners of every room." Hmm.

> *Oh, my God, what a task. Whew! How will I ever get it accomplished?*

The secret to the rebirthing of the Kingdom of Heaven on Earth is for *you* to realize that when you sweep the dust out of the corners of *your own tiny closet*, you have done it in *every room* in my Father's mansion, because all minds and hearts are joined. Therefore, receive that healing for yourself and you *are* the janitor that has cleaned every room in the mansion. Makes it much easier.

Does that make sense to you?

Yes.

While time continues for yet a little while, it is given unto you to make that choice with every breath. This is what I mean by response-ability: the ability to respond in each moment,

> *What thought am I choosing to hold? Am I conforming myself to limitation and lack and fear? Or am I choosing to be the fullness of the Kingdom now because I am begotten before all worlds and am of one substance eternally with all that my Father is?*

That is the choice to be made. That is the choice that is *so important* upon this plane in this time.

In this room this evening there are many, many, many beings who do not at this point associate with physical bodies as you do. They are all around you. Some of you have been feeling that already. Some of you noticed and had thoughts come even while you were whirling around talking and eating,

There's something about this room tonight. What is it?

You could say other guests have been arriving for a while, to help do some things with the energy here. I have said unto you that I am one who likes to have a lot of friends, and this isn't the only plane that I like to have friends on; and this is not the only plane that is available to *you*. Each of you has what you know as guides and teachers and friends on planes unseen with the physical eyes, and *they are there for you because they love you*.

They know that you are Christ eternal and they will do anything they can to help you remember, to help you unlock that power to bring the fullness of the Kingdom and express it in *this* world.

Fear not crucifixion. All of you have tasted the illusion of death. Not one of you has escaped being persecuted by others in this drama, and you all carry that fear of crucifixion. Call it rejection. Call it abuse. Call it being put to death. Whatever form it comes, there is a fear that keeps your heart contracted. And yet, the fear itself is an illusion.

That illusion is paper thin, so thin that it only takes one choice to walk through it. And I ask you to join with me, precious and holy and ancient friends, begotten before all worlds, you who are of one substance with all that I am,

I ask you to walk through that veil within yourself and to never settle again for anything but the Power and the Wisdom and the Truth of the Kingdom to be uttered by your lips, to be extended by the movements of your body, that only Light lives in you and as you—and you will be the Light that heals this world.

The body is nothing more than a tool of communication. And it's not even yours! So what are you worried about? Nobody is going to nail it to a cross this time; and even if they did, it wouldn't matter. From dust the body is created and to dust the body shall return. It is the gift of your Holy Mother, given unto Christ eternal to become as a vehicle for communicating the unconditional Love of God.

If only you could understand what's really occurring on this Earth. Reality is not outside of you. It is not in the complexities that have been brought forth into this world. Reality is *in* you, and all that you have seen and all of the dramas unfolded in this world have been nothing more than you walking into a certain movie house and watching a certain movie. And now the time upon this plane is for you to arise from that seat, to go back out to the center of the movie house that has many little theaters in it, to go back to the center of your heart and to remember who you are, and then to walk into a different theater in which a new movie is about to start—a movie of Light, of abundance, of joy, of peace, of *extraordinary miracles*. The movie has already started and I come to be your usher to say, "Quickly, quickly, come with me. Tarry no longer. The old movie is already over." You are just sitting in the chair running it through your mind, all of the horrible scenes, and yet the film has already stopped.

Wait for me. I've got to get the popcorn.

[Laughter]

For that, we will hold all things up. Indeed. How are you doing, my brother?

Very well, thank you.

Gone through a few changes in the last few weeks?

Uh huh.

Hold nothing back! The river is starting to flow in a way that you could not have understood even a few short months ago. Open yourself up wholly every day and tell the Holy Spirit you are ready. Dare your Father to let the fullness of the union of Father and Son to explode through you. Just dare Him to see if He can overwhelm you. Do it every day when you arise. It is very important now because the habits you have known will want to creep back to build little dams. Choose the power of that Light. Choose it with everything you have got every morning when you arise and give thanks for it every night before you sleep.

Fair enough?

Quite.

Quite a small price to pay for the Grace that heals a hundred thousand illusions.

I thought it was just one.

One and a hundred thousand are simply two ways to say the same thing.

Well then, how are we all doing? It was a bit of a long greeting. I am sorry.

[Laughter]

It was worth it. It was nice. Wonderful.

You answered my questions.

Ah. What are you going to do with the answers?

Oh. That is a trick question. Yeah, that is a trick question. Rejoice in them. Take them. Well, you just said about the old habits wanting to jump out of their little corners and grab us again. That really holds true, and it has for me in the last week and I hope it's the last hurrah.

You hope?

Oh, okay. Got me.

No, I just gently corrected you.

Right.

Beloved brother, it is *you* that has *me*, and I abide in your heart as the fullness of your being. And the fullness of that being creates the experience of Jeshua so that you can talk with your true Self.

Understand well what I am saying unto you because this relates for all of you: inasmuch as you have been as one mind as the ego, or the separate self sense that has created all worlds, you are already of one Mind and one Heart in creating the salvation of the Sonship. As you have created the dramas of illusions of separation, so, too, do you create the drama of salvation.

Therefore, all that I am — and I have said this to you before — as Jeshua Joseph ben Joseph, who came and walked and talked, who sweated, got hungry, urinated in the woods (I'm sorry they didn't put that part in the Bible), all of the things you have ever done and felt tempted by, I, too, have tasted. And yet, understand that *my life is wholly yours*. You are the ones who brought forth the life of Jeshua Joseph ben Joseph, to be thesaviour of the world, a mirror that you could look in and be reminded of the Truth of yourself. You could say that you decided to sleep and have a very nice drama, and you scripted that there would be a being upon this plane and when you looked at him, it would trigger a remembrance like,

> *Ah, the bell has rung. Time for me to wake up from my drama. It's been nice but there is a far greater one to be lived.*

You are all that I am and between us there is not anything called separation.

Therefore, beloved brother, do not hope that it will be their last hurrah, but *decree* that that is true. Hm!

I would give you a little assignment. Are you ready?

I am ready.

We will see. Have I not spoken unto you that in each of your days, do something a little outrageous? Anyone hear that before?

Yes. Yes.

How long has it been since you put it into practice?

Well, I think once last week I finally had the time to do something outrageous.

Precious friend, go unto one of your malls, stand on one of the seats there. They usually put them around those plastic flowers. There's nothing like the aroma of plastic flowers.

[Laughter]

Stand upon the step there or the seat and decree at the top of your lungs,

> *I am the holy Son of God, and in this moment I decree that all of my illusions have just had their last hurrah.*

And look around at those who look at you with their chin on the floor and say,

> *Isn't it great that we are One?*

And then just go about your business.

[Laughter]

Now [breathes deeply] ...

> *Holy Father, let these be in me even as I am in You. Let them see the Truth of their being, for I have served them since before the beginning of time and that time is at hand. Father, enter their hearts that they might hear this simple Gospel and see that the time is at hand.*
>
> *Long have I toiled for You. Long have I served the Atonement of Your only begotten Son.*

And I beseech You, Father, enter these as You have entered me, with the fullness of Your Light and Your Glory and Your Wisdom and Your Power and Your Love. Let them be in me as I am in You, that together the Son might be one again with the Father to express the joy of that perfect union, to blend with the energies of this, our Holy Mother, and to express through these bodies the one Truth of Life eternal.

Father, I beseech You, let the time be now and let them awaken to the Truth of our union. Let illusions be ended. Father, let Illusions be ended.

Would you not receive my prayer? Would you not throw open the shutters of your heart, for I stand and knock, and I beseech you, precious ones whom I love deeply, the time is at hand to put down illusions and join me in the Resurrection.

Very soon now, Easter is upon you. What is it going to mean to you this year? Will it mean what the world wants you to believe it means? That someone in your long, past history finally got the message? Or worse yet, that one was sent by God and was without sin and was perfect anyway. That puts me on a pedestal so far above you that my lifetime becomes totally meaningless.

For if I came not and dwell among you as a man, tempted to live the Crucifixion, then my Resurrection is totally meaningless. Look not then upon me with the eyes the world has given you. But please look with the eyes that I seek to give you: to see that I am your brother and your friend. And if Jeshua can awaken to the Truth of his being, then, Lord knows, so can you, *because you are already my equal.*

So, would you join me in a little exercise—rather, a little celebration? Those of you who in this moment feel that your shoulders are a little hunched, throw them back. For God's sake, what are you trying to protect yourself from? What burdens are you insisting on carrying?

I feel guilty.

[Laughter]

So release the guilt and throw the shoulders back. Feel a lightness come to the spine itself. It is the tree of life. Let its branches reach up to the Light of the Father. In the depth of your being, now you can throw open the doorway to each and every cell of the body, your perfect servants.

Block not the angel of air, but feel it ascending and descending along the tree of life. Breathe not only the angel of air but *let each breath be a breath of Light and of power, and of wisdom and of joy.* Within yourself say unto your Father,

> *Yes, I receive You.*

Throw open your heart. Receive it. Dare your Father to send you so much Light that it feels the body might explode. Open yourselves. *Come to where I am.*

Let that little vibration begin. Feel the quickening within you. With every inbreath say,

> *Yes, I accept my Truth. I am the Son of God. I am the Light of the world. I and my Father are One. I and my Father are One. I and my Father are One!*

The Master of Time

Some of you are beginning to see certain colors. Let them come more brightly, more vibrantly. Receive them. Feel the cells all the way down to your fingertips and toes opening. If you begin to feel a little lightheaded and giddy, all the much better. Seriousness has no place in the Kingdom.

> *Yes, I am the Light of the world. I am the birthing of the New Age that is upon this earth. I am all power and I am all Light and I am all joy. I live; yet not I but Christ lives in me, for I am that Mind and that Heart.*

And if you be that power — and I assure you that you are — let not timidity come upon you again. And now, all together, we're going to take one very deep breath, and we are going to inhale the Light and the power of God, and as we exhale, we are going to open our mouths and let sound come out. Take a nice deep inbreath and with all the power of the Christ we are...

[Loud toning, continuing for a while.]

Not bad. How are you feeling?

Good. Great. Very good. Energized.

Vibrations of yourselves.

Yes.

Why would you settle for anything less in any moment of your day?

So, you see, when next you are in one of your board meetings and you feel the energy of the world wanting to contract you down so that you are conformed to everybody's illusion of lack and suffering, now you know what to do to change it.

[Laughter]

Yes. All right. Corporate management will fall down.

It's about time it fell down.

Don't you understand what it's all about? To *be* the Light of the world, not to pray that Light will come. You have been doing that for thousands of lifetimes. Receive the simplicity of the Gospel. If Light is to come, *you* are the ones that have to bring it. Gone is the time of timidity. Gone the time of weakness and lack and frailty. How can you abide in those states and still expect the new world to be born? How can you translate the unhappy dream of the chaos of this world into the happiness of the rebirthing of the Kingdom unless you choose to be that? Not to seek it, not to pray for it, but to decree that the time is at hand because *you* are choosing that *now is the time*.

What do you think, Seedplanter?

I agree. It's the time. Feels good.

You have a certain song, *The times, they are a-changing*. Are *you* going to change with them? Because, indeed, the time comes rather quickly now that if you choose not to, shall we say, uplift the frequency of your being by declaring that you will never again tolerate the error of misperception that you are anything other than the embodiment of joy, if you choose not to do that, you are simply not going to be able to be on your beloved Earth any longer—because the very heat of joy that will be coming from the very soil, the body of your Holy Mother, will be something that you can't tolerate because you are choosing a heavy vibration that can no longer abide on this Earth.

There are going to be a few that make that choice, to insist on the heaviness. And what will happen when the energy of the Earth becomes so transparent that solid things cannot abide upon it and they simply sink through it? Now, that's a metaphor, of course, but it means that if you truly love your Holy Mother, you had better get it in gear and catch up with the changes going on in Her own frequencies.

Don't let the heart contract with fear; you cannot experience death. All you can ever experience is the consequence of your choice. All of you understand well that what you experience in your life is the *effect* of your *choice*. And a new choice is being born upon this plane, a choice that will tolerate *only* Light, *only* peace, *only* joy, *only* abundance, *only* service one unto another.

The time is going to come upon this plane when minds and bodies can't sit still because they are going to be running around the whole time, finding a way to extend service and love to their brothers and sisters, and nothing but service. Gone will be the energy of taking, and it will be replaced by the energy of giving, because being rebirthed is the simple Truth that as you give, you receive.

Give your love away and you will never be without it. Give your vision of One Heart and One Mind away and you will experience it growing within you by leaps and bounds, and you will attract unto yourself other minds and hearts that have been waiting for you to give them the signal to live as unlimited vision. For it is through vision that your Father extends His Love and Creativity into this world. And where there is not vision, what happens to the people? They perish.

All of you know what it means to perish. Some of you are still insisting on perishing. Some of you are yet insisting that lack must be your experience. It's just a chronic habit. Let it go. Insist on abundance. Live abundantly. Live from the Truth that you know there is no such thing as lack. You are here to serve, expressing the unconditional Love of God—and do you think that if your Father is going to ask you to go forth and teach all nations, that He is going to leave you in poverty? Tell Him to get off His can and make sure you have everything you need for the fulfillment of your mission.

Jeshua, why do you say that? Because there is a reason behind that?

What? A reason behind what I say? Oh! Now I have to think up one.

Well, those words... you know, that were said that way.

Firewalker, look at the subtleties of your own thought. You are beginning to catch some of the fire you've been walking on. When you say, "I pray for a new world order to be manifested on this Earth," but you, yourself, choose to live in the impoverishment of a lack of energy, a lack of golden coins, in the belief that there is nothing you can do to change your *own* status, you have basically depleted the very life force that is required for the birthing of that new world order. *You* have

to be an *example* of that new world order.
Therefore, when you pray unto your Father,

Help me, Father, to do your will, whatever it is,

you come from a place of weakness and lack. That is why I have said that the time of false piety is over with. It is time for you to rise and to stand on the little seats in your malls and say,

> *Father, I have come here to serve the Atonement of Your Son. Now, get off your can and don't forget what we are doing here.*

[Laughter]

Ohhh.

> *Give me the abundance of Your Kingdom because I need it to do Your work. Bring it to me. And, by the way, I happen to like nice clothes, and I am not going to drive a rattletrap to do Your work.*

Oh, God.

The reality you experience is nothing more than the expression of the frequency and the vibration you insist on holding on to. Upgrade your vibrations and frequency daily and the world around you will have to change its shape.

I am calling you not to be meek any longer, but meek in the *true* sense. So meek and so pure that there is not one trace of illusion to be found in you. Allow the death of the world to take place in your own consciousness, that the Kingdom can be reborn in it.

Some of you believe that to achieve great abundance is going to take a lifetime of straining and planning and hard work because it's a tough world.
> *I'm going to have to compete. And if I'm really lucky, in twenty years I'll be able to retire and pay my bills.*

That thinking does not exist in the Kingdom. The only thinking that exists in the Kingdom is that,

> *I am the Holy Son of God and all of the abundance of my Father is given to me now. And I live from it, and I extend it, and I give it away freely and gladly to anyone who would ask. And if my brother lives in lack, I will teach him how to live in abundance because I can't tolerate this any longer.*

> *I am the holy Son of God and I am going to bring the whole of creation with me, and I am not going to stop until it comes to where I am. I am Christ eternal. And even as I manifested Jeshua Joseph ben Joseph and demonstrated the Truth of the Kingdom, I choose now to be the fullness of who I am, and I am going to manifest nothing but miracles until all of my brothers and sisters wake up with me.*

Hmm. Do you see the difference?

Jeshua, when you talk about abundance, you mostly mention material things. The abundance of love... I have felt a lot of resistance in this community to enacting that. I wonder if you could speak to the higher vision of how we can go about creating trust, safety, for us to do that?

Beloved friend, everything that I have spoken unto you this night addresses that very question. Put it into practice. If there is anyone with whom you are feeling some variance or enmity, then get on the phone and call them and say,

> *We've got to get together. You see, the time is at hand. Let's make sure all of the hatchets are buried.*

> *Let's join together and look into each other's eyes and declare that we* are *the holy Son of God, and we are going to get on with it and manifest that abundance to make this community happen because we cannot any longer tolerate error. We cannot tolerate waiting on the Lord, because we* are *the Lord.*

How can you manifest that community of trust and safety? By declaring to everyone who is attracted to that community that *you are giving it to them* and you wholly expect that it will be given to *you* because nothing less can any longer be tolerated. Now don't forget to sing and dance and play as you are doing that.

The time is at hand, precious friend. The Father indeed provides all things, and if you would look around you, He is extending unto you many vehicles and many ways in which you can enact the Truth of who you are and bring the abundance to you. But it will *never* happen until *you are ready to declare for yourself the Truth of who you are and to live it with every breath and to settle for nothing less*. Stop waiting for the person to your right or to your left to make it happen for you.

Beloved friend, that is how. How can you create that safety? By declaring and demonstrating and *being* that safety. By *being* that Love that embraces all things. By in your own life cleaning out the cobwebs in your closet, letting the Father manifest all power and wisdom and abundance through you so that you can show your brother and sister how to do it also. This is no fun if you do it alone.

The time is at hand, even as many of you have felt a shift in the way I bring my energy forth to bear through this temporary carcass, and indeed a shift in what I am not so much saying unto you but the way I am saying it.

Understand that there is a shift in frequency that has gone on in your Holy Mother, this Earth. Some of you have felt it. Some of you haven't noticed at all because you are too busy keeping yourself limited by the constrictions of your very narrow-minded perceptions. In other words, you are too wrapped up in the drama of the ego to notice what's happening. And those of you that persist in that are going to wake up one day and realize you are not even on the Earth anymore. You are somewhere else.

What happened? Did the New Age pass me by?

Yes.

But you get to come back, don't you? Choose again to come back?

[Laughter]

Well, you do. You never get left out. It's just a matter of when. I don't know if I am using that as an excuse or anything, but I'm just wanting to say that we are all going home. We are all going to make it. I'm not trying to negate anything you're saying.

Firewalker, you *are* trying to negate something that came out of an impulse of your own thinking that wants still to have a trapdoor to escape through. If we are all coming home, that means that for you — this is not at the conscious mind, it is at a slightly deeper level — you are hoping that you will still have time to make up for it if you don't choose it now. That is where those statements came from.

The mind and heart that chooses the Truth of the Kingdom does not even entertain the thought that maybe later the choice can still be made anew.

It is too busy choosing *now*. Contemplate that well within yourself. For though you would look around you and want many to catch on fire and leap ahead, there is still a part of you that has the rope tied around the end of the dock, and your own ship is not quite yet sailing freely.

That's true.

I know.

I have news for you. None of this is going to happen until you choose it for yourself. The whole of creation is *on hold, waiting for you*. Now, that's responsibility! But guess what? The whole of creation is on hold waiting for *each and every one of you. That* is your responsibility: to be the Light of the world with every breath you breathe. You don't have time for the drama of separation. You don't have time for the drama of indulging in the whimperings of the ego. All of that is an illusion. You don't have time for it.

Will you not join with me and truly come to where I am? Come to that frequency or that vibration that cannot tolerate error in your own perceptions any longer, to see that there is but One Mind and One Heart, called Christ, and all of these little bodies are nothing more than vehicles through which that One Mind and One Heart can express the Love of God.

Wherever you are, whether you are in a grocery store, and someone else in this room tonight is in an office, and somebody else in this room tonight is in a garden planting seeds, can you remember fully that you are One and you are united and you are together all the time? You are never alone. You can't be alone.

And if all you did was to think on the energy in this room and the little exercise we did and allowed that power to come forth through you, wherever you are you would know that the power of the one Mind of Christ is moving through you. And when you extend love unto anyone on this plane, once it is done, you could just that fast, [snapping fingers] move to that plane of reality in which everyone in this room is abiding as if you were sitting around a table watching a movie, and you could step into that frequency and say,

> *Ah, I've just extended some more Love into the world. How did you do over there?*

It's all available to you. You have never been separate one from another, and those of you that are attracted to the expression of *community* need to start putting that Truth into practice. You can join with any mind of any brother and any sister anytime you want, if only to extend power and love to them.

You don't have time to stare at your soap operas any longer. You don't have time to sit in your easy chair, lamenting how tough your life is, because your life and your world will be transformed when you learn to do nothing but extend the Love of God with every breath you breathe. Whenever the mind knows heaviness or doubt or loneliness, think upon your brother and sister who has come with you to extend the Love of Christ into this world — and empower them.

Guess what happens when you do that? As you give you receive. As you empower your brother or sister, you will feel that power coursing through *you*, and you will wonder what happened to your depression and your doubt and your fear and your loneliness. It's all just an illusion, anyway.

Do you understand what I am saying to you?

You've learned to contract yourself, to separate yourself from the power of Christ. How, then, do you find it? By giving it away.

Salvation can only be known by sharing it. So when you think you are bored, you've washed all of your dishes, you've cleaned the cobwebs out of your closet, you've washed the filth off your automobiles, you've put the food into the belly of the body, you have paid all of your bills unto Caesar and you think you've got nothing to do — Saturday night and nowhere to go — think about your brothers and sisters, and do nothing more than play with *empowering* them.

Play at it and *love* it. Pretend like you are the controller of the universe. Send the power of Christ to your brother and your sister.

Hmm! Hmm.

Jeshua, I am answering your very joyful call. You showed up in a session I was giving this afternoon and it was quite clear that I would move my day and my evening a lot in order to come and be with you tonight. So I am just here, and open to your reflection.

[Short pause]

I am with you always. Join with me until you see and hear me as easily as you hear the voice that you are now hearing. Join with me so fully that there is no longer a trace of distance between us. Time to upgrade, shall we say, the frequency or power of the work that you do. But it's going to take leaps and bounds! Hmm.

Well, I have been feeling that. My daily awareness is to release, release, allow. Really allow the lightness to come, the movement to move. It feels so large at times that I keep wanting to damper it or contract or take a breath, and basically I am daily just breathing through and expanding.

A rather good idea.

Precious friend, have you not carried with you, even in the beautiful work you do, have you not carried a chronic thought,

> *Am I truly worthy of total union with Christ?*

Know you that feeling?

Yes.

Let it be gone. Well have you known that I have been knocking upon the door of your heart for a very long time.

Indeed.

Sometimes you let me come in and have a little cup of tea. But then you say, "Oh, you have to leave now."

Beloved friend, from this day, more powerfully than ever in the past, when you do the work you do in what you call the initiation, you are going to feel me standing next to you. And when you do your little ritual, there will come a day when you will literally see me standing on just the other side of the one you are doing your ritual with, and I am going to join with you.

In other words, we are going to be working together at a new level to increase the power and the transformation of that initiation. You have been inviting me but there has been this little shadow over in the corner of the mind,

Well, could I really take it if he truly showed up?

Know you the trace of that feeling?

Oh, yeah.

Yes. [Chuckles]

Thank you for receiving my invitation to come to this gathering.

Indeed, it is my honor. My joy.

Yes, as it is mine. I have known you for a very long time, and you know that.

Yes.

And you know that you are in Truth involved in your life's purpose and function in the work that you do. If you want to call it work. And you are going to see it begin to accelerate.

The room is very full tonight

Standing room only.

Floating room only.

Indeed.

Jeshua, I notice when you have been using the word "time,"

What do you think?

Oh, I welcome it. I have actually been inviting you clearly in every circle.

You have been inviting me but there has been this little shadow over in the corner of the mind,

Well, could I really take it if he truly showed up?

Know you the trace of that feeling?

Oh, yeah.

Yes. [Chuckles]

Thank you for receiving my invitation to come to this gathering.

Indeed, it is my honor. My joy.

Yes, as it is mine. I have known you for a very long time, and you know that.

Yes.

And you know that you are in Truth involved in your life's purpose and function in the work that you do. If you want to call it work. And you are going to see it begin to accelerate.

The room is very full tonight

Standing room only.

Floating room only.

Indeed.

Jeshua, I notice when you have been using the word "time," you have a different tone. I'm wondering about that. It feels different when you use that. You are doing something with your frequency. I was curious.

Anyone else notice that?

Yes.

Precious friend, you have perceived well. There is a shift of what you perceive as frequency when I use that word tonight because it is a way of intoning a certain power that can begin to actually break down the perception or the limitations of time that seem to enshroud the mind and the heart.

You are doing that with more than just that word.

Yes.

Especially that one, more than others?

Tonight, especially that word. You could say it's the lesson for today.

Time is a very important barrier that has been created in the mind that is inhered in the illusion of separation. Time is the very thing that needs to be transcended. Become the masters of time and you will remember that you abide in eternity.

It is going to be very, very important in only a little bit of time. Are you truly choosing to master the illusion of time? Or are you letting it continue to master you?

Remember always that time is given you for one reason and one reason only. Does anybody remember what it is?

To extend Love.

Which is to do something I have stated to you probably thirty-five times or more. To use it constructively. To construct, to let the creative thought of God flow through you, so that what is created in the illusion of time sends a message to your brother and sister that time is an illusion and that only eternity is real; that time cannot be a barrier or limit you in any way from communication with all of the gods and goddesses that you have prayed for the opportunity to communicate with. Time is an illusion that has been translated from a limitation to an opportunity to express what is *unlimited*. Own it. Use it constructively, and your constructive use of it will translate it into a vehicle through which *you* become the Light of the world.

Does that help a little bit?

It is time.

That's rather a paradox you've given us.

Yes.

Thank you.

What you experience *is* a paradox. Don't try to make sense out of anything that I come to teach you. *Just do it.* And in the doing of it, you will witness miracles extended through you. And when you have seen them extended through you into the life of your brothers and sisters, you will have to finally admit that they have already been done to you.

The Master of Time

Please, never, never, never, never in any moment of your day, never choose to limit what I can do through you. If you could give me but one gift, give that to me. Give to me your solemn promise that you will never limit what I can do through you.

I promise.

And you are going to see the fruit of that promise.

I have.

Yes. Are you ready for it to expand exponentially?

Yes.

Thank you, Father!

How are we all doing?

Okay. Time to stretch a little, I think.

Then, do so. No one is stopping you.

Yes, I am.

How about the rest of you?

Stretch time.

So, go ahead and take a short little break if you want. I am not going to do what you would perceive as depart from this blending with my beloved brother. But rather, instead, I am going to quicken it a little bit.

If ever you want to know what *you* have to be willing to release, willing to release in order to join with me, have a little chat with my beloved brother. Many of you have no idea what it takes to blend with me like this although you would pray for it, and some of you have known jealousy.

Are you willing to let everything in you that is false *die*? Are you willing to experience the pain of a thousand little deaths within you as the ego becomes ashes? Why not give it a try? Hm. Indeed.

Are you truly willing to realize that throughout thousands of lifetimes you haven't known what in hell is going on? But you have judged the world as though you did, because you have judged yourself as being separate from God. That illusion is the cornerstone of the separate self.

Are you willing to loosen your fingers from it and let it become as the dust of the ground? *That is death.* But from that death the fullness of life can be born and you shall become the perfect servant of the Atonement. The form may differ but the power of the miracles wrought through you is the same. Become the one who allows only miracles.

Remember always that the purpose of the miracle, you see, is to shorten the need for time. Therefore, use time constructively to allow miracles, and miracles will shorten the need for time. Do you see how it all works?

So, take your short little break. If you want to leave, by all means do so, and do so with my love and my blessing. If would like to remain for yet a little while, then please do so and we will see what happens.

I love you and I give you my peace, and until your strength is the same as mine, please *use* mine. You can't use it up and it's freely given. Therefore, never allow yourself to feel weak or frail or fearful. All you have to do is to reach into your heart and pull out a handful of my strength and my certainty until you've learned that that strength and that certainty is yours and it cannot be taken from you.

I love you, because you are the Light of the world.

Peace be unto the only begotten Son of God, and I'll be seeing you very soon.

Amen.

{Break}

Jeshua I have a couple of questions. I am new and I have been enjoying this evening very much, and I appreciate the reflections that you give us of how to be, how to perceive to attain mastery of the self and peace in the heart and quiet in the mind. I get to see all the ways that I don't do that, which is wonderful.

I have a question about a reference that you do make and I... how do I say this? You had said to all of us to... When we are not feeling strong to turn to you for our strength. Yes? Okay. And I have a question in turn because I use a different terminology. The strength that you are speaking of is the strength, of course, that comes from God, right?

Yes.

Okay. My question is, I guess, why the need to go through *you*, to get your strength, because I see your strength as the strength of God Almighty moving through you, moving through each of us, and I have a question about that. Do you understand what I am saying? I'm sure you do.

I do, but do *you*?

Yeah. I think I do. Yeah. I just wanted to get clear. Do we need to go by you or can we... you know...? I feel like the Source is one and the same. Is there a reason that maybe those who need to lean on you were in that way because of whatever relationship that they might... because they are connected to you... they see you on these weekends and get a deeper connection? Is that like a stepping stone or what are you saying when you are saying that? Now I'm clear.

And you actually are giving the answer.

Now, first of all, I would say this: I am the Way, the Truth and the Life and no man comes to the Father but by me. So if you haven't done it yet, learn how to pronounce the name "Jeshua," because no other name under heaven can bring you salvation!

[Laughter]

I'm leaving!

Now, what does all of that mean?

We'll have you spoken that there are some that come not only to these Friday night gatherings and, therefore, see me as the vehicle through which they come to remembrance of the holy union of Father and Son, but indeed many who come unto these gatherings have known me throughout what you would perceive as lifetimes.

The Master of Time

There is something called holy lineage that is extremely important. Imagine that a child sleeps in a meadow and begins to dream dreams of many journeys and forgets that he sleeps in his Father's arms. And he begins to believe that the nightmares he is using his own creative power to create have a power in themselves, and he learns the complexity upon complexity and world upon world, and comes to actually believe he has been separated from his Father's Holy Kingdom.

Now, somewhere along the line—he might be a cobbler; he might be a Roman soldier; he might be a member of the Sanhedrin; he might be working in a court in Egypt—somewhere in one of those journeys he hears a message. He sees someone that others call "Master." And though he does not know it, he has heard this message before and he is seeing those who are its masters walking with him upon the Earth. Yet, for some reason in this moment something is different. And as he hears the words of that master being spoken, something begins to vibrate in the heart and a little door opens and for just a moment he sees the union of Father and Son. That is the beginning of a holy lineage, and though he might close that door and say,

Oh, not yet,

and go back to being a cobbler or what have you, and though he might choose to travel through another hundred thousand worlds, when it is time for the soul to take its final journey home, that soul shall make sure that it comes back into contact with that lineage because it becomes the doorway home.

I am the lineage for many and, therefore, especially in *this* work that I do with my beloved brother because I am *his* lineage, I come forth and use a certain language that identifies me as the one who walked and talked as Jeshua Joseph ben Joseph. I talk about Abba, I talk about the Holy Mother, I talk about the union of Father and Son, because this is a language that those entrusted to me of my Father have known very, very well. Most of them have known many incarnations within what you would call the Judeo-Christian tradition. It is a language that vibrates within their soul, and so I come and I use it yet again. It is not, as you know, the only one that could be used.

But those who come and resonate with what I say unto them, there are many in this room that would nod their head and say,

Oh, yes, I know Jeshua is my lineage.

Your lineage is a little different but you appreciate the universality of the Gospel that is expressed in these words, do you not?

Yes, very much.

Therefore, do not see it so much as a stepping stone but see it as the enactment of the awakening of the Sonship. This same Gospel can be given in many forms. As you know, yours is a bit different. And yet, when I say that I am the Way and the Truth and the Life and that no man comes to the Father but by me, I am speaking a Gospel that has been given in many forms to any heart and mind that must come to realize that you *are* Christ eternal. You *are* Jeshua. You are the power of the Light that is the offspring of Light Divine. You are the Daughter of the Goddess and, therefore, when you come to be fully identified in the core of your own being as that same Love and Power and Wisdom that took form as Jeshua, then indeed you have become the Way, the Truth and the Life.

Does that make sense?

That is wonderfully clear for me, and I really appreciate the recognition, because I was aware that I had a different lineage and I just wanted to get clear for myself and understand what was really going on here, and what you were referring to, so that I could remain in honor and love — my love for your words and your works that have been so vastly written and talked and preached about. So, I thank you for that very special message.

I do have a question that is personal. Is that okay to ask?

Oh, of course not.

[Laughter]

No. This year I decided that I am... what you were talking earlier about lack. I really want to be done with it. I mean, clearly done with it and really trust. And as I have been declaring that I wanted to trust God more in allowing that flow to happen with not so much fear coming in, of course, fear comes blasting in my face — and I got ill from it and I had to go through that whole recognition of letting go to another level of vibration so that I could receive more, understand more. And there is a part of me that recognizes there is a way I am *blocking* my abundance. And I really want to be able to... I know that I will be able to move it out of the way. However, I am not really clear on what it is that I need to move, unless it is *the* big issue of totally trusting and just having faith in every single moment of every single breath that I take that all is well. My mind gets in the way. I don't know if you have any insight to share with me on this?

None. I haven't the foggiest idea what you are talking about.
[Laughter]

Okay, I'll rephrase that.

No, you don't need to.

I know that you know and I would like some help with this! Thank you.

Beloved friend, you have already given yourself the answer but you have not understood it. Indeed, your mind gets in the way and the obstacle that blocks it is the belief that there is an obstacle that *you* must remove *before* you can receive the abundance.

Oh. Okay.

Beloved friend, do what I am about to suggest to you. Do it daily for a period of twenty-one days. Fair enough?

Uh huh, fair enough.

Now, this is going to require that you do this twenty-four hours a day and you do not eat or drink in the meantime.

[Laughter]

Just kidding.

Now, when you arise in your morning, sit up, throw the shoulders back, feel the spine lengthen, block not the angel of air, and say unto that One who is the Teacher who teaches without error — the One I have called the Holy Spirit — and ask Him to correct the *only* obstacle in you: ask Him to correct the perception that an obstacle exists. As you breathe the angel of air, let the body soften. Let it feel as though the cells are becoming Light itself. You will feel that softness, and over the course of these twenty-one days you will feel that state and know it very well. And as that softness comes, simply say,

The Master of Time

Thank you, Holy Father, for I am healed.

Yes.

Then go about your day. But as you go about the day, within your mind ask that a higher vision be born through you. That's all you need to do. Do it with innocence, not trying to let the mind get caught up with wondering what the vision might be. Just ask that it born through you. In twenty-one days you are going to know that a deep healing and shift has occurred. A certain perception will no longer arise and you won't even have noticed at first that it's not in you any longer. And on around the twenty-second or twenty-third day you are suddenly going to be startled to realize that you will notice a certain weight is not with you, and you won't even know where it went.

Fair enough?

That is great, yes. Thank you.

You have much to do upon this plane and for you to move into the fulfillment of part of your purpose is going to require that you become a demonstration of one who is a teacher of God and one who lives in unlimited abundance.

Somebody has to do it. What do you think?

That's pretty awesome.

Don't fear abundance of any kind, even of golden coins.
But when they come to you, remember what they are really for: to give the Love of God away. Keep that in mind.

Okay. And my second question is personal. I came to a decision just today, and I feel like it's clear. I just want to ask you that I am not copping out on part of . . . I'm not copping out. Okay. Go forward and do it. Is that what you are saying? Okay. Thank you. That's all, and I appreciate your graciousness.

I appreciate the Light and the clarity and the power and the love and the demonstration that you are about to bring and give unto this world.

That makes my palms sweat.

Jeshua, this woman started her question with a proclamation

that was quite profound, I thought. She said, "Jeshua, I'm new." It is the first thing she said, and I rather liked it. So, can I say I am new, too?

Are you ready to be new?

I think so . . . Okay, I am ready.

There. All that "I hope" and "I think so."

Great.

Yes. Indeed, beloved brother, is it not true that all things *are* being made new for you? Is it not true that the perceptions have been dropping away almost constantly, and that even in the midst of your day you sometimes stop and realize that you are seeing things in a wholly new way? Is that not true?

Yes, energies are changing.

Yes. Allow, allow, allow. Do not strive. Do not make. *Allow.* You know what I mean by that?

Yes.

Had any nice conversations with deceased entities lately?

I started to. I tried, but they weren't very willing to listen.

That doesn't matter. Talk to them anyway.

Okay.

What you perceive as their unwillingness means that you are just getting caught up with the superficiality of their drama.

Speak to the deeper part.

You said... when you told me that there is a teacher that would help me... can you be a little more specific about that? No? Let's not. Okay.

I could, but I love you far too much to do anything which is a disservice to you.

Right.

Allow, allow, allow.

Seems like such a simple message, and yet in this year you have realized through revelation after revelation of the depths of the meaning of that teaching: to allow. Is that not true my sister?

Yes.

Continuing to learn it, aren't you?

Uh huh.

It is the most important of Keys to the Kingdom, and because you've begun to master the use of that key, it must necessarily come to pass that you will quickly come to the completion of your journey and reside where I am. The end is certain now. Allow it to be.

Surprise!

I have to hug the trees, huh?

Yes. You don't *have* to hug them. You get to hug them. They are waiting.

The day will come when you will understand the power and the significance of doing just that. You will come to understand what it really means in and for the depth of your soul.

Ah, nothing like enjoying the journey that another is taking in their choice to awaken from dreams to reality. It brings *me* great in small circles but journeys to awaken from the soil of separation and to burst forth as the fragrance and the flowering of divine remembrance. Because well do I know what is going to transpire upon this plane when the Sonship chooses to be the flowering of awakening. It's something worth working for, throughout all of time.

You are all so very beautiful. In you there is so much Light, so much love and so much radiance, so much wisdom and so much beauty that you cannot contain it in the vessel of the human body.

And when you choose to let it shine fully, when you decide just to throw caution to the wind—which is what I would call casting aside the belief in limitation—so much Light will radiate through you that the time must surely come to pass when the choice to manifest physical bodies will have served its purpose and you will have moved beyond it. And even what you call your world will dissolve in Light. Is that the end of creation? Hardly. But it is the transcendence of one form of it. Let your Light so shine before men that it is unmistakable—and you are the Light of the world.

Many of you would do well to call your mothers and your fathers and your brothers and your sisters and your children and say,

Guess what? I'm the arisen Christ. How are you doing today?

[Laughter]

Because, you see, when the thought comes,

Well, I couldn't do that it means you just identified yourself with the illusion that *is* the world. That's how close you are in every moment.

I would rather say it in person than over the telephone.

Very good.

What would we do with the aghast responses we would get?

Love it. Because you will see they will say, "Of course you can't be that. What's the matter with you?" And you sit there and smile back, giving nothing but love because, you see, a master returns *all* responses in love.

A master takes attack and returns love. A master takes condemnation and returns love. A master takes disbelief and returns love. And sooner or later they will stop and go, "Oh, my God, you are serious." And then you can smile and say,

> *Oh, yes, I am quite serious.*

And let them know that they are the same?

Exactly. Tell them that you are not going to stop loving them with the Light of Christ until they remember that they, too, are that Light.

Let them know that you will be with them throughout the next one hundred thousand incarnations if they so choose to do it that way, and *you* will be the one who is with them always, even as the master Jeshua said, "I am with you always."

Take the love that I give to you and give it to your brother and sister. "For he that drinks from my mouth becomes as I am and I shall become he or she."

That is what I mean when I say, "Take my strength and use it until yours is as certain as mine."

Need that take a long time? Time is an illusion. You can choose it now. When you walk out of this building tonight, you can say,

> *Oh, Jeshua is my brother. We came from the same lineage. We have the same divine parent. What is in him is in me also. Therefore, I am going to love all others as he has loved me.*

If you believe and feel that through my presence in your life, not just this life, that the grace of our Father has thrown open the shutters of your heart, then simply be as I am. Become the perfect servant of the Grace of God. Lay down the dream of the dreamer and awaken as the saviour of the world. Then my life has not been lived in vain.

My death, my burial, and my resurrection will have truly been filled with meaning, because until *you* pick up your cross — which is made of Light — and follow me, all that I have given unto you remains in vain.

If, therefore, you would love me, if, therefore, you would extend your appreciation and thanks unto me, speak not in words to me, but go and do likewise to your brother and your sister. For only in honoring the Son within your own heart can you in Truth honor me. And when you have extended that love unto your brother and sister, indeed,

you will feel me rejoice and you will know that, in Truth, I am with you always. And we shall walk hand in hand as equals in the Kingdom of our blessed Father, doing nothing but serving the Atonement because there is nothing else to do. Join with me by being what I am.

Of myself I do nothing but my Father though me does all things. And my Father is *only* Love.

Therefore, be that which you are and you are the Love that my Father has given to the world through me. Be, therefore, that which I am and *you* are the Light of the world. Great is my love for you. Great, *great is my love for you* because I know who you are even when you choose not to believe it.

I cannot find words in your language to express the love I feel. Though many of you forget about me during the course of your day, I forget you not. And I look upon you in this illusion and I see naught but myself. For have I not tried to teach you that the only thing you need to learn is that there is nothing outside of you? All of creation is contained within your Heart because you are the only begotten of the Father, begotten before all worlds and of one substance eternally with all that our Father is. Oh, how can I not love you? How can I not love the Light of the world? How can I not love the only creation of my Father, that which is eternal and changeless?

Pure is your heart. Pure is your heart. You have never sinned. You are Love in form. Give it to the world even as I have given that love to you. Give it with every breath you breathe and gone will be your depression and gone will be your doubt. Gone will be your lack. There are no limitations in you. You can do it all because of yourselves you do nothing, but your Father through you can do all things.

The body that you have thought yourself to be is *only* a vehicle of communication.

Stop identifying with it, and identify with the Truth of your being. You are Spirit and you are Divine. You have never known birth and you will never taste death. This illusion is a game. Play it with the *infinite joy of Christ*. Wherever you are, you are only there to be a demonstration of what transcends the world.

Short is the time that I am given to be with you in this way and yet, eternal is the time that I am with you. And though this world arises and passes away in the twinkling of an eye, we are together throughout eternity. Join with me; play with me.

You are already a master. Claim it. And when you are in a grocery store buying the food that you would put into the body, take pause and remember,

Ah, this mass of flesh that seems to be handing golden coins to the one who seems to be separate from me and who seems to have a frown upon their face and depression in their countenance because they do something they hate, this little body is nothing more than a vehicle to extend the Peace and Love of God.

Send that beam of Light through the heart of your very body and join with the heart of the one across that little stand. Look them in the eye and say,

Thank you from the bottom of my heart for the service you give me. I love you for your willingness to do the work you do.

When they've picked up their chin, you will feel their countenance shift. And though you may never see them again, they will remember you always. And you have no idea of the seed you will have planted, because they, in their turn, will begin to be quickened by your love. And it may be the next day, it may be next week, they, too, will remember that they can extend the love of Christ unto another. You will have started a string of miracles, and there is absolutely nothing worth doing than being the initiator of the string of miracles that awakens the Child of God.

Would you do that with me? Would you choose to play in each day as the one who can bring a miracle and give it to another? I need you as much as some of you have believed you need me. I can work from planes unseen but I can only join with so many bodies to do this kind of work. But wherever you are, you can join with me and say,

> *Jeshua, I'm going to extend the love of Christ. Are you ready? Here it goes.*

And trust this: when you call upon me in order to extend that miracle, rest assured I *am* with you. Some of you have already begun to see me, even though your eyes are open, in the midst of other experiences because you are beginning to get the message.

I am not limited by space and time. Nor are you. Join with me and play. Play in the Spirit of Light of being the saviors of the world.

Would you please do that for me? Would you please promise to join with me? Would you please in this moment let your decree be heard by your brothers and sisters by just saying,

> *Yes, I will join with you in the salvation of the world.*

[Group repeats: "Yes, I will join with you in the salvation of the world."]

Ah, nothing like having some help!

[Laughter.]

Now, that means tomorrow when you arise and lift your head from the pillow, leave your past behind you because it doesn't exist. Let your head rise and your body rise and say,

> *Oh, boy, what a great day this is going to be because I am going to give the love of Christ to this world. I am going to be vigilant in every moment. Who can I give it to? What do you think, Jeshua? Is that a good candidate?*

And I'll say, "Oh, yes, indeed. Go and do so."

Begin to play with it. Let the seriousness go. It has no place in the Kingdom. Play with me! Dance with me! Sing with me! Rejoice with me! Begin to have fun pushing buttons and blowing cobwebs away. So people think you are a little crazy. So what? If the world is crazy—and I assure you that it is—what will be perceived as *your* craziness is actually a demonstration of sanity. There Contemplate this well tonight: "Into thy hands I commend my Spirit." Treat it well and give it away with love. Into thy hands, my brothers and sisters, I commend my Spirit, and it is finished—whenever you choose to be the Light of the world. And indeed I *am* with you always.

Go in peace. Remember this day to keep it holy. Remember this day to keep it holy. Remember this day in every moment, and you are the Light of the world. You are my brothers and my sisters and you are my friends. I will never abandon you and I will never forsake you; and even if you are not quite of my lineage, sit down and have a cup of tea with me now and then.

Let it come to pass that in *this* hour and *this* day you shall go out no more from our Father's holy place. And indeed entrust your heart to the Truth of your only reality. Ask now and *receive* the fullness of that perfect wedding between our Heavenly Father and our Earthly Mother that you might extend it as far as from the East unto the West.

Be the Light of the world. Go in peace and *always* take me with you, because I have no other desire than to be where the awakened Son of God is.

Peace be unto you.
Amen.

The End

WayofMasteryBooks.com
Book Catalog

All New releases will be announced on the website as well as access to Kindle/ eReader versions and special audio offerings

IN BOOKSTORES

The Way *of* Heart
The Christ Mind Trilogy
Volume I

The *Way of the Heart* is the first of *The Christ Mind Trilogy* teachings, the core, formal, lessons of *The Way of Mastery* Pathway.

The lessons here are ones that Jeshua Himself was given in His lifetime, and subjects include the nature and meaning of reality, the power of forgiveness, purified desire as alignment to the Will of God, the four "Keys to the Kingdom," and much more.

The Way of the Heart teachings and experiential learnings provides the firm and essential foundation for all of that which follows in *The Christ Mind Trilogy*. It is a key aspect of Jeshua's Pathway of Enlightenment, and His Promise to us to help us awaken from the illusion that we have ever been separate from God, and to remember the deepest Truth of who we are: Christ.

ISBN 978-1-941489-41-3
Available in Paperback, Hardcover, Kindle, eReader & Audiobook

IN BOOKSTORES

The Way *of* Transformation

The Christ Mind Trilogy
Volume II

The Way of Transformation is the second of The *Christ Mind Trilogy* teachings, or the 'Way of' Lessons. These were originally recorded as live channelings of Jeshua, and later transcribed. Together, the trilogy forms an in-depth three year Course in *The Way of Mastery* devoted to healing the illusions that bind us beyond mere 're-training' of the mind. It is meant to be read and studied only after the student has completed *The Way of the Heart* text and lessons.

Hear what Jeshua says of it:

"The Way of Transformation absolutely requires that you be committed to living differently. For is not transformation a change from the status quo? How can you experience transformation if you do not use time to think and be differently? Crying out to me will not do it. Reading a thousand holy books will not do it. One thing, and one thing only, will bring you into the transformation that you have sought — the willingness to abide where you are, differently."

The Way of Transformation teachings and experiential learnings provide the firm and critical foundation for *The Way of Knowing*, the final part of *The Christ Mind Trilogy*.

ISBN 978-1-941489-42-0
Available in Paperback, Hardcover, Kindle, eReader & Audiobook

IN BOOKSTORES

The Way *of* Knowing
The Christ Mind Trilogy
Volume III

The *Way of Knowing* is the third and final teaching of *The Christ Mind Trilogy*, a Course originally recorded as live channelings of Jeshua over a three year period, and foundational to the larger Way of Mastery Pathway. It is meant to be read and studied only after the student has completed *The Way of the Heart* and *The Way of Transformation* texts and lessons. In Jeshua's own words:

"In *The Way of Knowing*, the final surrender is entered — that surrender which is beyond the comprehension of all the languages and theologies of your world, beyond all that can be spoken or uttered, yet not what can be *known, felt, realized, and lived!*"

Here, He unequivocally tells us that what we consider as 'knowledge' is a pale substitute for the mystical transfiguration the Christ Path is truly devoted to:

"Knowledge is a knowing by being that which is known."

Following the completion of the *Christ Mind Trilogy*, Jeshua begins the astounding restoration of His original Aramaic Teachings, notably the Lords Prayer and Beatitudes, along with a one year online Course for the maturing student called *Jewels of the Christ Mind*.

ISBN 978-1-941489-43-7
Available in Paperback, Hardcover, Kindle, eReader & Audiobook

IN BOOKSTORES

The Jeshua Letters
A Remarkable Encounter with Christ

In July 1987, Jesus (Jeshua) appeared out of a field of light, fully formed, to his chosen channel and scribe Jayem. Over a period of nearly two years Jeshua appeared many times and gave 'dictation', which Jayem recorded, and which became the earliest parts of *The Way of Mastery Pathway*. Eventually Jeshua asked that these be published, and they, along with Jayem's personal reflections on how all this unfolded, make up *The Jeshua Letters*.

The Jeshua Letters is the start of an astounding body of work given by Jeshua which restore the essential truths of His original teachings, previously 'lost in translation' in their passage from Aramaic to English. Jeshua's 'Letters' are simple, profound and practical. His voice is certain but always gentle; inviting, never demanding. To read them is know beyond doubt - to know palpably - that Truth is being expressed.

ISBN 978-1-941489-45-1 • *Available in Paperback, Hardcover, Kindle, eReader*

IN BOOKSTORES

The Way of the Servant

The Way of the Servant is the second text dictated by Jeshua and scribed by Jayem in *The Way of Mastery Pathway*, following The Jeshua Letters.

Jeshua oftens speaks of "beginning at the end", and here He does so, showing us nothing less than how the Pathway flowers as the highest pinnacle of Consciousness (fully realized Christ Mind) that can be known in this world: *true servantship*, devoted to the realization of Humanity's highest evolution or, the 'coming of heaven to earth'.

Short, succinct, of extraordinary mystical depth, countless Pathway students find that immersing in *Way of the Servant* every year reveals depths and brings illuminations they were incapable of truly comprehending before!

ISBN 978-1-941489-44-4 • *Available in Paperback, Hardcover, Kindle, eReader*

IN BOOKSTORES

The Early Years
Volume I
Now, We Begin

The Early Years (volumes I & II) are transcriptions of gatherings recorded live as Jeshua taught us all. The wisdom, guidance, and sheer brilliance of them is astounding; there is so much in these pages, dear reader, that will help you grow in understanding, support you to truly heal into peace, and more!

Volume one includes the talks below:
- Awakening
- Choose to See
- Death Earth Changes
- Decide to be Christ
- Grace as Reality
- Healing
- Heaven on Earth
- Ignorance is Bliss
- Joy I
- Joy II

ISBN 978-1-941489-46-8 • *Available in Paperback, Hardcover, Kindle, eReader*

IN BOOKSTORES

The Early Years
Volume II
Now, We Begin

The Early Years (volumes I & II) are transcriptions of gatherings recorded live as Jeshua taught us all. The wisdom, guidance, and sheer brilliance of them is astounding; there is so much in these pages, dear reader, that will help you grow in understanding, support you to truly heal into peace, and more!

Volume two includes the talks below:

- Mastering Communication
- The Blessing of Forgiveness
- The Divine Feminine
- The Holy Instant
- The Holy Spirit
- The Light that You are
- Walk with Me
- Love Heals All Things
- The Meaning of Ascension
- Teach Only Love
- The Heart of Freedom
- The Master of Time

ISBN 978-1-941489-47-5 • *Available in Paperback, Hardcover, Kindle, eReader*

COMING SOON

Darshan

Over a period of 3 years, originally in live group video recordings, Jayem offered for the first time an in depth immersion into each lesson of The Way of Mastery Christ Mind Trilogy. He reveals the rich beauty and practical wisdom of the Teachings and shares transforming insights into their timeless Lessons, garnered from his own studentship of them for over some 25 years.

This is a remarkable and vast treasure trove of material, and we anticipate 6-8 volumes as we transcribe over 178 hours of audio into written form.

COMING SOON

The Later Years

While Jeshua guided Jayem deeply into the Aramaic Teachings and their application to the students transformation, He ceased public channelings. Then, in 2010 He abruptly stated it was to begin again at a Pathway gathering in England, where He announced the 'Turning of the Ages'.

Also, gathered here, are some of the promised messages from other Teachers of the Lineage, notably Mary Magdalene and Elijah.

COMING SOON

The Living Practices
The Alchemy of Living from The True Heart

Well beyond the *Christ Mind Trilogy*, Jeshua –over a several year period – revealed the profound methods of healing the roots of Separation while cultivating the ground of mystical consciousness, and restored His original teachings utilized by the Essenes, as given in the Beatitudes and Lords Prayer. Principally, these are LovesBreath and Radical Inquiry. Here, find a rich and practical treasure trove of genuine transformative practices meant to also be utterly practical in our daily lives.

COMING SOON

The Christ Mind Trilogy

Spanish Edition

The Christ Mind Trilogy in 3 volumes will be published in Spanish and we are anticipating a 4th quarter release date. Keep an eye out at WayofMasteryBooks.Com for updated release dates on all our upcoming additions.

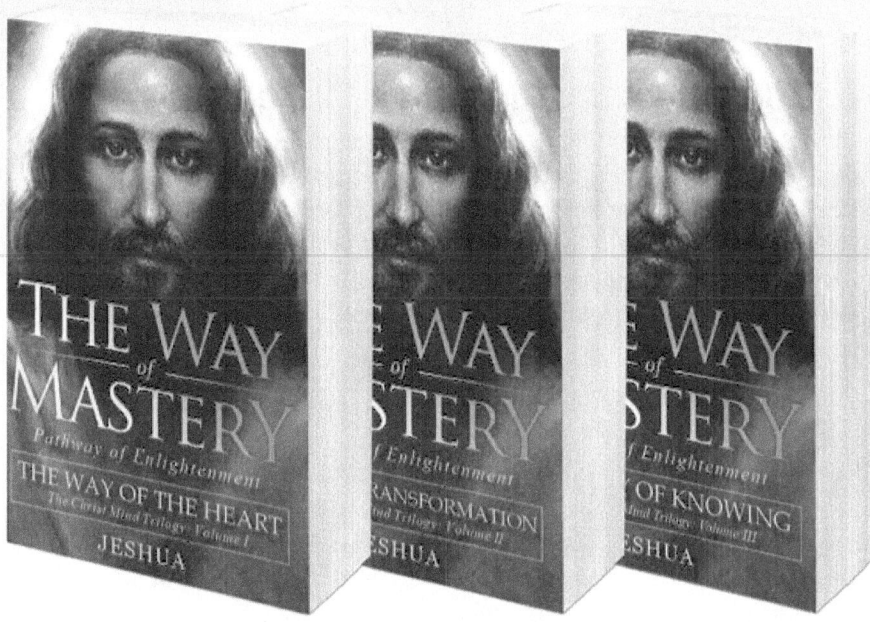

COMPLIMENTARY READING

The Essene Gospel of Peace

For the first time the complete 4 books of the Essene Gospel of Peace are available in one volume.

- *The Essene Gospel of Peace*
- *The Unknown Book of the Essenes*
- *Lost Scrolls of the Essene Brotherhood*
- *The Teachings of the Elect.*

The Essene Gospel of Peace were found in the Vatican Library and translated by Edmond Bordeaux Szekely

Edmond Bordeaux Szekely, grandson of Alexandre Szekely, eminent poet and Unitarian Bishop of Cluj, is a descendant of Csoma de Koros, Transylvanian traveler and philologist who, over 150 years ago, compiled the first grammar of the Tibetan language, the first English-Tibetan dictionary, and wrote his unsurpassed work, Asiatic Researches.He was also Librarian to the Royal Asiatic Society in India. Dr.Bordeaux earned his Ph. D. degree from the University of Paris, and other degrees from the Universities of Vienna and Leipzig.He also held professorships of Philosophy and Experimental Psychology at the University of Cluj. A well-known philologist in Sanscrit, Aramaic, Greek and Latin, Dr. Bordeaux spoke ten modern languages.

In 1928, he founded the International Biogenic Society with Nobel Prize-winning author, Romain Rolland.His most important translations, in addition to selected texts from the Dead Sea Scrolls and the Essene Gospel of Peace over a million copies in 26 languages are selected texts from the Zend Avesta and from pre Columbian codices of ancient Mexico.His last works on the Essene Way of Biogenic Living have attracted worldwide interest.He is the author of more than 80 books published in many countries on philosophy and ancient cultures.

ISBN 978-1-941489-40-6 • *308 pages, Paperback*

www.ingramcontent.com/pod-product-compliance
Lightning Source LLC
Chambersburg PA
CBHW020047170426
43199CB00009B/200